Gandhi's
HIND SWARAJ
A New Paradigm, Agenda and Programme

L.M. Bhole

SHIPRA

Rs. 650; US$ 32.50

ISBN: 978-81-7541-700-7

First Published in India in 2013

Gandhi's Hind Swaraj: A New Paradigm, Agenda and Programme

Published by:
SHIPRA PUBLICATIONS
H.O.: LG 18-19, Pankaj Central Market, Patparganj,
Delhi-110092, Tel: 91-11-2223 5152, 2223 6152
Br.Off.: 4617/18, Ansari Road, Darya Ganj,
New Delhi-110002, Tel: 9650028065, 9810522367
E-mail: info@shiprapublications.com
www.shiprapublications.com

Contents

Introduction

The philosophy of modernization is ruling the roost even today in the West as well as the East, including India, even though it has brought the present civilization to the brink of disaster or annihilation or extinction. That modernization is today's dominant ideology is quite clear from the instances or happenings like the following ones. In August 2007, the then Minister of Agriculture in India made a policy statement that development in India cannot be made agriculture-dependent, and that the Indian youth and job seekers should leave rural areas and seek jobs in cities.

Similarly, the United Nations Organization (UNO) is reported to have said that agriculture is harming and endangering the environment and bio-diversity on the earth. The signing of the Nuclear Treaty by India and USA in the year 2010, the policy of creating a large number of Special Economic Zones (SEZs) in India, China, and some other countries, the plan to build a Delhi-Mumbai industrial corridor, the fire-like spread of Information Technology (IT) and mobile phone technology, the policy of 'Bombay First', the talk of linking all the major rivers in India, and the national ambition to make India a global economic, political, military super power are only a few examples of the ideas, plans, policies, actions, projects, and programmes that are being incessantly contemplated and implemented to strengthen the modern industrial civilization and culture of India.

It is a shame that the present modern civilization is squandering at least 2000 billions dollars on arms and advertising every year when a very large proportion of the world population lives on less than a dollar per day, per person, and it suffers from destitution, hunger, nakedness, malnutrition, disease, and extreme privation.

Although the overwhelming majority of the world population is enamoured and won over by the modern civilization (MC), fortunately for mankind, there are still some wise, enlightened people who have come to know the devilish character of the MC, and have been always trying to wake up and alert the people to the diseased and pathological character of the MC. They have been engaged in a search for a 'new, alternative paradigm', or a 'just society' or a 'new society', or an 'economy of permanence' or a 'sustainable society', and the 'alternative world-view'. Mohandas Karamchand Gandhi (Mahatma Gandhi) occupies a unique position among them due to his vast, original, fundamental contribution in this context.

About a hundred years back Gandhiji or Gandhi, or Mahatma, or MKG, hereafter, wrote and published a 'seminal', 'revolutionary', 'spiritual', and 'classic' book (booklet) namely, *Hind Swaraj* (HS or the Book hereafter) through which he severely criticized the modern Western civilization, and presented a blueprint or contours of counter-civilization or counter-culture. However, inspite of its great depth and height, the Book has remained mostly unknown to students, teachers, researchers in India and abroad. It is an irony that the Book has received the highest praise among the world leaders of ideas, and yet it has remained a grossly neglected, ignored book the world over. HS contains Mahatma's seminal ideas and basic approaches to the problematique of contemporary civilization, and yet, it has not received the attention it deserves. The Book was ignored even when he was alive and at the helm of national affairs. After Gandhiji's demise, the Book became almost completely unknown, and in fact, the experiments, methods, approaches (*viz.*, Central Planning, Community Development Programme, Panchayat Raj liberalisation) adopted in India after 1950, for societal change, social and economic reconstruction were anti-HS i.e., they were largely counteractive to the spirit and central message of HS. Should this suicidal amnesia continue any longer? Certainly not. One of the central points of HS is that civilization is a disease but it is not an incurable disease. The Book shows the way towards curing the disease, it shows which way lies hope.

The present book, therefore, seeks to revive, to renew the interest of the public towards the message, insight, ideas, ideals, and programmes of HS. It attempts to spread widely the Gandhian vision and mission among the people so that the impending apocalypse or survival crisis or doom could be averted. We have contributed to some extent towards this end through hermeneutics and at places through intelligent compilation of ideas, facts, and views. While writing HS, Gandhiji appears to have anticipated by about 100 years certain important studies, such as Eric Fromm's, *Sane Society* and *To Have or To Be*; T. Roszak's, *Making of a Counter Culture*; Alvin Toffler, *Future Shock*; Stephen Bertman's, *Hyper Culture: the Human Cost of Speed*; and Ivan Illich's, *Deschooling Society*. The thought in HS has been subsequently elaborated, extended, amplified by Gandhi and Vinoba, and they have presented a complete, comprehensive Alternative Paradigm in the form of Sarvodaya or Gramaswaraj or Saamyayoga. The book, *Unto This Last* is the seed of *Hind Swaraj* which, in turn, is the seed of Sarvodaya or Gramaswaraj.

The organization of this book is as follows: Apart from the present Introduction, there are 13 chapters and nine sections in this book. The political, economic, social, moral, patriotic conditions in India under the British Rule, how India lost her independence, and how she could regain it are discussed in Chapter I. Similarly, Chapter II describes the conditions in England, Europe, Japan and other countries in the recent past. Chapter III presents a brief portrait of Gandhiji as the man. Chapter IV contains some facts about the Book, and quite a large number of statements of condemnation as also encominum made by various scholars and eminent personalities the world over. We have been quite liberal in giving these statements because we believe that they serve the useful purpose of enabling the readers to grasp the content and significance of the message of the Book. Chapter V is devoted to the exegesis of two crucial terms in the title of the Book, namely, Hind and Swaraj. Chapter VI dwells on the civilizational and cultural issues *vis-à-vis* Swaraj i.e. it discusses the nature of the current Western Modern Civilization (WMC), and the Gandhian Civilizational Alternative, which, in this context, has also been aptly called as 'true civilization' (TC). Chapter VII briefly discusses how Swaraj can be obtained by adopting and following the Ancient Indian Civilization (AIC). The Gandhian World-view developed so far is further extended and elaborated in Chapter VIII through discussing certain themes which are often taken up for debate in global discourses. These themes are: (1) Post-Nationalism, (2) Environmental and ecological crisis, (3) The question of speed and development of transport and communication like railways, (4)

Technology, Machinery, and Science, (5) Education, (6) Religion and Communalism, (7) System of Justice, (8) The Medical and Health system, (9) Economic Development, (10) Hind Swaraj and Pandit Jawaharlal Nehru. Chapter IX presents 'Swaraj Sutre' or the gist of HS as presented by Gandhiji himself. Chapter X briefly touches upon the questions of relevance and the Utopian nature of HS and the outline of the action programme for it. Chapter XI elaborates further the Tri-sutri programme for action. Chapter XII discusses how the philosophy and the programme for HS were developed in the post-Gandhi period. Chapter XIII contains a comprehensive Summary and Conclusions.

There are some differences in the HS text in Gujarati and English respectively. While the Gujarati text is written by Gandhiji himself, the English text is a translation of the Gujarati text into English text by Gandhiji himself. The discussion in our book is based on the English text (translated by Gandhiji) and edited by A.J. Parel. We have used much material in various chapters from the cited References at the end of our book. The positive and negative evaluatory statements presented in Chapter IV have been culled from the literature cited, particularly from Prasad (1985), Parel (1997), and Mathai and Moolakkattu (2009). Although it has not been always possible to acknowledge our debt to each of the sources/authors individually, we are happy to acknowledge our debt of gratitude to them collectively. The reader may also note here itself that if the reference or quotation in our text is followed by a page number, the said page number is from Parel, 1997.

I
India under British Rule

As a man of the highest scientific temper (one could even say, as a scientist), Gandhiji has first analysed the state of things in India and the West. As a 'doctor of civilizations', 'Gandhibhai' has first undertaken a diagnosis of humanity, and has then proceeded to offer his prophylaxis. While the conditions in India have been discussed in Chapters 1, 2, 7, 8, and 14, the conditions in the West have been highlighted in Chapters 5 and 15 of HS. Although Gandhiji lived in South Africa for many years, he appears to have studied the socio-economic and political history of India and other countries quite well. It also appears that he had kept himself very well informed about changes and developments in India while leading the struggles in South Africa. Chapters I and II of the present book give a brief historical account of India and Europe, respectively, during the period of the modern civilization. Needless to say that this is not an exhaustive history of the countries just mentioned. Only a brief account of history, germane to the theme of our book, has been presented here.

Gandhiji has raised certain important questions about India, and has tried to answer them in HS. What are the duties of newspapers and their editors? What were the conditions in India before and during British rule? Why had India lost her freedom? What do we need to do to regain that freedom?

During the ancient and medieval periods, India was an affluent, prosperous, wealthy society. It is widely known that India in those years was characterized as a 'golden bird'. It is said that symbolically, there used to be continuous smoke emitted from the burning of gold in India in that period. It is also said that India was so resources-rich that rivers of milk, curds, ghee, and honey, used to flow abundantly in the country in those years. It is because of her riches, wealth, prosperity that many marauders, plunderers, and merchants, traders from other countries invaded this land again and again. It is true that the above-given description of India is exaggerated, but it also contains a large extent of significant truth establishing that India once was a rich nation.

All this underwent a change during the period of British Raj. India became a country in which destitution, hunger, impoverishment, famines, and misery, came to rule the roost. She suffered from large—scale draining of resources to metropolitan centres in England and within India. The country suffered from de-industrialization also with its adverse consequences. In short, India became a slave nation of dependent villages. By the end of the middle ages, the economic, political, social organization, institutions, relations, underwent drastic decline and degradation. The *'varnashram dharma'* degraded into the curse of casteism and untouchability. The polity of village republics disintegrated. The system of basic democracy got undermined. The individual, social lifestyle which was founded on self-reliance, self-governance, swadeshi came to be destroyed. Vinoba has lucidly described that during the ancient period, India was a free nation of free villages. In the middle ages, she became a slave nation with free villages. In modern times, she has become a slave nation of slave villages. In other words, India has declined from near *'gramaswaraj'* to *'gram-slavery'*. The objective of HS is to take India back to the era of *'gramswaraj'*.

Why did this happen? Gandhiji has given a non-conventional answer to this question. As was his wont or in keeping with his habit of rejecting prefabricated notions, he did not blame England for India's condition. According to him, the blame lies with the Indians themselves. He argued that the English have not taken India; we have given it to them. If the British rule persists in India, it is because we keep the English in India for our base self-interest of becoming rich all at once (Parel, 1997, pp. 39-41). We made the East India Company a 'Company Bahadur'. The English did not have the slightest intention of establishing a Kingdom in India. We assisted them to do so. It is wrong to say that the English took over and held India together by the sword, because the sword is entirely useless for holding India together.

If the sad, bad, miserable conditions in India under British rule were not due to British rule, then what were they due to? In

Gandhiji's view, they were due to the singular fact that India had embraced modern civilization; that she had turned away from God; and that she had become irreligious. Gandhiji believed that between religion and modern civilization, the humbug, the number of victims, and superstitions of modern civilization are for greater than those of religion.

The uniqueness of Gandhian thought is its open, non-hesitant, confident, bold reference to God and religion along with spirituality, in its discourses. Unlike many of us, Gandhiji never shied away from taking a religious or theistic approach while explaining any phenomenon. The following position of Gandhiji illustrates this uniqueness. He has said, "It is my deliberate opinion that India is being ground down not under the English heel but under that of modern civilization. It is groaning under the monster civilization's terrible weight. Religion is dear to me, and my first complaint was that India is becoming irreligious" (Parel, p. 42).

The Euro-centric form of thinking has often charged us that Indians are lazy, fatalistic, superstitious, non-enterprising people. Gandhiji has rejected such a charge also. According to him, the Indian people appear to be so because true religion i.e. "religion which underlies all religions" has taught them that they should remain passive about worldly pursuits and active about godly pursuits; and while they should limit their worldly pursuits, their religious ambitions should be unlimited.

HS can be said to be, among other things, an essay in defense of religion. Apart from the above-given arguments in favour of religion, Gandhiji has impressed on people that humbugs in worldly matters are far worse than the humbug in religion. Further, the humbug of civilization and that of modern secular culture is not to be found in religion. The wars, fights, conflicts, burning, torture, cruelties in religion have been far more bearable than those of civilization. Similarly, the religious superstition is harmless compared to that of modern civilization. The humbug in religion has to be eliminated by strengthening the true religion.

As a part of stating and interpreting the conditions, events in India under the British Raj, Gandhiji has given us a peep into the early part of the history of the freedom struggle in India in two chapters (1 and 2).

In the last decade of the 19th century, and in the first decade of 20th century, the Indian National Congress was established, and it led the freedom struggle in India. In the first decade of 20th century, the demand for Swaraj, Home Rule, self-rule, and National Independence grew, and it soon became a big and strong wave. It, however, must be noted that the terms such as home-rule, self-rule, swaraj did not have the same meaning in the early 20th century which Gandhiji had in his mind when he used those terms in HS. The latter had a very deep and revolutionary meaning.

HS is a great essay on tolerance, humility, fairness, respectfulness. The leaders of Indian National Congress (INS) in the initial years were Dadabhai Naoroji, whom Gandhiji called, "grand old man of India", G.K. Gokhale, B. Tyebji, Hume, etc., and Gandhiji was very appreciative of the sacrifices, services, simple living, voluntary poverty, etc. of those leaders. They were the first authors of Indian Nationalism, and the pillars of Home Rule.

It is interesting to note that HS opens with Gandhiji's views on the objectives of a newspaper. It is certainly great that as an editor in real life, and as the 'Editor' in HS, Gandhiji was laying down the rules of the game for himself, as well as for others, in writing HS. According to him, the objectives of a newspaper are:

(a) To understand the popular feeling and to give expression to it;
(b) To arouse among the people certain desirable sentiments.
(c) To expose fearlessly popular defects (Parel, p. 13).

Today's media and which is engaged in the pursuit of only fame, name, and money would do well to take this advice in all seriousness.

Gandhiji has given very useful advice to the people regarding how they should behave with leaders and elders. He himself had a very high level of respect for the leaders like Dadabhai Naoroji, G.K. Gokhale, and others. He did not like showing disrespect to them. Certain views of these leaders (for example, Indian Governors will do justice; we have to learn a great deal from English, and so on) cannot undo or negate their great work. A nation that is desirous of securing Home Rule cannot afford to despise its ancestors and elders. Leaders like G.K. Gokhale, do what they do with pure motives and with a view to serving India. If we do not agree with their views, we should follow the dictates of our own conscience without being rude to them. It is a bad habit to say that another man's views are bad and ours only are good, and that those holding different views from ours are our enemies or the enemies of the country. The same rules hold good for the English as for the Indians. We who seek justice will have to do justice to others (Parel, pp. 16-17). This very simple advice is highly relevant, and we would realize this if we remember our own behaviour during election times.

Another development in the early period of the freedom movement which Gandhiji has discussed at some length in HS was the Partition of Bengal by the then Viceroy, Lord Curzon in 1905. This step by Lord Curzon was very much in keeping with the British policy of divide and rule. The demand for Home Rule and the Partition of Bengal resulted in

(a) a great awakening among the Indians,
(b) laying the foundation of Indian Nationalism,
(c) the realization of the need and importance of Swadeshi,
(d) the realization that the petition for independence must be backed by force and readiness as well as capability to suffer.

Another consequence of the Partition of Bengal, which Gandhiji alone could see, was that it made a rift in the English ship, or it partitioned the British Empire. Similarly, the Salt Tax proved to be an Achilles' heel for the British Empire. The very day on which Gandhiji made salt at Dandi in Gujarat without paying any tax, India became a virtually free nation.

One more important aspect of conditions in India under the British Raj which Gandhiji has discussed in HS is the important question of how to regain, secure, obtain India's freedom? Or how can India become free once again? Or how can one expel the British from India? Or what is the way to Swaraj?

Gandhiji was well aware that his views on this question, as on many other subjects, are different from those of others, and others may not accept and like his views. Yet, he thought it his duty to keep on airing his views with the hope that people would sooner or later live by his views. According to Gandhiji, for freeing India, what we need to do is to remove the cause(s) which resulted in her bondage or slavery. The cause of India's slavery was her acceptance or embracing of the modern civilization and the desertion of the Indian civilization which is the best civilization in the world.

This kind of argument raises the question as to how did India lose her freedom in the first place if the Indian civilization was the best of all? Gandhiji reiterated that the Indian civilization is unquestionably the best in the world. But she experienced a decline and fall or descend from it for a temporary period. The sons of India were found wanting in certain times which placed the Indian civilization in jeopardy. India was enslaved and she lost her freedom during those times. If the Indian civilization is revived and strengthened, India will become free again. This is certainly possible or workable because it is only the fringe of the Indian population, and not the whole of India, which has become degenerate due to the impact of the West's modern civilization. If we the individuals become free, or when the Indian people learn to rule themselves, India as a nation becomes free. For regaining our freedom, we do not need to expel the British out of India. If the English become Indianized, they can live with us. But there is no place for them in India, if they want to remain in India with their modern Western civilization.

II

Conditions in England and Europe in the 19th Century

As a part of his diagnosis of the present problematique affecting the human race, Gandhiji has highlighted the conditions in certain countries such as England and Japan, apart from India. He has also raised a pertinent question as to whether India should follow England or Italy, or any other European country.

After a deep study of the conditions and developments in the above-mentioned countries, he outright rejected the advisability or desirability of India following any one of those countries. While doing so, Gandhiji's language of expression becomes very sharp and at some places even very harsh indeed. Gandhiji took great pains to convince the readers by pointing out the defects, shortcomings, and failures of the English and other systems.

For a long time, England and particularly her parliament, have been regarded as the role-models for other countries. England has been known as the oldest democracy, and the English parliament has been known as the mother of parliaments. In Gandhiji's view, even then it functioned in such a manner that it was like a *sterile woman* and a *prostitute*; it was a *talking shop* of England, or a *costly toy*. It was a baby, and it was an institution with such a bad character that no true Christian would like to be its member. In Gandhiji's opinion, in general, the parliaments in the world are emblems of slavery.

The same was true about the highest office in a parliamentary democracy, namely that the the Prime Minister (PM). The parliament does not function steadily and in an orderly fashion under the leadership of the Prime Minister. The Prime Minister, in turn, is more concerned about his power than about the welfare of people or parliament. The Prime Minister's energy is concentrated upon securing the success of his party. *The Prime Minister cannot be considered to be really patriotic.* In order to gain their party ends, the people are bribed in many ways. *Prime Minister's have neither real honesty nor a living conscience.*

Gandhiji had a poor opinion about newspapers (media) also. In the light of what should be the objectives of newspapers laid down by Gandhiji himself (Parel, 1997, p. 13) it was experienced that newspapers were often dishonest. The English people even now use newspapers as their Bible; they take their cues from such dishonest newspapers. It is sad that all the four pillars of modern democracy, *viz.*, parliament (legislature or law makers), judiciary, executive, and the media are dishonest, corrupt, and without a conscience.

Not only English parliament was malfunctioning but also the overall conditions in England were bad, sad, miserable, pathetic, pitiable in Gandhiji's times. Child labour was rampant; the labour unions were banned; children were auctioned and carried off from their homes for work; unsanitary slums had proliferated; the thousands of children and the young starved; or worked to death, or were destroyed in ill-health or they were turned into ignorant slaves. The workers were flogged. There was extreme poverty and starvation on a mass scale (Ruskin, 1862, pp. vi-ix). It is ironical that such a pitiable condition should prevail in a country when its empire was at its peak, and "the sun never set on that empire".

This is a very strong indictment of English civilization, which Gandhiji has made with full sense of responsibility, and has illustrated his stand with examples and arguments (See Parel, 1997, pp. 30-33).

The Italian model was even less worthy of emulation, Gandhiji thought. In any case, both the English and Italian models are afflicted by the same disease, namely, modern civilization. Although from afar, the Italian Revolution and its leaders, such as Mazzini and Garibaldi appear to be great and adorable, that revolution never enabled Italy to gain self-rule, and it was extremely violent in which a large number of people were mercilessly killed in internecine wars.

Thus, all the countries of the world appear to be on the verge of collapse; the world civilization was on the brink of disaster and it may any time fall with a thud into the aby of oblivion. The only silver lining among the dark clouds of world civilization is the existence of Indian civilization.

According to Vivekananda, the Western nations are now almost borne down, half-killed, and degraded by political ambitions and social scheming. In spite of the sparkle and glitter of the Western civilization, in spite its polish and its marvelous manifestation of power, Western civilization is "a vanity of all vanities". The tide of world-weariness has come upon the West. The people over there are increasingly realizing that the rat-race for gold and power is all "vanity of vanities". They have now become weary of competition, struggle, and brutalities of their commercial civilization. The West is now finding that no amount of political or social manipulations, force, government can cure the evils of life and Western civilization (Vivekananda, 1969, pp. 1-52).

The conditions in India have been better, but not much better. The need to search for an alternative exists for both the West and the East. In India, aristocratic ancestors have been exploiting and treading on the common masses. There has been too much of an inactivity, too much of weakness, too much of hypnotism. The people have lost faith in themselves. Thus, in a way, civilization has begun nowhere and 99.9 per cent of the human race is more or less savage even now. There is tremendous religious persecution yet (Vivekananda, 1969, pp. 1-52).

Why is there such a crisis of survival in so many countries? According to Gandhiji, it is not because people are bad but because both the good and bad people have adopted modern civilization. A country after country has become ruined due to the impact of modern civilization. This civilization has been the real culprit or the real curse for mankind.

III

Gandhi – The Man

Hind Swaraj is a part of oceanic 'Gandhiyana' comprising more than 100 volumes of Gandhiji's collected works, and hundreds of books and articles (papers) on him written by various authors. Is it then justifiable to say that Gandhiji was not an intellectual or a genius?

One of the common traits of Gandhiji and also his book HS is that both of them have been received with both a highly hostile criticism and the highest level of acclamation or praise. He has been both revered and reviled. The range of epithets showered on him has been very wide indeed – sage, saint, prophet, genius, crank, faddist, humane. Before we begin the study of Gandhian thought in the form of HS, it would be useful to know about Gandhiji as a man, as a person, as a human being. This would help us to understand HS better or (correctly). It would not be wrong to say that Gandhiji was the embodiment or personification of HS, or in Gandhi, HS can be seen in flesh and blood.

Our forefathers have put forth before us many examples of the ideal person (*Aadarsha Purusha*). For example, there is the '*Stitaprajnya*' of the chapter two of Srimad Bhagavad Gita, and the ideal person described by Dynaneshwar (in Marathi) as a part of '*Pasayadana*' (giving Prasad i.e. giving part of the food prepared for God) in his Magnum Opus, *Dynaneshwari*.

'*Stitaprajnya*' means firm in judgement, or he who is unshakably established in super consciousness, firm in wisdom, and contented. In '*Pasayadana*', the ideal person is one who has intense and unshakable faith in God, who is like the moon without a stain, and who is like the sun without scorching heat. How far can Gandhi be called '*aadarsha purusha*' of Indian lore?

In order to enable the reader to form his own view in this regard, we present below Gandhiji's own views about himself along with the views of world-renowned leaders and scholars about Gandhi. What follows is 'About the Author' of the book, *Hind Swaraj*.

Today, Gandhi has remained just a name for young boys and girls in India, and quite often, they do not even know his name or are confused about it because his namesakes are being thrust upon the country. There has often been a destruction and desecration of his statues and Samadhi. There is a deep hatred for him in certain sections of the Indian population who even call him filthy names. There has been a systematic attempt to misunderstand, misinterpret, and misrepresent his life and work through books and other art forms. The dalits take a vehement objection to his calling them *'harijans'*. Some people question why he should be called the 'Father of Nation'. One sometimes feels like crying because so much suffering has been heaped on him by precisely those sections of society whom he had served the most. Today, his ideals have been buried alive. It is through his ideals that we have reached where we are today, but we are kicking away the very ladder with which we have climbed high.

On the other hand, many eminent scientists, literary persons (litterateur), enlightened political leaders the world over vouch for the effectiveness, the rightness, and redeeming nature of the Gandhi-Marg (Gandhian path). Some of the revered names in this context are: Leo Tolstoy, Romain Rolland, Arnold Toynbee, Nelson Mandela, Martin Luther King Jr., Obama, Einstein, Ho chi Minh and Dalai Lama. Let us note what they and Gandhi himself have to say about him:

(1) Fifty-three Nobel Prize-winning scientists have unanimously declared that it is only Gandhian thought and path which can halt the progress of mankind towards self-extinction.
(2) The UNO has announced October 2 as the *International Day of Non-violence.*
(3) According to the opinion poll conducted by the *Time Magazine*, Gandhiji has been adjudged to be the man of 20th century.
(4) The American house of representatives has declared

Gandhiji as the '*Yuga Purusha*'.

(5) Obama, the President of USA, and Martin Luther King Jr. are never tired of acknowledging their debt to Gandhiji across many cases.

(6) "You must watch my life, how I live, eat, sit, talk, behave in general. The sum total of all those is my religion" (MKG).

The reader may note the close similarity between what Gandhiji has asked people to observe in him, and the following question of Arjuna in the Bhagwad Gita.

Sthitprajnasya ka bhasa samadhisthasya Kesava
Sthitadhih kim prabhaseta kim asit vrajeta kim
(*The Bhagavad Gita*, Chap. 2, Stanza 54).

Arjuna's question, in short, is: How does Sthitprajnya speak, sit, and walk?

(7) "I claim to be no more than an average man with less than average ability. I have not the shadow of doubt that any man or woman can achieve what I have, if he or she should make the same effort and cultivate the same hope and faith. (MKG)

(8) "My life is an indivisible whole, and all my activities run into one another; and they all have their rise in my insatiable love of mankind". (MKG).

(9) "My life is my message. It has been my experience so far that wherever I go and settle down, my presence gives the poor and destitute a sense of comfort. If I could do even this much, I will be satisfied". (MKG)

(10) "I have nothing new to teach to the world. The truth and non-violence are as old as the hills. All my philosophy is contained in what I have said. No elaborate literature or propaganda is needed for it. The scriptures have been quoted against my position, but I have held faster than ever to the position that the truth may not be sacrificed for anything whatsoever". (MKG)

(11) "I am not a visionary. I claim to be a practical idealist". (MKG).

(12) "The best way to find yourself is to lose yourself in the service of others. Be the change you want to see in the world". (MKG).

(13) "We have to make Truth and non-violence not merely for

individual practice but for practice by groups, and communities and nations. That any rate is my dream. I shall live and die in trying to realize it". (MKG).

(14) Einstein, in a world-famous quote, has said that future generations of mankind would scarcely believe that such a man as Gandhi actually walked on this earth in flesh and blood.

(15) "If humanity is to progress, Gandhi is inescapable. He lived, thought and acted, inspired by the vision of a humanity evolving towards a world of peace and harmony. We may ignore him at our own risk". (Martin Luther King, Jr.)

(16) Gandhiji is the greatest man in the world (Kahlil Jibran).

(17) The Twenty-first Century belongs to Gandhi. It is Mahatma Gandhi's spirit which sustained me during 21 years of solitary confinement (Nelson Mandela).

(18) "I and others may be revolutionaries, but we are disciples of Mahatma Gandhi, directly or indirectly, nothing more, nothing less. (Ho chi Minh)

(19) Such was the greatness of this little man's love that as his body fell, nothing but the mantram which was deep within him came to his lips, Rama, Rama, Rama; it meant I forgive you, I love you, I bless you (Eknath Eshwaran).

(20) Gandhiji's whole life was an experiment with truth. His creed was the service of God through that of humanity. To him God was Truth and Truth was God. His simplicity of manner was captivating. His devotion to duty was inexhaustible, his sincerity of purpose was infallible, and sense of humour irresistible (Radhakrishnan).

(21) Historians of the future, I believe, will look upon this century not as the atomic age, but as the age of Gandhi (Eknath Easwaran).

(22) "More than a leader, he was a father to us all. We are today orphaned. He saw the moral degradation in us, and as a loving father, he pointed out the right way. With his infinite love, he was trying to quench the anger that raged in many breasts. He has won the martyr's crown. He had to offer the supreme sacrifice for us. Let us not forget our guilt". (Rajkumari Amrit Kaur)

(23) "The light which led us to freedom still burns and will

burn on till it conquers". (Sri Aurobindo).

(24) The murder of Mahatma Gandhi is something far more terrible than any political crime. It belongs to the supernatural realm of high religious tragedy. The hand that killed the Mahatma is the same hand that nailed the Cross. After the work of Gandhi, it is not presumptuous to hope for a miracle. The death of this leader will raise men to heights they have not attained hitherto. The example and teachings of Mahatma Gandhi have left an indelible mark upon our time (News Chronicle, 31-1-1948).

(25) "When all the kings and princes and great captains of our time, who make so much noise and occupy so a central place upon the stage, that when all these have been forgotten, the Mahatma will still be known and revered as the greatest Indian since Buddha and Jesus Christ." (J.H. Holmes)

(26) "Gandhi is unique. There is no record of a man of his position challenging a great Empire. A Diogenes in action, a St. Francis in humility, a Socrates in wisdom, he reveals to the world the utter paltriness of the methods of the statesman who relies upon force to gain his end. In this context, spiritual integrity triumphs over the physical opposition of the force of the state. That was Gandhi's triumph. That was his achievement. That marks his place in history." (Francis Neilson)

(27) Nothing more revolting has occurred in the history of man than the senseless assassination of this venerable man. In the evolution of civilization, if it is to survive, all men cannot fail eventually to adopt his belief that the process of mass application of force to resolve contentions issues is fundamentally not only wrong and useless, but also contains within itself the germ of self-destruction. Mahatma Gandhi, however was one of those prophets who lived far ahead of time (General D Mac Arthur).

(28) "The light has gone out of our lives and there is darkness everywhere. The father of nation is no more. Our beloved leader is no more." (Jawaharlal Nehru)

(29) "The voice of world has proved that Mahatma Gandhi was a world figure, loved and worshiped by all those who have a sense of ideals, of righteousness, right doing and peace." (Sarojini Naidu).

(30) The light has gone out. He has left as his heritage a spiritual force that must in God's good time, prevail over arms and armaments and dark doctrines of violence (*New York Times*, January 31, 1948).

(31) "Gandhiji is the greatest man in the world. He is a man of this century and all centuries to come. Whenever I think of Mahatma Gandhi, I think of Jesus Christ". (J.H. Holmes)

(32) "Gandhiji was the greatest spiritual genius of India since the Buddha". (Sudhir Ghosh).

When Gandhiji was assassinated, it was said that we have buried him and his ideals alive. Is this true? Gandhiji himself and many others think that his ideals are so important that they cannot cease to guide mankind on to the right path. As Nehru has said, the light which had shone was no ordinary light, and, therefore, it would always continue to guide us. Gandhiji, confident as he was, has said that he and his ideals cannot be buried alive, that even in the grave, he will remain alive and vocal. He has said, even after my death, I will continue to reiterate my credo from my grave.

Based on Vinay Lal (2008), Swaminathan (2007 and 2008), K. Raja (2005), Edgar Snow (2005) and other writings, let us understand further Gandhi's personality and character traits. Gandhiji was an extremely affectionate, loving, compassionate, human being. He was full of love for men which extended beyond India and time. He was essentially a humanist, and he was a great lover of humanity. More than the ideas and programmes, he was a lover of mankind. Rabindranath Tagore was amazed by the Mahatma's humanity. He oriented worship towards more humane purposes. None of his activities limited his humanity. The greatness of his personality lay in his unlimited humanity. In a way, he was an imperfect being with all his fads, foibles, idiosyncrasies and mistakes. At the same time he was a rare being who had reached, more than any one else, nearest to perfection. Even with his imperfections he towered like a colossus among his fellow-beings.

Gandhiji was a complete man in the sense that he was absolutely one with his ideas, and whose vision perfectly blended with his whole being. It is the life-force of a complete man that energized the nation. It is because of this completeness that he could boldly assert that "my life is my message".

It has been frequently debated whether Gandhiji was a spiritual being or a political being. Did he spiritualize politics or politicized spirituality? It can be said that Gandhiji was both a spiritual and a political being for whom spiritual matters were at the centre. They were the goals, while political activities were the means to an end. There should not be any doubt that he was a spiritual seeker or a lifelong '*Sadhaka*' whose goal in life was 'Moksha', liberation, Swaraj, and he sought to achieve this goal through "Nishkam Karmyoga" in the mundane arena of politics, the latter becoming a natural choice because of the state of the Indian nation in his times. Among the different paths to '*Moksha*', the widely practiced, widely advised, even widely prescribed path has been one of trying to attain 'moksha' or 'Paramartha' while doing 'Prapancha' (visible world) or 'Sansara' (worldly life). Gandhiji has accordingly said that there has not been even a single moment of his wakeful life when he has not been aware that God is within his and He is observing him. The mind has been fully aware of this, and it has happened due to constant practice and repeated study. He has further said that really speaking, he was a religious and spiritual being. I have made politics my medium and instrument or a tool. Any of my politics, sociology, economics cannot be separated from my spirituality. If my politics, etc. are separated from my spirituality, they are mere dust and garbage." Moreover, politics of Gandhiji's was no ordinary politics; it was not characterized by expediency or 'real politik'. Gandhi's politics was politics with morality, love and dignity.

Gandhi has admirers galore or legion. He is revered. He commands veneration from a vast multitude, but at the same time, he has been the target of severe, virulent opposition and criticism. According to Vinay Lal (2008), everyone likes to hate and everyone likes to love Gandhiji. He has been reviled, belittled, disapproved; his genuineness has been often questioned. However, this has never ever unnerved him, nor has it made him discard his openness or transparency. All the ridicule, criticism in the world has not made him swerve from the truth; Gandhiji has been all the more compelling in the face of opposition and criticism.

Gandhiji no doubt was a very fascinating man. One is wonderstruck by the long arc of his strenuous life. His life was extremely crowded, and it was full of tragic elements. For example, it was a tragic spectacle that ultimately he was forced to see the limits of his ambition to remake his world. His life has been full of scenes of agony and ecstasy.

Gandhiji was more an experimenter and a scientist than a *'Shastri'* or *'Pundit'* or a highly learned person. He regarded himself to be a *'bread labourer'*, a *'weaver'*, a *'farmer'*, and a *'harijan'*. He has said in one place that nursing the sick and serving the needy were works of his great liking. Therefore, he nursed Shri Parchure Shastri and his father in their illnesses with rapt attention and great devotion. Similarly, he raised an Ambulance Corps during the Boer War and Zulu Rebellion. He always endeared himself to one and all through nursing the sick and wounded, nurturing the young, furnishing solace, and providing a healing touch to all those who felt defeated by life. It has been nicely said that suffering and service wanted to be on earth, and Mohandas Gandhi was born. His greatest ambition in life was to wipe every tear from every eye. All this is beyond a person like Churchill who thrived on colonialism. Only an uncaring person like Churchill could call Gandhiji a "half-naked Faqir".

The following lines from Urdu poetry reflect quite accurately Gandhiji's ambition:

> *Yaha jindagi kitani choti hai, phir woosme itane AAnsu, itane gama kyo hai. AAnsu kisike bhi ho, Woonko pochana hoga̓, gam kisika bhi ho, woosko mitana hoga.*

It means: How short is this life! Yet why are there so many tears, so much sorrow in it? Tears may be there of anybody; they have to be wipedout. The sorrow may be those of anybody; it has to be ended.

Gandhi ji created a profound uneasiness among the many constituencies which had to deal with him—Brahmins and Shudras, Dalits, Hindus, Muslims, Marxists and so on. The paradoxes leapup from every page of his life. For example, Gandhi the Indian nationalist and believer in universalism, or a leader of the Congress, advocating its dismemberment through his last will or last testament (Vinay Lal, 2008).

Gandhiji was a very human man who was quite capable of committing human blunders. He possessed 'unlimited humanity'. To be aware of difficulties of individuals and remembering details even under severe stress was the characteristic human touch of Gandhiji. He was endowed with divine or unshakable courage also in times of adversity. In his lonely pilgrimage to interior villages in East Bengal in October 1945, he became extremely lonely, yet walked barefoot from village to village at the ripe age of 77 years and gave a sense of security to the frightened villagers. And on 15-8-1947, when his colleagues had occupied the seats of power and were celebrating Indian Independence, Gandhiji was on fast far away from New Delhi wondering what was there to celebrate on August 15, 1947? For him it was a day of fast and mourning.

Gandhiji's prayer meetings were a moving, unforgettable, amazing spectacle. On an average, 2 to 3 lakhs of people attended these meetings daily and people used to walk for miles to reach the venues of those prayer meetings.

Gandhiji was always concerned with the person and not with the so-called more important matters of the state. This brings into focus the humanity in the Mahatma. Why was Gandhi so popular? Why did he have such great power over people? It has been pointed out that he was tremendously popular because he had incredible capacity to care for others, and people considered him as their father. You were taken up by him because nobody else cared for you as he did. It was a miracle that he could find room for so many in his mind and heart. He was the father who cared for you. He was not a remote heavenly father. He was very much an earthly father with whom you could argue and disagree. Every Indian lost his father when Gandhiji died. S.C. Bose called Gandhiji the 'Father of the Nation', and it was so because he won freedom for India, and he created pan-India or a United India emotionally and destiny-wise.

Rabindranath Tagore has called Gandhiji 'an artist'. Tagore was highly impressed by the uniqueness of the mind of the Mahatma. This unique personality, however, was characterized by obvious contradictions. For example, although Gandhiji lived like an ascetic, he did not frown on the joys of others. He exalted poverty, but no one in India has striven more assiduously than him for the eradication of poverty. He oriented worship towards more humane purposes, yet none of his activities ever limited his humanity. He behaved with unbounded graciousness; he was greater than the party, greater than even his creed. The greatness of his personality lay in his unlimited humanity. Great as he was as a politician, as an organizer, as a leader, as a moral reformer, he was greater than all these as a man because none of these aspects limited his humanity. He was not just a patriot or ascetic, he was greater than his virtues.

Gandhiji was a great synthesizer of the old and the new, traditional and modern. He preserved the truth and essence of tradition and rejected the peripheral. He tried to preserve traditional institutions by giving them a higher and time-relevant meaning. For example, the varnashram system. He taught that this system was not only a sociological system, but also an economic, social, political and spiritual arrangement.

Gandhiji was not merely an individual. He was a symbol and personification of ahimsa and swaraj. Mankind got a good outline of a non-violent social order through him. About Gandhiji, Vinoba has said that while baba i.e. Vinoba was a 'poorna shunnya' (perfect, complete zero), Gandhiji was a 'poorna purusha' i.e. complete man. Both together made ten.

Gandhiji's emphasis, his insistence on the truth and purity of his means, from which he evolved his creed of non-violence, is the natural outcome of his personality, an aspect of his deep and insistent humanity. According to Gandhiji, men in their fight for their claims must only assert their rights but should never violate their fundamental obligation to humanity, namely, to respect life.

Gandhiji often referred to the 'inner voice'. He claimed that it is the inner voice which has made him take certain decisions. What is 'inner voice'? It is the voice of conscience. What is truth? The truth is what the voice within tells us. Inner voice is man's conscience, or moral sense. It is the voice of God.

Edgar Snow has said something profound about Gandhiji. He said that Mahatma was a mirror in which every one of us could see himself.

It has been frequently debated as to whether the method of satyagraha or non-violent resistance really worked? Can it really work? Did Gandhi himself succeed in applying, using it effectively? We think that the truth lies somewhere in between *'Failed'* and *'Succeeded?'*. It did achieve a lot. One shudders to think of what would have happened if this method was not available. But it is also true that it was not completely or fully successful. Gandhiji himself has said, "Our fight for independence was not entirely one without war. I was fooling myself to believe that all our actions for independence were non-violent. But God blinded my vision, and if I really believed that we were acting non-violently at the time, perhaps God wanted to use me for his purpose. Now I think that in reality it was nothing more than the passive resistance of the weak. But I think I have made a small contribution to the world. I have demonstrated that ahimsa (non-violence) and satyagraha (soul-force or non-violent non-cooperation) are more than ethical principles. They can achieve practical results". This assurance along with his other assurance (I will speak from my grave) should enable us to answer another question, namely: Can Gandhiji's technique be applied without Gandhi? The work of Vinobaji is the clinching evidence to give an affirmative answer to such questions (*Sarvodaya* 2005, p. 41). But if someone is bent upon insisting that Gandhiji has failed, one can retaliate saying! In that way, Buddha and Christ also failed in the past. If human beings are bent upon failing divinity, who can save it?

One discerns a wonderful synthesis of five civilizations and cultures in Mahatma Gandhi. We find in him the contemplation of 'Aatmatatva' (the supreme spirit or soul) of the Aryan civilization, the vastness of the Arabian-Egyptian civilization, the industriousness of the Chinese-Tibetan civilization, the scientific experimentation of the Western civilization, and child-like attitude of African culture.

As it is widely known, Martin Luther King Jr., Dalai Lama, J.H. Holmes, Aung San Suu Kyi, Nelson Mandela, Native Americans, Africans, Arabs, Palestinians in thousands have been inspired by Gandhiji. They regard Mahatma Gandhi as the 'kindly light', a leader, teacher, and 'Guru'. Everyone lost his 'Guru', the world lost its 'Guru' when Gandhiji died. In Dwapar Yuga, Krishna had become 'Shantidoot' (messenger of peace), 'dharmadoot' (messenger of dharma), and Jagatguru (the Guru of the universe). In Kaliyuga, Gandhiji came as 'Shantidoot and guru'.

There has not been a leader in the whole world so far who, while leading a political movement has defined the aim of the movement by taking it beyond political freedom. Gandhiji alone has been such a leader. At this point, one ought to note of the progress, advancements which the Gandhian genius wrought in respect of certain doctrines and methods. One is wonderstruck when one realizes the kind of leap of intellect Gandhiji has taken from time to time. We are referring to the fact that visionary as he was of non-violence, he made non-violence the foundation of a new or alternative social order. But he also thought that henceforth (a) Satyagraha must be based on satyagrahanam. (b) We must advance or progress from non-violence of the individual to the non-violence of collectivity. (c) There is a scope for both constructive and agitational non-violence. (d) There is a need for a combination of constructive work and agitations (sangarsha). Gandhi-Vinoba have defined ahimsa as follows: Non-violence = love + non-killing + not to cause sorrow to any one + non-accumulation + gifting whatever one can give (dana). They also taught that henceforth, individual and social life would have to be lived in the light of illumination of 'brahamsutre', 'samyasutre', and 'swaraj sutre' values. (e) Satyagraha is not only the ethical principle or only the practical instrument; it is both.

Gandhiji has been one of the greatest revolutionaries of all times. The ignoramuses call him a status quo, a capitalist stooge, etc. This, however, is a false charge. Gandhiji was a revolutionary *par excellence*. This is very well evident from a few examples from his life. There are many many incidents, events in his life which show his revolutionary nature. We will give only three of them here to save space and yet illustrate the point. (i) He suggested that a 'harijan' girl should become the first President of India, and the vice-regal Lodge should be converted into a public hospital. (ii) As his last testament, he proposed that after independence, the congress party should be converted to Lok Sevak Sangh. (iii) He advised that we should fight the British raj but love the British. *Mahatma Gandhi was a Mahavir*. That Gandhiji was one of the greatest revolutionaries in the world is well reflected in the revolutionary departure, in the definition of revolution which he introduced. Conventionally, revolution means changes in the physical environment, surroundings, and economic redistribution. According to Gandhiji, revolution means changes not only in physical surroundings but also in mind, thinking, views, and heart.

Thus, revolution means a change in values. It means the end of injustice. It means I pit my soul-strength against all the unjust powers in the world. Conventionally, revolutions were occasional, they do not have long term aims. As per Gandhiji the true revolutions will not create a need for another revolution. He visualized a peaceful revolution, and it should be for peace. A true revolution has a spiritual dimension. Unless the mind that has caused the present crisis changes, true revolution cannot occur. The goal of revolution is happiness (sukha), balance or equity in happiness (sukha-saamya), and progression of happiness to a higher and higher level (sukha-unnayan).

Although there were some differences between Nehru and Gandhiji, there was also mutual affection, mutual love, mutual respect between them. Nehru has called Gandhiji a light, a powerful light, which has illumined India for all these years, the light that presented the living truth, the light that gave solace to innumerable hearts, the light that showed us the right path and made the country free.

It is not easy to describe or portray Gandhiji because he was many things in one. He was a student, lawyer, leader, journalist, author and writer, politician, etc. and all these were integrated in him. He was a revolutionary, an intellectual, a scientist, an artist, a spiritual and moral being. He was a theist and devotee of Rama (Rama bhakta). He was not a dry person. On the contrary, he was a very much humorous person with an infectious smile and laugh. He constantly experimented with truth, ahimsa, diet, health system, khadi, education, and so on. As an author, his written output was vast, had a very high quality, and he wrote and spoke a scriptural language.

Gandhiji was a great patriot. He loved India from his inner depths, but there was not an iota of chauvinism in him. There was a perfect blend or balance between universalism and swadeshi in him. He loved India but between truth and India, he would choose truth because God was Truth and Truth was God for him. Gandhiji was an extremely loving, affectionate, compassionate, sensitive, and humane person.

He was in politics throughout his life but his spirituality was stronger and had overcome politics. He was a religious person, who knew the importance and limitations of religion. He was a "sadhaka" and, many would believe, the 'siddha' (self-realised person). In politics, he did not seek power for himself, but he exerted to gain power for people. His whole work was devoted to empowering the masses. He was a man of the masses, but he never tried to please people by giving promises. On the other hand, he constantly asked the people to make sacrifices. His ideal in this context was,

> *Na twam kamaye rajyam na swargam na punarbhavam*
> *Kamaye dookha taptanam praninam artenashanam.*
> (Do not desire rajya or heaven or rebirth. Desire to end or remove the affliction of living beings who are suffering).

He himself has said that his goal in life and in politics was self-realisation. He looked at himself as an instrument in God's hands, and there was not even a moment in his life when he forgot that God was watching him.

In hardly any respect, Gandhiji was only this or that. There was no 'either or' in his life. The two opposites lived in him harmoniously; his life was a good example of the 'middle path' or 'anekanta vada'.

Unlike any one else, he has been compared with many prophets, sages and saints, *viz.*, Christ, Buddha, etc. He has gifted many things to humanity, *viz.*, universal love, truth, ahimsa, ekadasha vratas, trusteeship, swaraj, suraj, sarvodaya, antyodaya, swadeshi, gramaswaraj, peaceful revolution, and so on. There was a remarkable unity of thinking, speaking, and practicing in his life. He was a personification of what Tukarama, a Maharastriya saint – poet (17th century) has said,

> *Bole taisa chale tyachi vandavi powale.*
> (We should respect and touch the feet of one who behaves as he speaks).

Gandhiji died at the age of 79 years. But he had a desire to live upto 120 years of age. The life which had devoted itself to *ahimsa* was cut short by intolerance and belief in himsa. It is full of pathos. It is also a great shame, and we are guilty that we did not respect, we did not fulfill the 'jijiwisha' (will to live) of the one who expressed a desire to live longer only to serve the people.

IV
Hind Swaraj: Some Facts

If the saying, small is beautiful, is applicable perfectly to anything, it would be to the book, *Hind Swaraj* by M.K. Gandhi. It is, of course, true that HS is not only beautiful but also heroic and revolutionary in the manner of its writing and in the nature of its message. As a person in the knowledge of the modern Western medical model, Gandhiji has offered a thoroughgoing diagnosis as well as prophylaxis of modern civilization and culture in *HS*. In other words, *HS* locates the causes and offers the cure for the sick, moribund modern civilization.

The present chapter gives certain interesting facts about the process of writing and publication of *HS*, and it also includes (unprecedently) a large number of statements by very eminent and not so eminent persons in the world which contain positive and negative evaluation of the book, *Hind Swaraj*.

As said above, the very process of writing *HS* has something heroic about it. Its composition may virtually claim epic status for it. It was written in 10 days between 13-22 November, 1909.

The manuscript of *HS* was written by Gandhiji (as Gandhibhai) at the age of 40 years in Gujarati, his mother tongue, by using his left hand whenever his right hand was tired and ached, when he was voyaging from the United Kingdom to South Africa on board the ship *Kildonan Castle,* in November 1909. The photocopy of this Gujarati manuscript was published by Ramdas Gandhi in 1923, through Navajivan Press, Ahmedabad, and it reveals that the writing by left hand was more clear or legible than that by the right hand. *HS* is thus a bi-handed or double-handed book, and it would be a pleasant exercise to find out whether the left-handed clarity was the result of the leftist leanings of Gandhiji!

HS was first published in 1909, serially, in Gujarati on 11th and 18th December 1909, in the multi-language weekly (Gujarati, Hindi, Urdu, English), 'Indian Opinion' which Gandhiji was then editing and publishing in South Africa, Urdu and English. It was published in the form of a book in Gujarati in 1910. Gandhiji himself translated *HS* into English at the request by a European friend, Mr. Kalenbach and published the English version in the book form in 1910. In its English edition, the book has the title, *Indian Home Rule* (or *Hind Swaraj*), while in its Gujarati edition, the book has the title, *Hind Svaraj*, and the sub-title, *Indian Home Rule* is absent. It may not be wrong to say that the title '*Hind Swaraj*' is more expressive and deeper in meaning than the title, '*Indian Home Rule*'. The book is in the form of a dialogue between Adhipati/ Editor and Vachak/Reader in the manner of the dialogues in the Gita or *Upanishads* or in the words of Plato or Socrates. The choice of the form of a dialogue, and the choice of the language reflect Gandhiji's belief in the value and importance of the mother tongue, and his belief in the necessity and significance of the discussion or two-way interaction among the people living in Swaraj. The form of presentation reflects Gandhiji's constant readiness to talk with others, including adversaries, in order to resolve differences in viewpoints, conflicts through negotiations or through non-violent means. In the dialogue in *HS*, the editor refers to Gandhiji while the reader refers to revolutionaries, militant Nationalists, anarchists, the Indian school of violence, and persons such as V.D. Savarkar, and Pranjivan Mehta.

The book has a total of about 30,000 words, 119 printed pages, 275 manuscript pages. Forty of the 275 manuscript pages were written by the left hand. In the entire manuscript, only 16 lines were scratched out, and only a few words were changed. The dialogue as it has been given actually, took place between Gandhiji and his several friends.

The claim to the book's heroic character can be claimed for by *HS* because it was meant to counter the violent beliefs, philosophy, actions of the revolutionaries. Around the time *HS* was written the cult of violence for gaining political independence had become widely accepted in India and abroad.

It may be useful to present here the chronology of the stages of completion of writing and publishing of *HS*, resulting in its 'five texts':

(a) Manuscript written by Gandhibhai in Gujarati during 13-22 November, 1909, on board the ship *Kildonan Castle* at the age of about 40 years.
(b) Gujarati text published in two issues (in two installments) of the weekly, *Indian Opinion* dated December 11 and 18, 1909, respectively.
(c) Gujarati text published in the form of a book in January 1910. This book was prescribed on 24 March, 1910, by the Government of India, Bombay, Madras, and Bengal on the ground that the book was seditious. The seizure or proscription of the book constitutes grounds for a condemnation Western (English) civilization.
(d) The English translation by the author himself was published as a book in April 1910.
(e) A photocopy of the Gujarati manuscript was published in 1923.

A look at the contents of the book gives one a feeling that various chapters in the book do not follow any appropriate or meaningful sequence. The chapters may be said to have been randomly arranged. Structurally, 20 chapters in the book can be grouped in the following seven parts, each part dealing with a given theme:

(i) The condition in India; why India was lost; and how India can become free. (Chapters 1, 2, 7, 8, 14)
(ii) The condition in England, Europe, Japan, and other countries (Chapters 5, 15).
(iii) The meaning of Swaraj (Chapter 4).
(iv) On Civilization (Chapters 6, 13).
(v) Technique of Passive Resistance or Satyagraha (Chapters 3, 16, 17).
(vi) Some special themes such as railways, doctors, lawyers (Chapters 9, 10, 11, 12, 18, 19).
(vii) Conclusions and Programme (Chapter 20).

Why was *HS* written? Whom it is addressed to? What were Gandhiji's intentions or motivation or objectives in writing this book? What was the background or context for writing *HS*? What life-mission did Gandhiji want to convey through *HS*?

Parel has given six exalted aims behind writing *HS*? We would like to summarise them below (see Parel, 1997, pp. xiv-xvii):

HS is addressed to a mixed audience. Although Gandhiji sometimes has said that the book is meant for the illiterate masses, it would be more true to say that it is addressed to the mixed audience of classes, masses, elites, activists, i.e. to everybody. The expatriate Indians who were greatly attracted to terrorism and violence, extremists and moderates in the Indian National Congress, the Indian nation as a whole, and the English people who were meant to be reached by Gandhiji through *HS*.

(i) The first reason why he wrote *HS* was a sort of inner compulsion or inner illumination and the urge to communicate with others. He wrote to Henry Polak, "I feel that I should no longer withhold from you ideas which are not new but which have now taken violent possession of me ... I have written because I could not restrain myself."

(ii) Secondly, Gandhiji wanted to clarify the meaning of Swaraj. The real swaraj is self-rule and the quest for self-improvement, and not the quest for self-government or the good state alone.

(iii) Thirdly, he felt that he should respond specifically to the ideology of political terrorism adopted by the expatriates. He wanted to show that they were following a 'suicidal policy'. He wanted to counter the philosophy of 'Indian school of violence'. He wanted to show that violence was no remedy for India's ills, and that Indian civilization required the use of a different and higher weapon for self-protection.

(iv) Fourthly, he wanted to convince the Indians that it is modern civilization and not colonialism which threatened them. Colonialism is the product of modern civilization. Therefore, India should never aspire to be a part of modern civilization.

(v) Fifthly, he wanted to contribute towards the reconciliation of Indians and British.

(vi) Finally, Gandhiji believed that through *HS*, he would be able to give Indians a practical philosophy, and an updated conception of '*dharma*'.

Thus, to repeat, Gandhiji wrote *HS* because his heart was full, and he could not restrain himself from writing. The book is a gist of his thinking over several years. It is not a mere political book. Though he has used the language of politics, he has really tried to offer a 'glimpse of dharma'. For Gandhiji, *HS* means a rule of *dharma* or *Ramaraj* and he often used the word *Ramarajya* for Swaraj. He was provoked to pen down his approach to India's freedom following his interaction with fiery revolutionaries who struggled for India's political freedom, but whose approach implied India's continuous bondage in modern, Western, industrial civilization.

To put it differently, one of the chief motives behind writing *HS* was to question and condemn strongly modern civilization. *HS* has been written to show that the Indian people are following a suicidal path by thinking that the shortcomings of modern civilization are due to the faults of the English people and not due to the inherent character of the modern civilization. The central concern and theme of *HS* is to uproot the modern civilization and to offer the outline of the alternative civilization. Gandhiji wanted to transmit his mighty message of ahimsa to the rest of the world through *HS*. It was written in order to demonstrate the sublimity of satyagraha. The greatest motive behind writing *HS* was to serve our country, to find out the truth and to follow it. The central concern of *HS* is to convey that civilization is a disease, but it is a curable disease. It seeks to impress upon the people of India that they would be following a suicidal path if they adopt modern civilization and that they should revert back to their own glorious civilization.

The initial reception of *HS* was hostile. It became widely known in India only in 1919. It continued to be under scathing or blistering attack in India by the leftists and the rightists. In contrast, the reception in the USA was warm and enthusiastic. The first serious appraisal of *HS* by scholars occurred in 1938, and their reception for the book ranged from enthusiasm to (respectful) criticism.

Hind Swaraj has journeyed from proscription to prescription. The British Government in India had proscribed the book in 1910, on the ground, that it was seditious. Subsequently, the ban on the book was lifted and now it is one of the prescribed texts in the Cambridge University for post-graduate political science students.

If we are to grasp firmly the message and relevance of *HS*, we should always remember its symbolic, emblematic, and metaphorical approach to discourse. As in the case of the Mahabharata, Srimad Bhagawata, Ramayana, etc., in the case of *Hind Swaraj* also, many people take an antagonistic view of the book because they forget that when Gandhiji criticized certain developments, institutions, and events, he condemning something deeper. Apparently, it does appear crazy to criticize the railways, but if one remembers that, apart from their harmful impact the railways represent the modern system of transport and communication, one begins to see the validity of criticism of a railways by Gandhiji. Gandhiji's critique of the railways is equally relevant and valid today when pitted against cell phones, tele-communication, jet aeroplanes, internet, and so on. It may be noted that Gandhiji has criticized the modern system of medicine through hospitals; the modern system of justice through lawyers, courts, and judges; the modern system of production through machinery; the modern system of education through universities; and the modern state through Parliament, and so on. *Hind Swaraj* tries to alert the Indian people that they would be making a blunder if they did not reject modernism and the Western world-view. *HS* advises Indian people against lapping up Western institutions, systems and their world-view uncritically, avidly, and adoringly.

In adopting a symbolic approach, Gandhiji was taking a great risk of being misunderstood, being misinterpreted, being misguided. But he did take that risk because he wanted to reach the masses. Simplicity in everything was the hallmark of Gandhiji's approach.

HS is a book whose reading may so completely disorient and unsettle some readers that they may call the book a big mistake, and may demand its withdrawal from circulation at once. This is exactly what happened in the case of G.K. Gokhale, the political 'guru' of Gandhiji. After reading *HS*, Gokhale was so upset that he wanted the book to be withdrawn from circulation at once. But Gandhiji was so certain and confident of his vision, had such a remarkable courage of conviction that he responded to Gokhale's criticism by changing not more than one adjective in later editions. Gandhiji's convictions in *HS* grew with the passage of time, and he did not think it necessary to change more than one word even in 1940s from what he had written in 1909.

HS is a book which is not only a tract for the time-being; it is also a treatise on modern politics for long-term use. It is the product of Gandhiji's contemplation and rich, varied experience of life which he gathered from historical and intellectual contexts. Indian philosophical thought enabled Gandhiji to integrate ideas which he gathered from the West. In his long introduction to the 1910 text of *HS*, Gandhiji has discussed the historical and intellectual context of (a) modern civilization, (b) the politics of South Africa, (c) the politics of expatriate Indians, (d) politics of the nationalist movement, (e) Western and Indian intellectual sources (see Parel, 1997, pp. i to xii).

After having presented some interesting facts about *HS*, we now turn to its contemporary evaluation which comprises both condemnatory and acclamatory characteristics. The book has received strong criticism from some thinkers, while it has received rich encomiums or highly laudatory testimonies in superlative terms from others. Gandhiji himself once said that he had produced an original work by writing HS. Of course, sometimes, under the influence of humility, he has also said, "I lay no claim to originality" (Parel, p. 10) in writing this book. We present below an unprecedently large number of statements, which we have culled and assembled from various sources because we believe that such statements are very much useful for understanding properly the message of *HS*. These statements are not to be taken as words of praise or otherwise. They contain truth, which is more important. Unfortunately, we could obtain the names of sayers or authors of only some of these statements, and, therefore, we have to present certain statements without the names of their authors. The readers are requested to bear with us. We think that it would have been too great a loss to the readers if we had not reproduced below certain statements about *HS* merely because we could not get the names of their authors. Our discretion has guided us in this context. Moreover, is it not true that what is said is more important than who has said it?

(A) Critical Statements

(i) The views expressed in the book are crude and hastily conceived, and, Gandhi himself would destroy the book after spending a year in India (G.K. Gokhale).

(ii) Gandhi was trying to put into practice the extreme

Christian theory of suffering through *HS* (Shyamaji Krishnawarma).

(iii) *HS* represents Christian piety and mere humanitarianism, and it is ignorant of class struggle (M.N. Roy).

(iv) *HS* is an unrealistic book (Jawahar Lal Nehru).

(v) Only a noble slave could have pronounced such doctrines as are contained in HS (Nirad C. Chaudhury).

(vi) *HS* is an anti-science, anti-machinery, anti-civilizational crude text.

(vii) *HS* is a backward looking book.

(viii) *HS* is a Conservative book.

(ix) *HS* expresses the fads and fancies of Gandhi.

(x) *HS* is too idealistic a book.

(xi) *HS* is an absurd book.

(xii) Gandhi went off the rails in *HS* and indulged in the emotions of a machine-smashing Luddite.

(xiii) *HS* is all a Ruskin-Tolstoyan rodomontade (boastful or bragging talk). It is as unreal as Rousseau's discourse.

(xiv) If Gandhiji had not achieved what (all) he did after he wrote it, *HS* might have been a forgotten text.

(xv) Gandhi's views on the railways are outlandish and they are of a person who is an inveterate enemy of any attempt to improve human lives.

(B) Statements of Encomium

(1) It would be appropriate to begin this section by briefly referring to Gandhiji's own evaluation of *HS*. Although *HS* was strongly criticized, Gandhiji was totally convinced about his analysis and stand or position presented in it. He believed that by writing *HS* he had written an original tract or treatise, and he always discussed the ideas and ideals in *HS* with a complete courage of conviction. However, as pointed out earlier, sometimes, humility made him say that he has made hardly any original contribution by writing HS.

He believed that *HS* was a *"total vision of life"*, or a *"whole theory of life"*, and it taught us *"the art of living"* and *"the art of loving"*.

He informed us that *HS* was written in order to

demonstrate the sublimity of satyagraha, and the book is a true measure of his faith in its efficacy.

He admitted that *HS* was an incredibly simple book; so simple as to be regarded as foolish. It is the work of a fool.

(2) *HS* is one of the *spiritual classics* of the world, and the greatest that has been written in modern times (J.M. Murry).

(3) *HS* is one of the best modern *handbooks of the real revolution* which must happen in us all, if we are to fulfill the creative purpose of life (High Fausset).

(4) *HS* contains ideas which would result in the beginning of a new world order. It is superior to Rousseau's social contract, and Das Capital of Karl Marx (Gerald Heard).

(5) Gandhi's case against the West in *HS* is quite strong. The book has a deep power to disturb (G.D.H. Cole).

(6) *HS* is an enormously powerful book and by its tremendous honesty forced me to search my own honesty (Irene Rathbone).

(7) The underlying message of *HS* is love (Claude Houghton).

(8) The merit of the book lies in its emphasis upon moral issues, and opposition to the pursuit of private wealth and power (Delisle Burns).

(9) Anyone who wishes to change the world would do well to study *HS* (Fredrick Soddy).

(10) Read *HS* if you love the human family and this earth which is our home. Read it if you wish to do your bit to halt man's mad rush (mad race) towards self-extinction (T.K. Mahadevan).

(11) *HS* is rather an incendiary Manifesto (Erik Erickson).

(12) *HS* is the most important book written after Tripitak (Samdok Ringpoche).

(13) *HS* occupies in the Gandhian story much the same place as Chapter IV of St. Mathew, or St. Luke in the *New Testament* (Swaminathan).

(14) *HS* is on par with the book, such as *The Spiritual Exercises* of St. Ignatius Loyola (Catlin).

(15) *HS* shares with Ramayana, Mahabharata, and *Meghdoot* the ability to cross boundaries, bridge distances, and integrate self and others. All of these books have usefulness

as a way of imagining, understanding, and acting for Swaraj of the nation and the self (Sitanshu, Y.).

(16) I have read *HS* with great interest for I consider the question dealt with (in it) to be of very great importance, not only for India, but for the whole humanity (Leo Tolstoy).

(17) *HS* depicts the clash of civilizations (Gavaskar, M.).

(18) *HS* is a performative text (Nigam, A.).

(19) *HS* is the most prophetic book of the 20th Century (Lunine, M.J.).

(20) *HS* is Gandhi's seminal work. It is the seed from which the tree of Gandhian thought has grown to its full stature (Parel, A.J.).

(21) *HS* is a very basic document for the study of Gandhi's thought (Chatterjee, M.).

(22) *HS* is Gandhi's confession of faith (Nanda).

(23) *HS* is a proclamation of ideological independence (Dalton).

(24) *HS* is an intensely spiritual and intensely practical book. It may be said that Gandhiji, through *HS*, has given Indians a practical philosophy, a new "Yuga Dharma" for the creation of sustainable moral civilization (Parel, A.J.).

(25) *HS* is a highly antagonistic book. It is all crusade and war. It defines the enemy in unmistakable terms; asks us to guard against it, propagates against it, boycotts it, and finally destroys it. It disturbs the status quo in every field, and individual and social life. The natural corollary of *HS* is non-co-operation, nay rejection of the extant arrangements or life style (Pattanayak, Kishen).

(26) *HS* is a Green Manifesto, Counter-Culture Manifesto, and Sarvodaya Manifesto.

(27) *HS* is a Counter-Civilizational discourse, a post-nation vision, and a radical Utopia.

(28) *HS* is an all-inclusive paradigm, and a dynamic model for spiritual development.

(29) *HS* teaches neither globalization nor nationalism. It is a model of 'Glocalization' i.e. a combination of universalism and localism, or universalism and swadeshi, or jai-jagat and gramaswaraj.

(30) *HS* is a post-modern, post-liberal, post-neo-liberal thought. It anticipated 'limits to growth', 'sustainable

development', and 'environmental and deep ecological' approaches.

(31) *HS* is a rebellion against Western culture: It is an utter condemnation of the modern civilization.

(32) *HS* expresses Gandhi as a prophet of a new civilization and a new society.

(33) HS is a penetrating, compelling, unsettling book. Gandhi does not condemn only certain aspects, faults, and defects of modern civilization but also condemns and rejects its very foundation and the world-view.

(34) *HS* has the effect of decolonizing the reader. It is a rare book. It rejects, dismantles prefabricated, borrowed intellectual and cultural horizons. It makes most of our referential terminology and conceptual frames inadequate and non-functional.

(35) A good reading of *HS* can completely disorient, unsettle some readers so much so that they may call the book a big mistake, and that the book should be put out of circulation.

(36) *HS* coolly subjects to scrutiny by long-held new or old, traditional or modern notions about human civilization and asks the reader to discard them for swaraj.

(37) *HS* is a written sermon on the sea.

(38) *HS* combines Bhagavad Gita and Das Capital.

(39) *HS* has a depth of the ocean and the height of the Himalaya.

(40) The unit of Gandhi's protest is civilization, and not mere state and market, or capitalism and communism.

(41) The *HS* model anticipated post-modernist thought; it is a post-modern model.

(42) *HS* is a seminal text in the intellectual history of modern India.

(43) *HS* is a paradigm and an agenda for 21st century global swaraj.

(44) *HS* was written under a profound experience of illumination.

(45) *HS* is the manifestation of Gandhi's crystal-clear mind (Vinoba).

V

Meaning of Hind and Swaraj

The two terms namely, 'Hind' and 'Swaraj' need to be explained because the author of *HS* has not closely defined them in any one place in the book. Although Chapter 4 in the book is titled as 'What is Swaraj', in all humility, we may point out that the said Chapter 4 is not very useful in understanding 'What is Swaraj'? The meaning of Swaraj would unfold to the reader as he reads chapter after chapter in *HS*.

Does Hind in *Hind Swaraj* refer to India only? Certainly not. Although as an Indian, swaraj of India was of first and special interest and concern to him, as the seeker of Sarvodaya (upliftment of all) MKG must certainly have been interested in the freedom or liberty of all nations and the whole of humanity.

Being a critique of modern civilization, *HS* is relevant for all countries and societies. Its message is certainly that India should follow a different path than the one followed by the West and that she should be decolonized. But it also asks the West to "rethink about its own development", or to seek its own "redevelopment", and to free itself from "internal or developmental colonization". The universality of the message of the book should not be doubted, undermined, overlooked, and lost sight of; HS is a post-nation vision, it is a decidedly far more comprehensive world-view than a 'Hindu Swaraj' or a 'Hindu Raj'. *HS* argues for liberty, autonomy, freedom of not only India but also of nation and every man.

It has been rightly pointed out that HS challenges not only the British colonial power in its historical specificity, but also any power, particularly the one that exploits societies. The relevance of *HS* lies beyond Hind. Similarly, being a post-national paradigm, its relevance also lies beyond any international colonial situation. *HS* is relevant as much internationally and inter-socially as intranationally and intra-socially. Due to its ability and usefulness to cross boundaries like Indian Epics, the swaraj that *HS* offers is not only for Hind; the offer is universal and place-free (Sitanshu, 2008, p. 267). The book, therefore, may perhaps be retitled as '*Global Swaraj*'. At the same time, it can also be said that the word Hind might have been used by Gandhiji to indicate that he was arguing in the book in favour of the Indian or Asiatic world-view.

Before we delve deeper into the meaning of swaraj, let us note and remember the grand feature of Gandhian thinking namely Gandhiji's ability to take the *ideational quantum leap* while coining and using various words. 'Swaraj' is such a term, other such terms being development, swadeshi, trusteeship, socialism, revolution, etc. The terms used by him have often been hijacked by people, even adversaries, to serve their political, ideological, narrow vested interests, the terms notably gramsabha, panchayat raj, and decentralization.

The term 'swaraj' has not been used by Gandhiji alone; it has been used earlier and elsewhere also. For example, Shivaji, a great warrior who lived in 17th century Maharashtra, and who established or founded a kingdom (or enlightened kingship) in India, very often used the expression "Hindavi Swaraj". Swami Dayananda had also often used the term Swaraj in the 19th Century. B.G. Tilak's clarion call, "Swaraj is my birthright and I will definitely obtain it," is known to everybody throughout India. V.D. Savarkar had also used it in his book, the *Indian War of Independence: 1857*. But in all these uses, the target was primarily political independence from the British rule. Till the arrival of Gandhiji on the scene, the term 'Swaraj' was used in a limited or narrow sense. Even the term, 'Poorna Swaraj' used in the 'Complete Independence Resolution' passed by the INC at its Lahore session in December 1929, did not include the meaning which Gandhiji had in mind. Gandhiji alone appears to have used the term 'Swaraj' in its widest and deepest sense.

The terms expressing different meanings of Swaraj can be arranged in the ascending order i.e. from the term with the narrowest meaning to the one with the deepest meaning. The discussion on *HS* suggests the following order: expulsion of alien rulers, political independence, parliamentary swaraj, poorna swaraj, i.e. self-rule or Home Rule, grama-swaraj, Hind swaraj, and global swaraj.

Gandhiji has explained the meaning of swaraj in two stages. First, by telling what swaraj is not. Second, by explaining multifarious nuances of what swaraj is, and what swaraj is not:

(a) Mere physical expulsion of the Britishers from India is neither the necessary nor the sufficient condition of Swaraj. A very good example of how mere political freedom does not necessarily result in democracy and Swaraj is the mindless, autocratic, despotic repression of citizens' constitutional rights such as freedom of assembly, freedom of speech, freedom to strike work by the Government of India against Anna Hazare and his colleagues, or Ramdeo Baba in July-August 2011. The Emergency imposed by the Government of India in 1975, also proves the same point.
(b) Expulsion of the British but keeping their political, military, and economic institutions.
(c) Keeping English rule (in its nature) without English people. In other words, to have proverbial tiger's nature but not the tiger.
(d) Make India English. India would then be Englishstan and not Hindustan.

What then is Swaraj? One of the striking or unique features of the Gandhian approach to Swaraj is the primacy, priority given to the individual and the need for his mental and spiritual progress for founding Swaraj. In Gandhian thought, Swaraj belongs more to matters internal than matters external. Thus, swaraj and its namesakes or 'conceptsakes' such as Home Rule, Self-Rule, grama-swaraj, parliamentary swaraj, global swaraj, and "Gandhi Swaraj" mean inner freedom or positive freedom. As Gandhiji has often said, "Without Swaraj as self-rule, Swaraj as self-government would degenerate into the State oppression even in liberal societies."

Swaraj no doubt means political independence or the end of alien rule or the arrival of home rule. But more than that it means self-control, self restraint, self-rule, mastery over body, senses, emotions, passions, emancipation from the power or hold over mind and desires. To use the language of the *'shastras'*, Swaraj means becoming *'muktaha'* or *'atimuktaha'* which means attaining *'moksha'* while living on this earth, or to attain transcendence of mind, or to become *'amanha'*. It is instructive to note that the concept of swaraj has become progressively subtler, deeper, wider, and taller, ascending from political freedom to mental and spiritual freedom i.e. from external to internal freedom or liberty. From this perspective, swaraj is experiential i.e. it is something that has to be experienced internally, giving rise to an internal moral transformation of the individual. One can never know what is swaraj merely through armchair speculations.

To restate, before *HS*, swaraj meant only political freedom, and it was regarded as the right of the people. After *HS*, swaraj means self-control and it is a duty rather than a right. In swaraj, the state and all its functionaries work as trustees. Gandhiji has tried to explain the meaning of swaraj in Chapter 4 on 'What is Swaraj'? However, he has discussed what Swaraj is not rather than what Swaraj is in this chapter. The explanation of what is swaraj is spread over the entire book. His idea of Swaraj is very different from the widely held view. Generally, swaraj is meant to convey driving away the English from India. The physical expulsion of the English is regarded necessary and sufficient condition for Swaraj ordinarily. Generally, it was thought that it was enough for swaraj if the British left India; even if English institutions continued to remain in India, but if the British left, Swaraj was obtained as per general view. According to Gandhiji, India would not be free if British institutions remained in but the British left India.

It may help to get a good and clear understanding of the meaning of Swaraj if one notes that in Gandhiji's mind Swaraj and *Ramaraj* are one and the same things. In both, there is a rule of *'dharma'*, and moral authority and moral power is the basic foundations of the sovereignty of the people. Swaraj, like Ramaraj is a kingdom of righteousness, a divine raj, a Kingdom of God. It is not the *'Hindu Raj'*. Gandhiji often used the words Swaraj and *Ramaraj* interchangeably. He has said that HS was addressed to the illiterate Indian masses. Now, if one were to be successful and effective in conveying to these masses the meaning of swaraj, the best way had to be to tell them that Swaraj was like *Ramaraj*, or Swaraj is *Ramaraj*.

The letter Gandhiji wrote on April 2, 1910, to his nephew, Maganlal Gandhi, clearly shows that Gandhiji regarded internal freedom to be more valuable than the external freedom. He said, "Please do not carry unnecessarily on your head the burden of emancipating India. Emancipate yourself. Even that burden is very great. Apply everything to yourself. Nobility of soul consists in realizing that you, yourself, are India. In your emancipation is the emancipation of India. All else is make-believe" (See Reference in Parel, 1997, p. 96). Swaraj, like honesty, begins at home.

The idea of Swaraj as self-rule, self-governance occurs in the Mahabharata and in the writings of Swami Vivekananda also. Swamiji in one of his lectures has said, "If a country is inhabited by men and women who have killed all selfishness, who live and work to acquire wisdom and the power of love, who are spiritual and moral and good, that country is above and beyond all law. Police and military are not necessary to govern them" (Vivekananda, 1969, pp. 48-49).

In the Mahabharat, broadly, it is said by the Sage Vyasa that in Swaraj and ideal society, there is no state, king, punishment, and executor. The people protect each other by observing dharma. Thus,

> *Naivam rajyam Na raja assit Na dando Na cha dandikaha* |
> *Dharme naivam praja Sarvam rakshanti Sma Parasparam*

It is interesting to note that the idea and ideal of Statelessness or "withering away of the State" or "*Shasan-mukti*" are not the monopoly of Marx or communists. The Indian people have been inspired by this ideal of statelessness since ancient times.

Is the idea or the goal of this type of Swaraj practicable? It appears that perhaps Gandhiji himself had some doubt on this subject. He had two objectives while writing HS. One the long-term objective of presenting a picture, a model, a blue-print of a pure, highly idealistic social order enjoying *poorna* or *total swaraj* or *Ramaraj* or the rule of *dharma* and *swadharma*. But the 'practical idealist' as he was, he knew that in the short-run it was perhaps not possible for the most of ordinary people or the masses to live by the value system of the *poorna swaraj*. He did say that he knew that India was not yet ripe or prepared for a complete self-rule. Therefore, he put forth the aim of "parliamentary swaraj in accordance with the wishes of the people of India" which can be achieved even in the short run. He further informed us that his corporate activity was devoted to achieving this goal. Thus, he has stated, "I am individually working for self-rule, but today my corporate activity is undoubtedly dedicated to the attainment of parliamentary swaraj in accordance with the wishes of people in India".

Unfortunately, this is a rather weak, vague, and worrisome point in Gandhiji's analysis of Swaraj, and it has remained unexplained in HS. What could be the exact meaning of "parliamentary swaraj in accordance with the wishes of the people of India"? Gandhiji has not explained the meaning and nature of the system of "parliamentary swaraj" anywhere in *HS* (and anywhere in his other writings). Given Gandhiji's trenchant criticism of the British parliamentary system, his goal of 'parliamentary swaraj' appears to be confusing and contradictory. Similarly, "his passion for loyalty to the British constitution" remains an enigma for the same reason. It is difficult to reconcile the ideas of parliamentary swaraj, loyalty to British constitution, and the criticism of the British parliament.

The way out of this tangle may perhaps be to say that "Parliamentary Swaraj" is not the same thing as present form of 'parliamentary system'. While the latter 'does not work in accordance with the wishes of the people', the former would do so. Thus, the character of the former is different from that of the latter. The latter form parliamentary swaraj may be expected to be an advance over the parliamentary system. One wishes that Gandhiji had avoided soaring up and up in defining swaraj almost to the level of 'Moksha' and then descended to define swaraj as parliamentary swaraj. In defining swaraj as parliamentary swaraj, Gandhiji perhaps allowed the purity and ascension of the concept of swaraj to be compromised.

One finds that the attempt has been made to explain the meaning of Swaraj by answering four related questions, *viz.*, what is swaraj? What are the obstacles to swaraj? What is the relationship between swaraj and modern civilization? What is the way to swaraj? The most fundamental and crucial meaning of swaraj is self-control. Swaraj is self-realization. There can be no true Home-Rule or Self-Government without self-rule or self-control. The most formidable and visible obstacle to Swaraj is not British rule because even if the British left or they were expelled from India since their institutions remained, it would not be a true swaraj. As long as India remains under the sway of modern Western civilization, she cannot be said to have obtained self-rule or self-control which is the master key to swaraj. The way to swaraj is to make proper use of non-violence by both individuals and the society. If India adopted the doctrine of love as an active part of her religion and politics, Swaraj would descend upon India from heaven. The way to swaraj is Satyagraha or to be satyagrahi, i.e. non-violent in thought, word, and deed and to nurture values of celibacy, voluntary poverty, truthfulness, and fearlessness (Mathai, 2009, pp. 154-157).

Swaraj is overcoming self-will, self-love, and self-interest, and all these equally for both the individual as well as the society. It has been a great contribution of Gandhiji's that whatever has been applicable to the individual has been made applicable to society by him. This is true in the case of spirituality also. One school of thought in India has always argued that religion, spirituality are personal matters (affair). They are for the salvation, "mukti" of the individual and society has little to do with it. Gandhiji proved the falsity of such a philosophy: he made spirituality a concern of both the individual and social domains. He socialized and spiritualized the individual and the society.

If it is so, a moment of contemplation will reveal that in HS, the meaning of Swaraj does extend to 'Moksha' (release, liberation) or 'mukti' (liberation) or self-knowledge (aatmadarshan) or manifestation of the soul (aatma sakshatkar) at both the individual and social levels. The collective spiritual practices (samuhik sadhana) can result in collective liberation (samuhic mukti). Collective 'sadhana' is that 'sadhana' in which the whole collectivity or the whole society tries to transcend the mind; it make effort to reach a state of 'beyond the mind', and intaking so does transcend the mind.

This is the need of today because only my liberation is a kind of spiritual individualism. After successful collective 'sadhana', a society attains collective 'moksha'.

The point bears repetition that for Gandhiji (and his disciples like Vinoba) there is no strict divide, separation, wall between the individual and social or collective. Gandhiji insisted that the satyagraha method should not remain confined to individual, the society. Also one should be able to use it effectively. With this approach, they worked for social development and reforms, constructive works, reestablishment of Indian civilization and culture and social order. They were actively involved in mundane, worldly, political activities, but their sight was always set on spirituality and 'Moksha' for both the individual and the society. They had the quest for filling the whole universe with joy, happiness, and peace. In the words of Dnyaneshwar (12th Century saint-poet of Maharashtra) their goal was to make the whole universe joyful (*avaghachi sansar sukhacha Karin, aanande bharin tinhi lok*).

In modern times, individualism has increased but dependence psychology also has increased, while the spirit of freedom has declined. Modern times are also times for flattery, sycophancy, servility, slavishness, fawning, cringing nature, obsequiousness all of which reflect a loss of freedom in its subtle nuances. In both religions and temporal domains, man has been taught that his deliverance does not depend on his own 'purushartha', it depends on obeying, serving the temporal and religious authorities. Gandhiji, through his ideas of decentralization, self-rule, production by masses, public participation, development from below tried to reduce dependence and promote swaraj of the people. *HS* challenges the hegemony of the State, organized religion and life-long he exerted himself to liberate, free man from slavery, serfdom, thralldom of the capital, state, and religion.

In summation, swaraj means the following:

1) It is swaraj when we learn to rule ourselves. It means self-control, self-restraint, self-discipline, self-realisation, control over desires, emotions, sentiments, passions; mastery over one's body, mind, intellect, senses. The outward struggle for swaraj is at once an inner struggle towards truth, self-realisation or "*moksha*". Gandhiji's approach to defining swaraj makes swaraj and *moksha* nearly synonymous. Swaraj means spirituals freedom. The socio-economic political goal and spiritual goal become one. This is the widest sense in which term swaraj has ever been used by anyone anywhere. Thus, swaraj means "swashasan" or "atmanushasan" or "atmashasan".
2) Political, economic, social, cultural and moral freedom, and freedom from alien rule.
3) Independence from modern, industrial, Western material civilization and culture. Respiritualisation of India and resumption by her of role of world teacher and guide.

4) Swaraj is the quest for self-improvement and not merely self-government.
5) The key to swaraj is that human beings realize that it is unmanly to obey laws that are unjust. If this happens, no man's tyranny will enslave human beings.
6) Swaraj is real and deeper freedom. It involves political independence, economic independence, social independence, and moral independence. Swaraj comes not by the acquisition of authority by a few but by the acquisition of capacity by all to resist authority when it is abused. Swaraj exists when new life is given to dumb millions living in villages (village swaraj), when the cow is not killed, and when all welfare schemes of the state are abolished.

VI
Civilization and Swaraj

As Gandhiji has said, the central concern of *HS* is to uproot the modern Western civilization. One of the chief motives behind writing *HS* was to strongly question and condemn modern civilization, and this forms the broad historical context of *HS*. Gandhiji's critique of modern civilization is one of the main contributions to modern political thought. Although Gandhiji rejected most of the things of modern civilization, he also welcomed certain contributions of modern civilization, *viz.*, civil liberty, equality, rights, prospects of economic improvement, liberation of women, and religious toleration. It is, therefore, necessary to discuss below matters civilizational in relation to swaraj.

According to the concise Oxford Dictionary, civilization means those peoples in the world who have crossed the primitive and barbarious stage of society, and who have attained an advanced stage of social development. The term 'modern' means things which are of the present or recent times, and which are not simple. For example, modern history begins from the end of middle ages. Modern English is English from the year 1500 AD. Modernism refers to modern ideas or methods. Modernize means to adapt to or adopt modern needs or habits, ways, and views. Gandhiji has defined civilization as that mode of conduct which points out to man the path of duty.

Various civilizations are known to have existed on this earth during different periods of human history. For example, Oriental and Occidental civilizations; Ancient and Modern civilizations; Roman and Greek civilizations, and so on. Most of these civilizations, except the civilizations like the ancient Indian civilization, came into existence, prospered for some time, and then they collapsed and vanished. Gandhiji, in his *HS*, has rightly pointed out that most of the countries in the world experienced pitiable conditions during the past two or three centuries (18th, 19th, 20th centuries). In his view, the basic cause of this has been the choice of modern civilization by these countries, and not so much the faults of the people residing therein.

In order to explain this point, it is necessary to know Gandhiji's views on the nature, consequences, characteristics, ailments and cure of modern civilization which form the broad historical context of *HS*.

According to Gandhiji, civilization is a disease, but it is a curable one. Modern civilization with its progress has been questioned; many doubts and objections about its validity have been raised by great men like Tolstoy, Ruskin, Romain Rolland, Toynbee, etc. Gandhiji tops the list of contestants of modern civilization. Gandhiji's critique of modern civilization has been the most scathing, and his alternative to it has been the most thorough and comprehensive (Rudolph, p. 421).

One of the great positive features of Gandhiji's thought is its balanced nature. Among Western civilizations (WC), modern civilization (MC), and Western modern civilization (WMC), his condemnation was reserved for modern civilization or western modern civilization because he recognized that a part of WC is a good and healthy part. He contested the values and moral and practical validity of western modern civilization.

The modern civilization is a young civilization (200-300 years old) and it is amazing that in such a short period of time, it has amassed a legion of vices and shortcomings, and has acquired a horrendous character. People in modern civilization have been reduced to a state of cultural anarchy. Most of the people in modern civilization are 'intoxicated'. Gandhiji has called modern civilization a "kingdom of Satan", and an ancient civilization a "kingdom of God". The "spirit" of modern civilization is evil. It is a greedy, myopic, hedonistic civilization.

Modern civilization is a cancerous pathological civilization; it is an "illusory structure" and a bad "dream". It is a self-destructive civilization with compulsive suicidal propensity. Modern civilization is an inhuman and monstrous civilization (Parel, pp. 16-38). It is "truly a God of war" and a genuine irreligion. Those who live in it appear to be half mad; they lack real strength and courage. Modern civilization is a Black Age (Parel, pp. 34-38). It makes bodily welfare or bodily happiness the object of life. People are enslaved by the temptation of money and luxuries that money can buy.

Modern civilization takes note neither of morality nor of religion; it teaches immorality in the name of morality. It seeks to increase bodily comforts and fails miserably in even doing so (Parel, 1997, pp. 16-38).

The western modern civilization has been strongly criticized by the wise and saintly men of the West also. A leading critic in this context has been the French Litterateur, Romain Rolland. He has denounced the West in very clear and unequivocal terms. He believed that Europe never had any hero of the stature and caliber of the titanic soul of India. The European mind and temperament have been deformed, and they are no longer aware of the incalculable forces of the soul. Europe was treading a suicidal and tragic path and that she was threatened to be crushed by the forces of violence with no hope of recovery (For extended description, see Bhole (4), pp. 59-60). A few more hallmarks of modern civilization are as given below:

1. The pursuit of stark materialism.
2. The physical side of life overstressed compared to the ethical, moral, spiritual, religious side.
3. Primacy to pleasure pursuit, enjoyment, merry-making, Epicureanism, myopic hedonism, and little importance to sacrifice, service and suffering.
4. Individual and collective violence is rampant; the "will to live" of other beings is not respected; and there is a wanton, wholesale destruction of all life on this planet. Modern civilization has been the most violent civilization so far.
5. Life-corroding, cut-throat competition (rat race) exists and it leads to exploitation and domination.
6. Belief in '*might is right*', and the "*survival of the fittest*".
7. Annihilation of time and space; the obsession with speed; ceaseless, incessant activity which results in the absence of a real or true leisure.
8. Suffers from continuous discontent, unrest, conflicts; lacks "culture of peace and non-violence", violence addiction.
9. Degenerated into "physical and intellectual voluptuousness".

10. Anthropo-centric, self-interest-centric, self-centric. Lacks respect, compassion, and love for nature and other beings.
11. Obsession, worship of machine, mechanization, automation, and modern technology-enthusiasm and technology optimism.
12. Prevalence of militarism in international politics; industrialism, urbanism, and gigantism in the world economy; alienated and aggressive relations with the nature; and exploitative and dehumanizing relations with others.
13. Euro- and USA-centrism, and State- and Market-centrism.
14. Legitimization of economic growth and increasing global poverty, plundering and degrading the environment, and incipient biological collapse and ecocide.
15. The culture of terror is all-pervasive.
16. Modern civilization is like a terrible wolf; it is irreligious, satanic, monstrous, cursed, wretched, self-destructive, suicidal, illusory, dehumanized, alienated; it is Kaliyuga.
17. The modern man has elongated his life-span but he has brought about the regress in the goal of life, and a decline in health, physical, mental, emotional. He now appears to have a long life only for earning and spending more money. Modern civilization has created a mad, mad, mad world.
18. The Modern civilization has been described as disoriented, endangered, wounded, dying, satanic civilization.

The mode of living in modern civilization is devoid of the destiny of man (which is self-realization) and the motivation for universal solidarity. It is important to know that all human beings are connected by their common destiny which, as said above, is rediscovery of one's own self, total contentment, total self-fulfillment, or self-realization. However, modern material civilization has no teleological purpose; it is without the concept of common destiny of man. It is obsessed with the physical or gross, and believes in "bigger the better", "more the better" which is reflected, for example, in the love for giganticism, highly stilted, loud, noisy, expensive religious and other celebrations and functions.

The newer and newer diseases like HIV and cow fever are the

result of modern civilization and "affluenza". The modern civilization is characterized by what the psychologist Eric Fromm has called "pathology of normalcy". Modern civilization is a cruel, satanic, insane civilization as reflected in many examples two or three of which are: (a) The land is kept uncultivated even by giving subsidies so that prices do not decline, but it does not matter if millions go hungry, die of hunger. (b) Under "operation Flood" or "white revolution" in India, the milk is actually, literally poured into the sea so that milk-prices do not decline, but it does not matter if millions of children and even adults are suffering from malnutrition and diseases caused by it. (c) In 1985, European Economic Community killed four million dairy cows so that milk prices would not decline. (d) In the middle of the 1990s, the millions of cows were slaughtered and disposed of in England because they developed some unknown, new disease.

In Chapter XIII, we have referred to seven deadly sins which Gandhiji had asked the people to avoid. The modern civilization has given birth to two more following deadly sins: First, the failure to regard land as mother, and agriculture as a way of life. Second, to hold that literacy or formal education is a great virtue and the good society depends on literate people.

One of the worst realities of modern civilization is that it squanders mind-boggling sums on arms and armaments and on advertising every year. Modern civilization believes that what is economic is also moral, ethical, spiritual. Modern civilization is obsessed with creation of wealth out of the thin air, *viz.*, market capitalization on the share market, and creation of "wealth under the wheels."

The nature of modern civilization as discussed above clearly shows that modern civilization is anti-Swaraj. If we want to create Swaraj, it is imperative to dismantle, wind up modern civilization.

The Modernity has the quest for plurality, the ancients had the quest for unity. Modernity believes that world perfection can occur without individual perfection but this is not true. Civilized, modern man has walked and left deserts in his footsteps. Modern development has proceeded leaving behind scorched, parched, desertified, devastated, desolate land. The modern dominant belief is that the soundest foundation of peace is universal material prosperity or universal mass affluence. Modern industrialized economy is driven or propelled by a frenzy of greed and orgy of envy. Myopic hedonism and consumerism characterize it very well. The motivational foundation of modern civilization comprises, self-interest, economism, greed, envy, and the lust for power.

If modern civilization is a curse, if it is satanic, if it has the worst pathology, has humanity chosen it as an alternative paradigm? Why has it sustained and survived, and why have the overwhelming majority of people in the world continued to embrace it?

This is so because, as indicated earlier, it has a certain good side also. As Wyberg, a theosophist has written in his letter (dated May 3, 1910) to Gandhiji, "European civilization has many defects and I agree with many of your criticisms, but I do not believe that it is the Kingdom of Satan or it ought to be abolished. It appears to me a necessary step in the evolution of mankind ... while I recognize that the highest ideals of India are in advance of this civilization, yet I think also that the bulk of the Indian population requires to be roused by the lash of competition and the other material and sensuous as well as intellectual stimuli which 'civilization' (MC) supplies. The Western ideals are necessary for India, not to supersede but to modify and develop her own culture. The civilization (MC) is both necessary and useful, if it grows naturally and is not forced and it cannot be avoided" (Parel, pp. 140-141).

Gandhiji did not agree with this viewpoint. In his reply to Wybergh (dated May 10, 1910) Gandhiji wrote that it may be possible to show that some of modern civilization's features are good, but if we examined its tendencies in the scale of ethics, it would be difficult to exonerate modern civilization. Gandhi informed Wybergh "that I have tested the life which modern civilization has to give, as also that of the ancient civilization, and I cannot help most strongly contesting the idea that the Indian population requires to be roused by the lash of competition. I cannot admit that these will add a single inch to its moral stature (Parel, pp. 145-146).

The Indian public has ignored the advice as well as the warning given by Gandhiji and Swami Vivekananda. The Indian population has done this at its own risk. Developments in India during the past century show that consequent to embracing the modern civilization, India has gained cowries and lost the gold, and this should be regarded as the most pathetic development.

India was warned that if she chooses Western civilization, she is likely to face another period of slavery. The state of the Indian nation and Indian society today is extremely worrisome in terms of higher level of criteria or indicators. This is because India's elite has never recovered from their colonial hangover. At the official level, India did not adopt or choose HS paradigm. India is still a country which is dominated by foreign thinking. The native elite still admires and apes the ways of the West. India still follows the Western economic thinking. When socialism was in fashion, Indian leadership, particularly Nehru, had rejected the Gandhian path. The elite who dominate modern India believe that all that is good comes from the West. The theory and evidence show that this is a wrong thing to do because the West itself does not have answers to poverty and the Western path increases poverty and instability.

In the recent past, there has been a discussion on the clash of civilizations. It appears that there is a great confusion in the minds of many in this connection. In this discussion, the failure of communism in the former Soviet Union and Eastern Europe is taken to be a superiority of the capitalism. Here capitalism and communism are posed as different civilizations which is a wrong thing to do. Both capitalism and communism belong to the same civilization namely Modern Civilization.

VII
Towards Swaraj through Counter-Civilization and Counter-Culture

After having delineated the nature of modern civilization which has come in the way of progress towards Swaraj, we now discuss the contours, the features, hallmarks of the alternative or 'true civilization'. Let it be recalled that Swaraj requires independence from the modern, industrial, Western material civilization and culture. Gandhiji has over a lifetime of thinking and practice evolved a moral and practical alternative to modern civilization, alternative which has come to be known as counter-civilization and counter-culture.

The widespread and popular view has been that the evils of modern civilization in India have been due to the bad nature and faults of the English people, and not due to the (devilish) nature of modern civilization. Generally, Indians are not prepared to think that the modern civilization is the source of evils and vices. Due to this twin belief, the Indian populace is generally in favour of acceptance, adoption, and promotion of modern civilization in India. They are also keen to use modern methods of violence to drive away English from India.

HS has been written in order to show that the Indian people are following a suicidal path by thinking in this manner. Instead, if the Indians would revert to their ancient glorious civilization, they would successfully and effectively deal with the crisis of survival of mankind. Another benefit of such a choice would be that the English people would adopt Indian civilization and become Indianised, or alternatively, they would find that their work in India is over (Parel, 1997, p. 7).

HS is a blueprint for survival of the present civilization or the whole humanity and Nature. The wisdom it contains has been qwll-recognized as shown by a number of evaluatory and adulatory statements about HS given in Chapter IV of the present book. Recently, about 33 most distinguished and renowned British scientists issued a 'blueprint for survival' in which they stated that now it is only the Gandhian values and methods which can halt the inexorable march of human kind towards self-extinction.

HS does not advise the promotion of Indian industrialism. Gandhiji has warned that capitalism, colonialism, imperialism of the communist countries is to be as much shunned as that of capitalist countries because both the capitalist and communist countries are actually capitalist countries; while the former have private capitalism, the latter have State capitalism. Gandhiji never dreamt of India as a super power, nay, in fact, he was positively against India becoming a super power, and he was genuinely worried over this prospect. He did say in one place that God forbid that India should ever take to industrialism after the manner of the West. The economic imperialism of a single tiny island is today keeping the world in chains. If an entire nation of 300 million (1200 million now) took to similar economic exploitation, it would strip the world bare like, locusts.

As said earlier, the central concern and theme of *HS* is to uproot modern Western civilization, and to offer the picture or outline or content or profile or contours of the alternative civilization which would be a pure civilization with high moral stature. It does not seek to take humanity back to the ignorant *dark ages*. It teaches one to appreciate beauty in voluntary simplicity, voluntary poverty, and slowness. *HS*, paradigm is devoted to the task of restoring man to his true self or true state. *HS* also discusses the kind of governance or the "system of Government" India should have.

The alternative of this nature, fortunately for mankind, exists in the form of the ancient Indian civilization (AIC), and it should be accepted as a starting point of the next phase of India's growth. Thus, to repeat, Gandhiji in *HS* offers a concept of a normal society having its roots in India's past, and its values. *HS* is a critique and rejection of western modern civilization, and acceptance of ancient Indian civilization as the alternative world-view or paradigm with truth, non-violence, satyagraha, or soul-force, or Truth-force, or love-force, and compassion as the foundation, and rural civilization as its framework. In other words, the value foundation and organizational structure of the alternative civilization would be '*Ekadasha vratas*' and village republics, respectively.

Following Gandhiji, we now briefly discuss the nature, the contours, the content of the alternative world-view, or the alternative "true" or "pure" civilization.

Basically, Gandhiji believed that Indian civilization is by far the best civilization it has really very little to learn and follow from other civilizations, and it has to teach and guide and lead other civilizations. If India were an under-developed nation, it was so by her choice; she was capable of modern development, but chose to remain under-developed by her volition. India should never imitate or copy Western civilization. She should build on ancient civilizational wisdom, and lead the whole world in the right direction. If India makes the mistake of imitating the West, both the Indian civilization, and the whole world civilization will perish. It was by choice that India's ancestors disfavoured modern development, urban living, and modern machines and technology.

In this context, Gandhiji has given a resounding call to all Indians which is worth memorizing. He told the people that it behoves every lover of India to cling to the old Indian civilization like a child clings to the mother's breast. We must restore India to her pristine glory, and one effort that is very much required for this purpose is to drive out Western civilization from India. All else will then follow. Gandhiji has said, "O! ye lawyers, doctors, traders, caste off your alien acquisitions and attitudes. Stand in your own boots. Be Indian, feel Indian, live Indian, return to India's civilization".

At this juncture we need to elaborate on two points. One: why we should not imitate the west. Two: while reviving, resurrecting Indian civilization, should the 'Kshatriya varna' and functioning also be revived? In respect of the first question, Toynbee has said that since the second century B.C. to the end of the 15th century, the intellectual atmosphere in the West was passive and submissive. It took its mental furniture from the canonized authorities. It was an atmosphere of complete or blind faith in the church and religious authorities. Dogmatism, intolerance, fanaticism, irrational insistence about one's own religion, have been true of the most of Christianity, Islam, Judaism, and also of the modern (post-16th century) ideologies of Communism, Nationalism, Individualism, and Scientificism which supposedly came up to oppose religious dogmas. When this was the situation in the West, many great changes, intellectual and spiritual developments, were taking place in India. Only Indian civilization, the *Sanatana Dharma* was free from dogmas. They were promoting universalism, unity, Catholicism, openness. Hence, the future of mankind has to be reconstructed only on the basis of Hindu culture and the Hindu world-view.

The second question too is very important, and the answer to it is both yes and no. If *'kshatriya varna'*, *'Kshatra dharma'*, *'Kshatriya vritti'* would continue to involve taking up arms, killing people, using physical and mental violence, etc. The *'Kshatra dharma'* would not be a part of the revived Hindu civilization. On the other hand, if *'Kshatra dharma'* would come to mean the development of *'soul-force'*, *'love-force'* in the place of *'body-force'* or violence or *'brute force'*, it would be a part of the revived Indian civilization. The revival of Indian civilization and culture would involve renunciation, rejection of the use of arms and violence even by the *'Kshatriyas'*. The efforts to redefine *'dharma'* or *'swadharma'* of the fighting *'varna'* were made earlier also and they are stated symbolically. The three examples in this context are as follows: (a) One of the names of Krishna is 'Ranachoddas' because he ran away from battlefield when the Yadvas were fighting with each other. (b) The idol of Shree Vitthala in Pandherpur in Maharashtra symbolizes the renunciation of arms and wars and any violence. (c) The motive of Parashurama in making the earth sans any *'Kshatriya'* 21 times suggests that he wanted to redefine the duties of people belonging to different *'varnas'*.

The nature of 'True or pure' revived Indian civilization would broadly be defined by the following basic elements or attributes, or characteristics, or features or the fundamentals:

(i) Belief or faith in God, divinity, religion, spirituality.
(ii) Founding and functioning of the society on the basis of non-violence, love-force, or soul-force.
(iii) Individuals living with self-control or self-mastery.
(iv) Harmony exists between individual, society, Nature, and God.
(v) The society functions on the basis of a moral foundation or moral duty rather than individual rights, and altruism, rather than self-interest.

(vi) The social order works on the basis of values such as co-operation, co-existence, the survival of the weakest or the last man (unto this last) the preaceple of live and let live, and not on competition or survival of the fittest.

(vii) There is a desire for slowing down; high speed is frowned upon. The things change but only slowly, and not through 'future shock'.

(viii) Society runs on the basis of minimization of wants, contentment, a ceiling on desires, absence of myopic hedonism, and the absence of greed.

(ix) Bread labour is regarded as a great virtue.

(x) Such a social order would shun cities and urbanization. The centre and backbone of the economy of the new civilization would be natural, organic, non-commercial, self-consumptive agriculture. It would promote small-scale, home, village, cottage, tiny agro-industries. It would help to sustain the countryside.

(xi) There would be political, economic, social, administrative, industrial, decentralization. India would be a loose federation of self-sufficient, self-reliant, self-governing village republics.

(xii) There would be minimization of the state, whatever the state that needs to exist. It would be decentralized. The best government is the one which governs the least. and the community or society overshadows the state.

(xiii) The economy would largely be a 'closed economy', and it would celebrate the importance of Swadeshi. It would be an 'anti-globalization' social order.

(xiv) The 'true civilization' would have a grass roots, face-to-face, all-inclusive, village democracy. The direct, rather than representative democracy, fits well here. Decision making would be by full agreement or consensus, and not by a majority.

(xv) Socio-economic, political organizations would be interconnected in the manner of "oceanic circle" with Man at the Centre, and not in a pyramidical manner.

(xvi) Man and civilization are interdependent; if one grows, the other also grows.

(xvii) The alternative would help to free man from enslavement to money and to luxuries money can buy.

(xviii) Rural, village development would make the Arcadian civilization an '*effective defence measure*' and also a '*peace potential*', and not 'war potential'. This would lead to the creation of '*culture of peace*'.

(xix) In his alternative, Gandhiji has envisaged a healthy civilization and culture wherein there is progress with purity and development, with creativity which is expressed or reflected in nation-building or national reconstruction. There would be prosperity with peace of mind, and where progress would be measured by *happiness*. In this alternative, the aim is to establish moral values and not material values.

(xx) This civilization would reject private capitalism, state capitalism, industrialism, and materialism.

(xxi) The alternative Arcadian civilization would be a civilization for all or *Sarvodaya* with *antyodaya* first. There would be an establishment of *Gramaswaraj* and *Ramaraj*. The aim of the new civilization would be to bring back the age of truth (satayuga) and not the age of gold (swarnayuga). The new or true civilization would establish the truth or Swaraj or Gramaswaraj or Hind-Swaraj or Dharmarajya or Ramaraj or Rama sanskriti or Sarvodaya.

Decentralization has been mentioned above as one of the elements of the alternative civilization. It can be said that there are two models of decentralization, namely the Indian model and the Greek model of the Greek city civilization or City State or City Republics, and the Indian Arcadian civilization or village kingdoms or village republics, respectively. Among these alternatives, the Indian model has been said to be superior to the Greek model. The nearest approach to civilization based on non-violence was the erstwhile village republics in India. There was no real democracy in Athens and other city states in Greece. The Greek city states had a large slave population who had no political and other rights. It is only from a part of the population (from freemen) that the Assembly with a limited number of members was elected by rotation. The rulers were intolerant of any dissent. Plato and Socrates tried to find a way out of this sham democracy but could not succeed. *Socrates suggested the alternative of the rule of 'wise aristocracy', and Plato suggested the rule of a 'philosopher King'.*

Both had contempt for people, masses, or the 'crowd'. Therefore, the Gandhian model of Arcadian civilization alone is suitable and favourable at the present times.

As part of the building blocks of the Indian world-view, there are two points which may be elaborated at this juncture. One of them is the assumption about the nature of man, and the second one is the role of the state in the New Society. About the second point, Gandhiji's ultimate aim was the withering away of the State. But in the mean time, he recognized the need for a 'minimum state' as a practical goal. He wanted a social order that is free from government (shasan-mukta) and free from exploitation ('Shoshana-mukta'). It has been rightly argued that minimization of the State is a natural thing. The animal-kingdom and birds kingdom do not have any state; they do not need one. The 'minimum State' doctrine is in keeping with Nature. We need not think about the nature of the State if we live in a state of Nature. J.B.S. Haldane and Einstein have said that authority, any authority, any government is bad. As to the first point, quite often man behaves so cruelly that one wonders whether man is the most vile and venal. Therefore, Gandhiji taught man his humanity, while Vivekananda taught him his divinity.

Is Gandhiji being over patriotic or over nationalistic in offering ancient Indian civilization as the only alternative to the western modern civilization? It does not appear to be so. Almost all great minds in India also have taught, advised mankind that the ancient Indian civilization alone can be a guide, a teacher (Guru), and lighthouse for mankind. The names of a few of them are: Vivekananda, Sane Guruji, Tagore, Aurobindo, Vinoba, and Rajagopalachari. There is a remarkable concurrence in their and Gandhiji's thinking on the ancient Indian civilization as the only alternative world-view.

Among these wise and great minds, we give below the viewpoints of Vivekananda, Sane Guruji, and Tagore by way of illustration. It would be found that the strongest, the most vigorous, the most forceful, the most inspiring, and the most stirring case for ancient Indian civilization as the alternative has been presented by Vivekananda. After he returned to India from the USA after attending and conquering the Parliament of World Religions, he gave a clarion call 'To the youth of India' in which he explained certain vital matters (see Vivekananda, 1969, pp. 1-52).

For Vivekananda, "India is our most beloved, most sacred, most dear mother land, a *punya bhumi* (virtuous land) and a *land of Karma*" (land of action). It is a land where humanity has attained the highest towards gentleness, towards generosity, towards calmness, and towards purity. She is the land of spirituality, service, sacrifice, and renunciation. India is not hedonistic or epicurean. Her method is *"conquering through love"*. Her message is "spiritualise the material civilization of the world." Her other message is "That which exists is one, sages call it by various names." (*Ekam Sat Vipra Bahudaha Vadanti*); and 'unity in diversity' (Avibhaktaha vibhaktashu); and "Thou art that" (*Tata twamasi*). The idea of the oneness or unity of all, the idea of the impersonal, the idea of the eternal soul – all such grand ideas have come to us from the Vedanta.

In India, religion is the one and only occupation of life. Political greatness, economic power, military power has never been the mission of India. It never was, and it never is and it will never be India's gift to our race. India's gift is the 'Light spiritual'. India has never preached her thought with fire and sword. The Indian nation's life was and is religion. The little toleration that is in the world, the little sympathy that is yet in the world for religious thought is practically in India, and nowhere else.

Further, according to Vivekananda, civilizations have arisen in other parts of the world also, and great wonderful ideas have emanated from those civilizations. But all this has taken place there always with the blast of war trumpets. Each idea had to be soaked in a deluge of blood. Each idea (for example, communism) had to wade through the blood of millions of our fellow beings. In comparison, India has existed peacefully for thousands of years. India has never been a conquering race and it is, because of this, that India continues to live. India has not vanished through fall and collapse like ripples on the face of the water.

Explaining further as to why ancient Indian civilization still lives, Vivekananda has said that the secret lies in the fact that India is the motherland of philosophy, of spirituality, of ethics, and love. In India, the foundation, the backbone, the nation's life or life-center. the vitality, the life-principle, bedrock, the basis, the very soul has been religion and religion alone. Touch the Indian mind on religion, on spirituality, on God, on soul, on the infinite, on spiritual freedom, and that mind becomes live and agile. The characteristic of India is transcendentalism, the quest for going beyond the phenomenal, and being religious. We can certainly learn a few things from other civilizations, but we should at once reject anybody's advice "to apotheosize the material world into God."

Vivekananda has taught us that the message of ancient Indian civilization is that God alone lives, the soul alone lives, spirituality alone lives, hold on to it fast. He, like Gandhiji, has warned India that if she also gives up that spirituality, the result will be that in three generations, India and her civilization will be annihilated; it will be extinct.

For the survival of Indian and world civilizations, we must come to believe in spirituality, stick to it fast, never forsake it. It should never be forgotten that if we give up spirituality, leaving it aside to go after the material civilization of the West, the ancient Indian civilization also will be extinct within three generations, and there will be annihilation all round. Everything must be subordinated to that one ideal of life. Out of this, a wonderful, glorious future India will emerge, greater India than ever was; India rejuvenated, more glorious than she ever was.

It is the spiritual and ethical culture alone which can change wrong civilizational realities. The Westerners are also discovering that Indian philosophy, the ideals of ancient Indian civilization, Vedanta alone can help them to save their civilization. As Vedanta is perfectly rational, rationality and spirituality, rationality and religion go together in Vedanta. No civilization can long exist unless the grand idea that universal religion, universal tolerance enter into it. Ultimately, it is the change in the soul itself for the better that alone will cure the curse of civilization.

Vedanta and freedom (swaraj) are closely related. In all the literature voicing man's struggle towards freedom, Indian vedantic ideas come out prominently.

Is this not a one-sided vision? Have there been no faults in the Indian civilization? Why have there been so many reforms and reformers in India? If there are certain shortcomings, what is the best way to deal with them? Vivekananda has categorically argued that there has been too much ado about nothing as far as the so called Indian renaissance is concerned. Reforms are not enough; they have not achieved much because they have been too much denunciatory and imitative of the West. Most of our reform movements have been inconsiderate (thoughtless, rash).

Vivekananda did not want any momentary social reforms. His aim, goal, ideal was improvement of the mind, growth, expansion, development, and rational life.

Sane Guruji has the following to say about Indian civilization and culture (ICC). He is overwhelmed by the ICC, and his humble wish is that he should become a small worshipper of the ICC. He likes that ICC worships both heart and intellect, combines generosity and pure knowledge, and also combines knowledge and science with the heart. ICC is a living example of bringing together karma, knowledge, and devotion; it aims at using the body, mind, heart, and intellect for the service of mankind. ICC is about sympathy, vastness, truth-experiments; it has grown by partaking of whatever beautiful, sacred, and truth found in the world. ICC is inclusive. It works on the principle of "no opposition to anyone" (Sarvesham Avirodhen). It abhors any narrowness; one remembers the sky and the sea, light and lotus, sacrifice, self-control, service, love, knowledge, discrimination, and dispassion whenever a reference is made to the ICC. ICC means a journey from the finite to infinite, from darkness to light, and from difference to non-difference (from separateness to unity). ICC means bringing together all religions and all castes to establish unity among them (Sane Guruji, 1937, p. 6).

Vinoba, in his inimitable style has often said that America is only a baby of 300 years, while India is an ancient person of 10,000 years. There may be much to learn from Europe and America in science and technology, but they are in a state of infancy in the areas of social science, political science, science of health and healing (quoted by Kanti Shah, p. 77).

Since ancient Indian civilization is being suggested here as the alternative to Western civilization, as much clarity about the comparative nature of these civilizations as possible is welcome. Therefore, at the cost of some repetition, we give below their features in a comparative style.

Ancient Indian Civilization (Features)	*Western Modern Civilization (Features)*
1) Founded on Advaita philosophy	1) Founded on dualism
2) Believes that the world is a family	2) Believes that the world is a market.
3) Based on sacrifice	3) Based on enjoyment

(*Contd.*)

Ancient Indian Civilization (Features)	*Western Modern Civilization (Features)*
4) It is a civilization that gives	4) It is a taker civilization.
5) Gives importance to spirituality	5) Gives importance to science.
6) It is ancient	6) It is modern.
7) Based on equality	7) Based on inequality.
8) Gives importance to spiritual joy or happiness	8) Gives importance to material happiness or joy.
9) Stresses self-knowledge	9) Stresses knowledge of technology
10) Follows path of live and let live	10) Follows path of self-interest.
11) Society or social centered	11) Individual centered.
12) Respects Nature	12) Does not respect Nature.
13) Nurtures Nature	13) Exploits Nature.
14) Culture of permanence or eternity	14) Culture of non-permanence.
15) Individual, society, and Nature progress in it.	15) Individual, society, and Nature perish in it.
16) Its root is non-self-interest	16) Its root is self-interest.
17) Path of non-violence. Its ideals (Aadarsha) are wonderful)	17) Path of violence. Its ideals are common place.
18) Gives importance to intellect, emotions, and soul. Regards material world to be "maya".	18) Gives importance to mostly the body. Regards physical world to be real.
19) Gives importance to self-restraint.	19) Gives importance to indulgence.
20) It is a true civilization.	20) It is a disease.
21) It leads to Sarvodaya.	21) It leads to all-destruction.
22) It is agriculture oriented.	22) It is industry-oriented.
23) It gives importance to joint the family system.	23) It gives importance to the divided family system.
24) It is based on sympathy	24) Absence of sympathy
25) The rich and deep diversity in everything (languages, food, clothing, singing, dancing, etc.) is the sine qua non of this civilization. But diversity is bound by unity (avibhaktaha vibhakteshu)	25) The lack of diversity.

Source: Compiled from Sane Guruji's Book on 'Bhartiya sanskriti'.

In Rabindranath Tagore's view, the word civilization is a European word, and although it has been used widely in the East as well as the West, there is a very high level of ambiguity about its real meaning; the word has largely been used on trust. Further, civilization stands for not merely progress in wealth, knowledge, and power, it also stands for redeeming the philosophy of life and the art of living. Civilization cannot merely be a growing totality of things and happenings. It must be the expression of some guiding moral force. Hospitality, simplicity are the hallmarks of a healthy civilization. It remains healthy and strong as long as it contains in its centre some creative ideals. Such a civilization has been called a *"living civilization"*. For Tagore, civilization means "dharma" which, in turn, means that principle which holds us firmly together, and leads us to our best welfare; it also means the essential quality of a thing. Civilization is the expression of man's *"dharma"* in his corporate life (Tagore, 1980, pp. 42-57).

In actual life, the definition of civilization as *'dharma'* has been ignored, and material progress alone is taken as the expression of civilization. In the recent past century or two, the West has made a phenomenal material progress, and that progress is taken to denote the advanced, developed, rich civilization of the West. But the enormous progress in the West has made man diminutive. It has smothered man. In the last two centuries, the inner ideal of the Western civilization has been pushed aside by the love of money and power. The aggressive force of greed has taken possession of the Western mind. Consequently, all that was human is being broken in to fragments. There is no greater calamity than greed (Tagore, 1980, pp. 42-57).

In support of the claim that ancient Indian civilization is superior to WBC, we reproduce below some testimonies from some Western scholars themselves (see Shah Kanti, 2009, pp. 75-79).

- It is becoming clear that a chapter which had a western beginning will have to have an Indian ending if it is not to end in self-destruction of the human race. At this supremely dangerous moment in history, the only way of salvation is the Indian way (Arnold Toynbee).
- India is the mother of our race, and Sanskrit the mother of Europe's languages. She was the mother of philosophy, mother of Mathematics through Arabs, mother of ideas through Buddha, mother of self-government and democracy through the village communities. Mother India is, in many ways, the mother of us all (Arnold Toynbee).
- Western civilization had nothing to offer to a people who were so endowed in terms of human values, were socially and culturally rich. Western civilization, in comparison, seemed pretty undeveloped (Alfred Webb).

- When we landed in India we found there a hoary civilization that was not perfunctory, but universal and all-pervading. Perhaps there are no other people in the world who show so much in their character the advantageous effects of their own civilization. They are shrewd in business, acute in reasoning, thrifty, religious, sober, charitable, obedient to parents, amicable, law abiding, compassionate and patient under suffering (Seymour Keay).
- When we read of the poetical and philosophical movements of India, we discover there so many truths so profound that we are constrained to bow the reverseace before the East, and do see in this cradle of the human race the native land of the highest philosophy (Victor Cousin).
- If a good system of agriculture, unrivalled manufacturing skill, schools established in every village, the general practice of hospitality, and, above all an equitable treatment of the female sex are among the signs of a civilized people, then the Hindus are not inferior to the nations of Europe (Thomas Munro).
- The Indian village has for centuries remained a bulwark against political disorder, and the home of simple domestic and social virtues. No wonder, therefore, that philosophers and historians have always dwelt lovingly on this ancient institution which is the natural social unit and the best type of rural life: self-contained, industrious, peace-loving. There is much that is both picturesque and attractive in the social and domestic life of Indian village (William Wedderburn).
- As for myself, India from now on is not a foreign land; she is the greatest of all countries, the country from which once I came. I find her again deep inside me. I have sought to nourish my cosmic dreams at the springs of clairvoyant India.... India can and should resume the great place of seniority which belongs to her in the world's social and moral life.

  To the land of glory and servitude
  Of transitory empires and eternal thought
  To the people that defies time
  To India resurrected (Romain Rolland)

If we still doubt the central thesis of *HS* that is at the present juncture of civilizational crisis, it is India's responsibility to serve as the Alternative, that she definitely has the potential to take up and fulfill this responsibility, and if India now shirks this responsibility, she will definitely die along with other countries. One can try to dispel the said doubt by giving some more highly simple but the most persuasive arguments which Gandhiji has expressed on this subject.

Gandhiji has said, among all the nations, I like India the most. This is so not because she is my country but because I have seen in her the best merits or goodnesses. Any person who has the highest inspiration to develop himself can get in India whatever he needs. I am devoted to and I worship Bharat because whatever I have today is given to me by Bharat. I believe that the goal, the aim of Bharat is different from that of other countries. Bharat has certainly such a suitability, such a fitness that she can become the greatest nation in the world. There is no other example of a country like Bharat which has attempted self-purification. She does not need the arms of steel, she has fought with divine arms, and she can fight with those types of arms today also.

I would like to think that through her faith in non-violence, India should become a messenger of peace (shanti-doot). I want Bharat to become free and strong because I want that she can even sacrifice herself voluntarily for the good of the universe. I am asking Bharat to embrace non-violence not because she is weak, but because I have faith in her strength and power. Therefore, I want her to walk on the path of 'ahimsa'. If Bharat embraces or accepts violence or 'himsa', I would not like to live in India. In the same vein, Vivekananda has said that India is immortal if she persists in her search of God, but if she goes in for politics and social conflict she will die.

In India, in all ages there has been a quest for Sarva (all), poorna (complete, infinite), truth, swaraj, swadeshi, swadharma. This is well-reflected in the following words or "Shlokas" in full or their parts:

Om! Poornamadaha poornamidam |
Poornat poornmudachyate
Poornasya poornamadaya
Poornmevavashishayate, Om! Shantihi, Shantihi, Shantihi.

(That is poorna or complete, this is complete. Poorna results from poorna. When (if) poorna is taken away from poorna, poorna only remains in balance or the remainder is also poorna. peace, peace, and peace.)

> *Sarvatra sukhinaha santu, sarve santu niramayaha*
> *Sarve bhadrani pashyantu, ma kasyachit dukham Aapnuyat.*

(All should be happy. All should be healthy. All should see auspicious things. No one should be unhappy.)

> *Sarveshwar, sarvatmaka sarvanarayan, sarvam shanty, sarvadharma, sarvodaya, twameva sarvam, sarvapape bhyo, asato ma sadgamaya, satchidananda, satyam bruyat, satyameva jayate, Sri sat akala, Vishveshwaraha, Vishvadevata, Vishwamanushha.*

(These are only a few examples of words which beautifully and succinctly express or reflect the vision, the mission and the quest of India).

We conclude this discussion on "towards Swaraj" by referring to Roszak's (Western sociologist's) study namely, Making of a Counter Culture, Reflections on the Technocratic society and Its Youthful opposition. Apart from HS, some other writings are available about the criticism of modern civilization and the case for counter-civilization (For example, Rudolph, 1992). Among these, the book by Theodore Roszak is of great interest (1970). Roszak has argued that the present civilization or culture in the West can best be designated as "*Technocratic totalitarianism*" or "*technocracy*". Certain youth groups like Hippies in the West refused to accept this civilization; they refused to live within this civilization. There was a Great Refusal of the present culture by the youth in the USA and Europe. These alienated young tried to give a shape to something that looked like the saving vision which the present endangered and disoriented human civilization required. For this they turned to the East or Orient, particularly India, for help. However, at some stage of their growth, they became corrupted; they succumbed to vices, indulgence, and immorality. Ultimately, they also were sucked by that invidious sponge called Technocratic totalitarianism as a result of which a cultural revolution petered out. Their vision needs to be developed further.

But, in fact, their approach and vision had been already developed in HS. HS had anticipated this vision long ago.

VIII

Hind Swaraj on Some Important Themes in Global Discourse

The exegesis of the world-view of *HS* would remain incomplete unless certain major global themes or issues related to *HS* also are discussed. Therefore, we now turn to the discussion, albeit briefly, of the Gandhian perspective on themes such as post-nationalism, environmental and ecological decay, means of transport and communication (railways), machinery, mechanization, and technology, communalism, religion and racism, system of justice, medical model, education, and economic development. This discussion should help readers understand better the discussion in this book.

1. Post-Nationalism in *Hind Swaraj*

Over the years, various schools (groups) of thought have emerged in the world and they have been debating various themes. Some of them are post-modernists, deep ecologists, greens, deschoolers, post-nationalists, historicists, historiographers, post-colonialists, subalternists, and nativists. Post-nationalists, among them, question whether a particular geographical area (*viz.*, India) is a nation at all. The phenomenon of a racial or ethnic Balkanization of the Nation-State is taken to be the arrival of the post-nation. Similarly, the marginalization of a nation in a new transnational federation is also taken to signify the arrival of the post-nation. The changes from below, minorities, other marginal groups, international mobility have all tended to render the concept of a nation anachronistic. Nations or national identities have tended to become irrelevant in the wake of large-scale diasporic movements and resultant hybridities. The reality of supra-national military alliances and the competing multi-culturalism have tended to result in the irrelevance of the idea of a nation, and in pushing the modern civilization into the post-nation world.

Another meaning of post-nationalism is to recognize the importance of localism. The local is real and tangible and any construct larger than the local is unreliable and vague.

The thinking about post-nation emphasizes the '*native principle*' which refuses to receive standards other than those we have evolved ourselves. This would naturally demand concentrating on one's own street, village, taluka, and district. Post-nationalism argues that the local landscape is the only landscape of cultural contact, and it alone provides a definite context to one's being. Nationalism is a false (planted) ideal and internationalism is still a bigger lie (Akshaya Kumar, and others, 2000).

Now, Gandhiji greatly valued universal solidarity. Although, he led the freedom movement to emancipate a given nation, it was not because he regarded India to be superior to England. In fact, his quest for universal oneness must have made him ensure the security and welfare of India. As pointed out earlier, Hind in Hind Swaraj refers to all other countries and not to India alone. Like Arnold Toynbee, Gandhiji regarded nationalism, communism, individualism as ideological dogmas or modern orthodoxies. Like Tolstoy, Gandhiji might have said that National Flag is a piece of cloth tied at the end of the stick. Gandhiji's readiness to go beyond Nation is well reflected in the difference in thinking of Gandhiji and B.G. Tilak also. Between Truth and India, while Gandhiji was on the side of Truth, Tilak was on the side of India, if the choice had to be made.

Gandhiji has anticipated or foreshadowed all the major schools of thought mentioned earlier. He has transcended them in terms of depth, breadth, radicalism, and humaneness. Gandhiji's concept of *swaraj* is much more a total vision than the other scholars' idea of post-nationalism. This argument needs to be elaborated further.

Gandhiji was committed to the ideas of minimization, decentralization, and withering away of the state. He never believed in the viability and benevolence of the Nation-State. "That government is the best which governs the least", and "minimize the Government and what Government you need, decentralize it", he used to say. This clearly is a position of the post-nation or metastate or porous state. His concept or nature of swaraj enables him to herald the arrival of the post-nation.

In the Gandhian model, the basic or fundamental units for governance or functioning are the 'self' and the 'villages' which are self-sufficient, self-reliant, self-governing, self-defending, self-sustaining and viable republics. As a result, he distrusted, or questioned the need, relevance, and efficacy of large nation-states. His vision of a village as a self-republic is a highly radical, or revolutionary thought as compared to the theory of localism in the post-modern school.

There are a number of ideas and concepts in Gandhian thought which make that thought post-nationalistic. For example, the important place which panchayats occupy in the Gandhian model results in decentralized decision-making. Then there is the replacement of the pyramidic organization by the scheme of the 'oceanic circle'. Further, Gandhiji would prefer anarchy to foreign or external or outside rule. The discussion in the remaining part of this subsection draws liberally from Akshaya Kumar, *et al.*, 2000.

Gandhiji is post-nationalistic also because he does not regard the rule of the English-educated Indian elite (i.e. internal colonizers) to be *ipso facto* superior to the rule of foreigners. Gandhiji's vision rejects the rule of 'white sahibs' as well as 'brown sahibs'. The consideration of nationalism cannot be used to prefer the rule of the latter to the rule of the former. Similarly, Gandhiji rejected the view (and practice) that the act of the majority can bind the minority; it is ungodly to hold such a view. Therefore, he found the Western concept of democracy extremely faulty. We very often quote very approvingly Lincoln's definition of democracy namely, "the government of the people, for the people, by the people", but in reality, democracy everywhere has turned to be the government of the majority, by the majority, and for the majority. The unprecedented trust in people and distrust of the institutionalization of democracy is the most unique feature of swaraj.

HS exposes the tyranny that is in-built in the so called liberal model of Western democracy. The sterile nature of parliament, the rule of representative rather than direct, grassroot, participatory democracy are the faults of today's democracy. At present, there is a nexus, collusion, collaboration, co-operation between the State and capitalism. There is a subtle presence of Nazism, Fascism,

Colonialism, and Imperialism. *HS* puts forth the ideal of *'total swaraj'* or *'poorna swaraj'* in place of the present parliamentary democracy which is at best truncated, and at worst dictatorial.

Gandhiji's post-nationalism requires liquidation of nation-centered democratic world order. It appears that Gandhiji is not for 'absolute independence' of the nation; he prefers interdependence, instead. Swaraj is a concept of the post-nation rather than that of the nation. Although the Gandhian concept of Swaraj is highly indigenous, the concept, the place, the role, the importance, and the responsibilities of the individual, the family, the village, the society, the nation or the State, and the world are beautifully interwoven in it to create an unique and remarkably consistent paradigm which integrates the traditional and modern. How does this happen?

Firstly, the concepts such as self-rule, self-discipline, self-sufficiency, and Swadeshi in Gandhiji's thought precludes or forecloses large-scale immigration of or diaspora of people, and they also avoid culture hybridization, cultural mutation, and demographic mutation as visualized by the post-modernists.

Secondly, *HS* is a counter-civilizational, and not a national discourse. The unit of Gandhiji's protest is the civilization and never any nation. He criticizes modern civilization which has corrupted basically good people. The corruption could occur because of the loss of religious moorings in and due to modern civilization. The implication here is that if civilization is to survive, its reformation in the form of respiritualisation and re-religionization ought to take place.

Thirdly, Gandhiji's post-nation is rooted in the concept of *dharma,* which is the principle of freedom as much as responsibility.

Finally, Gandhiji's post-nation rules out the emotionally charged and proud goal of making India a super-economy and superpower.

2. Environmental and Ecological Crisis and *Hind Swaraj*

One of the factors that have endangered our planet earth and the human civilization on it, is environmental degradation and destruction and ecological decay, and ecocide. In other words, the crisis of the survival of modern civilization has been caused by, among other things, global environmental crisis. And yet, there is much misunderstanding of environmental issues. Many current approaches to environmental protection are grossly inadequate. There is a need to adopt bold, serious, unconventional approaches to save the earth. Mankind needs to take up the right action for environmental protection, preservation, conservation, regeneration, and renewal. Environmental degradation on a wide scale began and has reached life-threatening or survival-threatening dimensions only during the days of modern civilization. The crisis has now become worldwide and all-pervasive.

What are the major examples of environmental crisis? The evidence in this regard is quite well documented. In brief, the manifestations of the crisis are: greenhouse effect, unexpected and unpredictable climatic changes, depletion of the ozone layer, widespread deforestation, acid rains, phenomenal increase in toxic waste, dying rivers and seas, the erosion of top soil, desertification of land on a large-scale, destruction of coastal ecology, and the extinction of species and species of animals, birds, plants, trees, and the threat to the existence of many of the species, and the end of biological diversity.

The author of *HS* had anticipated, foreseen these developments about 100 years ago and he had suggested suitable, effective, integrated strategies or approaches (philosophy and policy measures) to halt mankind's race towards self-extinction due to environmental crisis. *HS*, ideals are compatible with the broad concerns of the 'green movement'. It provides a strategy for 'green development'. HS holds that the only lasting solution to the crisis under discussion is to build, create a 'sustainable social order'.

As per the Gandhian perspective, environmental crisis goes much beyond the physical aspects. The social, cultural, and moral environments also have become dangerously degraded and polluted. The ecological crisis is an inseparable, integral part of the violent social order or the modern civilization. Its solution, therefore, demands far more fundamental changes in societies than those which have been conventionally contemplated.

Now, many thinkers on sustainability have been influenced in their thinking by the philosophy and life of Gandhiji. He had prescribed a panacea comprising minimization of wants, ceiling on desires, voluntary simplicity, reigning in greed, minimization of production, conservation of resources. The essential elements of the Gandhian world-view with a focus on environmental protection are as follows:

(i) Nature does not exist merely for man's conquest and exploitation. Nature is *'mother-nature'*, and the earth is *'mother-earth'* or *'good earth'*. There ought to be an inter-generational and inter-special balance or equity in all activities of man. He must conserve all life-supporting systems and preserve genetic and biotic diversity on this planet.

(ii) Human-beings should achieve holistic development and happiness for all.

(iii) The best consumption ethics for eradicating poverty, achieving equality or social justice, and protecting the ecology is the minimization of wants or voluntary simplicity. There is no scarcity of resources if austerity is practised by all. As Gandhiji used to say, "There is enough for everyone's needs, but not for everybody's greed". The individual and social lifestyles should not be resource-intensive, energy-intensive, capital-intensive and technology-intensive. The satisfaction of basic needs is the necessary and sufficient condition of economic activity.

(iv) Mankind needs a food-clothing-shelter-led development with focus on "unto this last" and not steel-cement-power-led development for the affluent. The economic, social, political systems should operate within an ethical framework.

(v) There should be an integration between science, technology on the one hand and spirituality on the other hand. The crucial functions for civilizational survival are: (a) Non-violence + science = Sarvodaya, (b) Violence + Science = All round destruction.

(vi) The life of the people should be governed by the 'Ekadasha vratas' laid down by Gandhiji [For elaboration see Bhole, L.M. (3)].

3. *Hind Swaraj* on Railways and Other Means of Transport and Communication (The Question of Speed)

The modern man is obsessed with speed, and he is pre-occupied with invention, production, and use of modern, highly speedy means of transport and communication (MTC). The world has come to be characterized as the global village living in the Jet Age and in which the ICE (information, communication, and entertainment) and FIRE (finance, insurance, and real estate) sectors pre-dominate.

In a rather short period of time, there has been a phenomenal development and widespread use of automobiles, railways, aeroplanes, radio and television, telephones, cell phones, etc. in all the countries. Gandhiji has questioned these developments or trends. He has used railways as a representative symbol of such developments. Given the fact that railways are mostly regarded as good, desirable, necessary, it was heroic on the part of Gandhiji to use railways as a symbol to condemn certain products and services of the modern age. It may not be a mistake to say that Gandhiji's critique of modernization would not have invited such a strong disapproval if he had not opposed railways.

It may be noted that many thoughtful persons like Dadabhai Naoroji, R.C. Dutt, A.V. Joshi also had drawn the attention of the people to the fact that to employ the available resources to develop the railways at that point of history was a wrong priority. India at that time needed irrigation, wells, etc. more than railways.

Gandhiji criticized rail development because in his view, it would not help to reduce poverty in India, which was a more important and urgent matter. Gandhiji had studied quite well the economics of Dadabhai Naoroji and R.C. Dutt and broadly he was in agreement with them. R.C. Dutt used to argue that for the reduction in poverty, the development of irrigation was more important than that of the railways. It was true that the railways facilitated the movement of food in times of famine, but it was equally true that the railways did not produce food. For the production of more food, irrigation was critical. Railways without irrigation did not solve the problems of poverty and famines.

Dadabhai Naoroji also had used the example of the railways to demonstrate his theory of internal and external draining of resources. Gandhiji, in turn, argued that railways, like lawyers and doctors, had impoverished India, and if we did not wake up in time, India would be ruined. Moreover, railways helped the British to increase their hold on India. Railways also resulted in spreading bubonic plague. Without railways, masses of people could not move from place to place; they are the carriers and spreaders of plague germs. Railways have also increased the frequency of famines, because, with the availability of the facility for travel or transportation, people sell out their grain which is then sent out to the dearest markets. The people become careless, and so the pressure of famines increases.

As was his wont, Gandhiji has drawn our attention to the mental dimension, along with the physical dimension of the growth of railways in India. The increasing famine pressures, to which railways contributed, accentuating the evil nature of man. Bad men fulfill their evil designs with greater rapidity. The holy places of India have become unholy. Formerly, people went to these places with very great difficulty. Generally, therefore, only the real devotees visited such places. Nowadays, rogues visit them in order to practice their roguery. The railways can become a distributing agency for the evil one only. It may be a debatable matter whether railways spread famines, but it is beyond dispute that they propagated evil (Parel, 1997, pp. 46-47).

What about the contribution of the railways towards creating a new spirit of nationalism in India? Gandhiji rejects such a claim outright. It is a mistake to think that railways have made India a nation. Such a thinking is the result of propaganda by the English rulers. According to Gandhiji, India was a one nation before the British came to India. We have been a nation since long ago, and this is shown by the facts that one thought inspired us, our mode of life has been the same, and our leading men travelled throughout India spreading the message of oneness or unity or Advaita (Parel, 1997, pp. 48-49).

Like Gandhiji, Thoreau also had thought that the "tools" such as railways, telegraph, post-offices, etc. do not represent a real advance of mankind. They are positively harmful because their foundation is the lives of many men. The man becomes, in the process, a tool of these tools. Therefore, the nation really need not bother to have them, which are a mere sham and delusion. The people should abandon the life of hustle and bustle, speed, etc. Self-realization is the important goal in life.

There is evidence which shows that the introduction and expansion of the railways in India had many adverse, deleterious effects in line with the apprehensions and skepticism of Gandhiji, Naoroji, and Thoreau. The layout of the railways was such that it upset the river flows and the natural drainage system. It was partly responsible for the ravages of flood and epidemics in India. While the railways did not boost the economy of the countryside, it played apart denuding them. It led to the decay of the old market and commercial centres and concentrated all resources in the metropolitan cities. The railways contributed to unequal exchange as existed between the imperial metropolis and its satellites. The long arm of the colonial cities reached the countryside but only to plunder them. There was no reciprocity between the town and the country. The colonial cities remained parasitic and did not play any regenerative or active role.

Thus, although railways are now widely accepted and widely used by the masses and the elite, and although they are looked at in wonder, this itself should not lead us to accept in outlook that the railways are a part of this civilizational change. This outlook should be determined by the beneficial and harmful effects of the railways per se, by consequences of the speedy or fast means of transport, and by the fascination or craze for speed. Gandhiji opposed railways because they increased the frequency and spread of famines and epidemics. Similarly, he opposed railways because he liked the beauty of slowness, and disliked the negative effects of speed. Gandhi was highly skeptical about speed. As against the beauty of speed, he posited the beauty of slowness (see the poem 'Slow me down Lord' given below). The increase in speed in modern times has speeded up death through environmental destruction, climate change, phenomenal increase in accidents, pollution, and so on.

We close this sub-section on *Hind Swaraj* perspective on speed and related matters by quoting below a very expressive, relevant and beautiful poem by an unknown poet:

> Slow me down, Lord!
> Ease the pounding of my heart by quietening of my mind
> Steady my hurried pace with the eternal touch of time
> Give me, amidst the confusions of my day,
> The calmness of the everlasting hills
> Break the tension of my nerves with the soothing music
> of the singing streams that live in my memory
> Help me to know the magical restoring power of sleep
> Teach me the art of making minute vacations of slowing down

To look at a flower, to chat with an old friend, or to make a new one
To pat a dog, to watch a spider build a web
To smile at a child, or to read from a good book
Remind me each day
That the race is not always to be swift
That there is more to life than increasing its speed
Let me look upward to the towering oak and know that
It grew great and strong because it grew slowly and well
Slow me down, Lord, and inspire me to send my roots deep into the soil of life's enduring values
That I may grow towards the stars of my greater Destiny.

4. Hind Swaraj on Machinery (Technology), Industry, and Science

In this section, we learn more about Gandhiji's views, perspective, position on science and technology, particularly the latter. Gandhiji's views on this subject are available in Chapter 19 in HS plus they are scattered over the whole of HS. We are living in the age or era of science and technology (ST). The modern civilization and culture has been called technological civilization and culture, or a technocracy (see Chapter VII in this book). Gandhiji's views on ST ought to be given a great weightage because he had a very keen scientific, experimental, and experiential mind.

Machinery is a chief symbol of modern civilization, and in Gandhiji's views, it is a great sin. Machines, machinery, technology, mechanization, automation, and engineering are the watchwords which broadly convey the same idea or phenomenon in this context. Technology has become a new orthodoxy, a new religion, a new God. Bertrand Russel had to lament that Machine was an object of adoration as the modern form of Satan. Machinery makes man a slave; it helps people to exploit other people. In the terminology of *HS*, machinery is thus 'anti-Swaraj'. And yet, the overwhelming majority of the people in the world are on the side of more and more, sophisticated, complex, gigantic, and costly technology. Technology enthusiasm and technology optimism are all-pervasive in the modern civilization. The most of the people in the world belong to the category called 'forward stampede' (see Schumacher, 1973) in technology. It refers to the views that whatever the existing use of technology, it is still less, and also that the adverse (evil) effects of technology can be tackled by more technology.

In *HS*, Gandhiji has mostly used the term machinery and not technology. He himself has raised the question: "What is a machine"? and has answered it in *HS*. In its wider sense, man is the most wonderful machine in creation, and it can neither be duplicated nor copied till date. In another sense, a machine is an appliance that has three distinguishing characteristics. First, it displaces human and animal labour. Second, there is no limit to its growth or evolution. Third, it seems to be possessed of a will or genius of its own (Parel, 1997, p. 169).

It is quite widely known that Gandhiji was highly skeptical about technology's potential to do good. Since technology is anti-swaraj, he was bound to be critical of technology's role or place in the life of humanity. He had sought to establish that a non-violent social order was superior to a society that is founded on violence. Now, the success of such a social order depends on appropriate technology, apart from an appropriate educational system. As in the case of many other matters, there has been a great difference in viewpoints on technology, between Gandhiji and other people. Quite often, Gandhiji's views on technology have been regarded as 'strange'. They have also proved to be highly controversial. It appears that no other question treated in HS has provoked as much controversy as has the question of machinery. The most of the other people have been fascinated by high technology and modern civilization, but not so Gandhiji.

Gandhiji held a balanced view, not a one-sided view on technology. He agreed that machinery has a potential to do good, that it can make a positive contribution. However, this depends on certain conditions which may not be always fulfilled in actual life. He also knew that more often than not, machinery can generate negative, harmful effects; it can create cultural diseases. Whether technology will have positive or negative effects will depend, as said above, upon whether (a) competent "doctor" (like Gandhiji) is available or not, (b) technology used is appropriate or not, (c) the use of technology is informed of a moral vision of human good or not. In other words, the nature of consequences of technology will depend upon whether the use of machinery is according to "*dharma*" or not.

When can we say that technology is being used according to *dharma* or truth? Technology can be said to be dharmic if it is appropriate for India, and it meets the needs of the masses of India. Modern technology does not meet these conditions; it has mostly rewarded the skilled and the powerful, and marginalized the poor and the weak. Gandhiji wanted to modify this historical trend; he wanted technology for India that would improve the material welfare of all without undermining the goal of self-rule or *swaraj*.

Let it be noted clearly that Gandhiji was concerned not so much about whether India needed technology or not? He was more concerned about as to what kind of technology and how much of technology India should develop and use? Was Gandhiji anti-technology? Those who are critical of Gandhian thought tend to say, without deeper and dispassionate study, that yes, he was anti-technology. Even the partisans of Gandhiji are not able to answer this question without hesitation and ambivalence. They are ill at ease while dealing with this issue. One feels that such a hesitation is not necessary; Gandhiji's position on this issue is quite clear. He did not preclude the use of technology or machines altogether, but he wanted that at least we in India stating that one should minimize the use of machines; that technology used should be appropriate technology; and that it should benefit all. Gandhiji very clearly saw the connection between technology on the one hand, and, dharma, truth, swaraj, the moral vision of the human good, non-violence, sin, evil, on the other. It is amazing how refreshing, unique, deep, non-conventional, multi-dimensional an approach Gandhiji had to the issue of technology!

Was Gandhiji then anti-technology? We reiterate and reemphasize that he had a qualified stand or position in respect of this issue, and this is quite clear from his statements made at different points of time, and in different contexts. There is no scope to label or brand Gandhiji as anti-machinery because he has repeatedly denied that he was against machinery. This has clearly been shown in his following statements. (These statements are from Parel, 1997, and the number at the end of each statement refers to page Nos. in Parel). Responding to a Japanese correspondent, he has said, "I am not against machinery as such, but I am totally opposed to it when it masters us" (p. 168). "What I object to is the craze for machinery, not machinery as such" (p. 166). "I am not opposed to machinery as such. I am opposed to machinery which displaces labour and leaves it idle" (p. 170). "Machinery is a grand yet awful invention" (p. 167). Having said this, if we had to make a final judgement in respect of the issue under discussion here, we will have to say that Gandhiji was anti-machinery if it was accompanied by certain things, and that he was not anti-machinery if certain things were fulfilled. On balance, one may say that he had a very reserved welcome to give to technology, if he was not anti-machinery. As he has said on the next page, "I am aiming, not at an eradication of all machinery, but at a limited minimum use of machinery".

Generally, people regard every invention, innovation, and discovery (IID) as a progress in science and technology (ST). Similarly, it is often lamented that India is backward, that it is worrisome that she is lagging behind other countries in ST progress. Actually, it is not so. Gandhiji has argued that our forefathers and rishis used their discretion and intelligent judgement to determine which IIDs are good for humanity and which are not. In modern civilization, a plethora of experiments is undertaken, quite often, to no purpose. These experiments and researches may add to information but not to knowledge and wisdom.

Gandhiji has said in *HS*, "... it was not that we did not know how to invent machinery, but our forefathers knew that if we set our hearts after such things, we would become slaves and lose our moral fibre" (pp. 68-69). In the same vein, in another place, he said, "Our ancestors had realized that just as the riches are not the cause of the happiness of the rich, so also the poverty is not the cause of sorrow of the poor. Therefore, they have preserved the plough and cottages extant since thousands of years. It is not true at all that we were unable to invent machines. But our ancestors had realized that if we get involved in the search for newer and newer machines, we would lose our freedom. Therefore, we choose to stop where we could do our work with hands and feet" (p. 68).

It is interesting that the poet T.S. Elliot also has highlighted the futility of more and more IID in the following poem:

> Endless invention, endless experiment,
> Brings knowledge of motion, but not of stillness,
> Knowledge of speech, but not of silence
> Knowledge of words, and ignorance of the world,

> Where is the wisdom we have lost in knowledge?
> Where is the knowledge we have lost in information?

HS has given a clear direction for undertaking IID. As Gandhiji has said, "scientific truths and discoveries should first of all cease to be the mere instruments of greed. Then labourers will not be over-worked, and machinery, instead of becoming a hindrance will be a help. I am aiming, not an eradication of all machinery but limited, minimum use of machinery" (p. 166).

It is interesting to find that Gandhiji has always connected the question of machinery with many other issues. For example, one of them has been machinery and health. This is a unique perspective, and it is typically Gandhian. Gandhiji could develop this perspective because man is the ultimate measuring rod, or man is the supreme consideration in the Gandhian world. Machinery in this world must not make the limbs of man atrophied. The real happiness and health consisted in the proper use of our hands and feet. We would do what we can with our hands and feet. In other words, the Gandhian approach to machinery is based on the concept of bread labour (earn thy bread by the sweat of thy brow), and it is guided by the prayer, "sarve santu niramayaha" (let all be healthy). This indeed is a very important and relevant approach to machinery because dependence on machines, the craze for machinery, pursuit of automation, and obsession with technology have made modern man an extremely sick being. The coming up of newer and newer diseases *inter alia* has made man himself an endangered specie. Modern civilization is now a disease, and man living therein is also a disease. There is no escape from this situation unless the mankind adopts the Gandhian approach to the use of machinery.

The subjects of machinery or technology and industrialization are closely inter-related. Gandhiji was often asked whether he would not industrialize India? Or would you close down all cloth mills?

As in respect of machinery, in respect of modern industrialization also, Gandhiji's response was always a qualified one. For him, the industrialization of India would necessarily involve the revival of village communities, and village, cottage, home, tiny, small-scale industries. The industrialization of India must occur within the framework of *swadeshi* in all its senses.

Many quotations by Gandhiji assembled and presented below would further explain Gandhiji's position on science, technology, and industry.

- "Opposition to mills or machinery is not the crucial point. What suits our country is the point. I am not opposed to the movement of manufacturing machines in the country...." (p. 165).
- "India does not need to be industrialized in the modern sense of the term" (p. 165).
- "I have nothing to say against the development of any other industry in India by means of machinery, but I do say that to supply India with cloth manufactured either outside or inside through gigantic mills is an economic blunder of the first magnitude" (p. 165).
- "It is time we realized that, where there is unlimited human power, complicated machinery on a large scale has no place. We cannot industrialize ourselves, unless we make up our mind to enslave humanity" (p. 165).
- "I would indeed industrialize India in my sense of the term" (p. 168).
- "I am not opposed ... to making improvements in machinery ... but I would penalize the manufacture of labour-saving machines and protect the industry which manufactures nice ploughs which can be handled by every man" (p. 165).
- "I want to save time and labour, not for a fraction of mankind, but for all" (p. 166).
- "Machinery impoverished India. It was due to it that India's handicrafts have all but disappeared" (p. 107).
- "Machinery is the chief symbol of modern civilization, and it is a great sin" (p. 107).
- "Instead of welcoming machinery as a boon, we should look upon it as an evil" (p. 111).
- "Machinery is a grand yet awful invention" (p. 167).

From these quotations, we get an idea of the structure of industry which Gandhiji favoured. In such an industrial structure, the spinning wheel will have the highest priority and importance. The adoption of spinning wheel (hand spinning) would have two consequences. First, it would solve the problem of unemployment. Second, the country adopting hand spinning would imply that she has no intention to exploit any other nation. It would also imply the commitment to end exploitation of the poor by the rich. Gandhiji had pointed out long ago that India can never be industrialized unless she could reduce her population from 350 to 35 million, which is an impossibility. India must realize that where there is unlimited human power, complicated machinery on a large scale have no place; we cannot industrialize unless we make up our mind to enslave humanity (p. 167).

While dealing with domestic problems, Gandhiji always wanted a conflict-free, equitable, just, exploitation-free world. He abhorred colonial, imperialistic, hegemonic relations and designs vis-à-vis other countries. Further, policy measures suggested by him are superior to those suggested by mainstream economists. For example, given the problem of unemployment due to "unlimited human power" (Gandhiji's words) or "unlimited supplies of labour" (the words of the economist, A. Lewis), Gandhi and Lewis offered vastly different policy measures. While Gandhiji suggested policies to strengthen agriculture, village or rural small-scale industries, Lewis suggested transfer of population from agriculture/rural areas to large, heavy, capital-intensive industry/urban areas.

Gandhiji's analysis and policy prescription were based on his observations and knowledge of the real India after seeing which he literally wept. He discovered that the misery and poverty in India were due to the use of machinery or imported goods which were made in big industries. He rejected that the substitution of Indian mills was an alternative to imports. He found the theories of import substitution and export promotion by conventional economics hardly of any use. He was convinced that it is the use of machinery which is the cause of 'deindustrialization' and impoverishment in India. The policies to promote modern industry resulted in the deindustrialization of traditional industries. The real solution lay in *Swadeshi*.

The appropriate technology for India consists of small-scale, human-scale, human-faced, simple tools, equipment, instruments, implements, etc. As far as appropriate industrial structure is concerned, there will a primary sector or prime activity of agriculture at the centre which will be supplemented by a cotton textile industry which would have three sub-sectors: Composite, machine-driven spinning and weaving mills, handlooms or hand-woven industry and the spinning wheel-industry. Gandhiji was not opposed to the growth of all these three textile sub-sectors, but in his heart of hearts, it was hand spinning which he really and very much wanted to spread and help prosper. The industrial (economic) structure in India would thus be formed by agriculture, hand spinning (spinning wheel) and weaving, and by mills in a descending order of importance. In hand weaving, or handlooms and the spinning wheel, Gandhiji preferred the latter over the former because while hand spinning can be installed in every home, handlooms cannot be so installed. He had a tremendous faith in the power of the spinning wheel to tackle many of the problems of India. No wonder, he once called the spinning wheel 'sacred' and the 'lung' of the nation. Vinoba went a step ahead and said that the khadi produced with the 'Takali' was the only true khadi. Gandhiji has said in one place, "It would be a blunder of the first magnitude to supply cloth to the vast Indian population made in huge mills." (p. 164-165).

The modern industrialization and technology saga in India has been a saga of misery of such a magnitude that it made Gandhiji weep when he saw it. He saw that the male and female workers in industry had become impoverished, famished, enslaved, and shocked. He impressed on people that if the craze for machinery grew, India would become an unhappy land. How correctly prophetic! The condition of the mill industry and mill workers in Mumbai in the recent past is a very good example of the Gandhian approach and viewpoint. What was the solution? To close down the cloth mills? This is the solution which was put through during the cotton textile mills crisis in Mumbai towards the closing of the 20th century. It led to unemployment, suicides, uprooting and disintegrating of families, and impoverishment of the mill workers.

It is to be noted that Gandhiji did not suggest such a remedy because of his compassionate nature. Instead, he asked the mill owners (a) not to increase further the number of mills, (b) to contract the mill business gradually, and (c) to establish or install in thousands of households the ancient and sacred spinning wheel. Simultaneously, he asked the people not to use any machine-made goods (pp. 108-109). If machinery was anti-swaraj, the absolute minimization of the use of machinery would support swadeshi, and it would help to attain Swaraj or Home-Rule, or Self-Rule (p. 110).

It is amazing to see how crystal clear and firm Gandhiji was about the negative nature of machinery. He once told his interlocutor that there was no alternative but to go without railways, trams, cars, electricity, mill cloth, and almost every machine-made product. Gandhiji had said, "I cannot recall a single good point about machinery. Books can be written to demonstrate its evils. Instead of welcoming machinery as a boon, we should look upon it as an evil" (pp. 110-111). More explicitly, he has said, "the railways, telegraphs, hospitals, lawyers, and doctors have all to go, and the upper classes have to learn to live conscientiously and religiously, and deliberately the simple peasant life, knowing it to be a life-giving true happiness" (p. 131).

In one of his interviews, Gandhiji has explained the relationship between his concept of Oceanic circle and machinery. According to him, in the ideal social order based on the ideas of oceanic circle, there would be no room for machines that would displace human labour, and which would concentrate power in a few hands. Labour has its unique place in a cultured human family (pp. 188-190).

Gandhiji's thinking on technology as stated in *HS* (and as discussed above) has certain features. It is based on a serious study of the state of the Indian economy, society, and polity. It has evolved over a period of time. The highest point in his thinking on technology is that we as a nation must adopt the spinning wheel more than even the handlooms. The non-violent Sarvodayi social order has to be founded on faith in manual labour. The spinning wheel alone can be the means available for this, and accessible to everyone. There cannot be a better emblem of revolution than this. In *HS*, he has preferred to use the word machinery to the word technology, but the two words mean the same thing. He has generally taken a qualified or balanced stand, position on technology, modern industry, and so on. Many have regarded it as a strange thinking, and it has generated very high controversy. Gandhian thinking on technology is one of the deepest thinking means in which technology is connected to non-violence, swaraj or Home Rule, resources-drain, dharma, etc. In his view, technology is acceptable as a servant, not as a master. Machinery is not an unmixed blessing, it has many limitations. The differences in conditions in different places must be taken into account while deciding a stand on it. Technology helps to concentrate wealth and power in a few hands; it leads to exploitation and injustice.

Let us now discuss Gandhiji's views on modern science. It is alleged that Gandhiji was anti-science just as he was anti-machinery. This again is a misrepresentation of Gandhiji's stand. He was keenly aware of both the contributions and limitations of modern science. He was neither a science-pessimist nor anti-science nor science-optimist nor science-enthusiast. In modern times, science and religion have been counterposed with each other. Gandhiji did not accept that science and religion were in conflicting positions. He believed in the need for synthesis of the two. How can the man who titled his autobiography as 'Experiments with Truth', be anti-science? The view that Gandhiji was anti-science must have gained currency because of our defining science narrowly. If we keep in mind that people have meaningfully talked about spiritual science or the science of spirituality, one would automatically hesitate to level a false charge that Gandhiji was anti-science. Gandhiji, apart from the above, called his work in Naokhali and Kolkata in 1946, as his "greatest experiment in non-violence". For him, rishis in India were as much scientists as Newton. He established ashramas and conducted many experiments in eating and drinking, khadi, and sex life. Vinoba experimented in spinning on the *takli*, freedom from money, wages from spinning, complete liberation from money, complete renunciation, complete *grama-seva* and *grama-vikas*.

The various experiments in personal, social, and political life (in respect of diet, health, sex, education, agitations, satyagrahas) which Gandhiji conducted show that Gandhiji valued science, that he had a very fine scientific temper. Gandhiji has offered an 'alternative science'; he has put forth the idea of a 'satyagrahi scientist'. Gandhiji's own self-image was not that of a politician or a saint but that of an experimenter or scientist. He no doubt was not an unmixed admirer of science; but he was not a sentimental proponent of this tradition either.

Gandhiji's views on and his attitude towards science were influenced by his views on modern civilization and the relationship between science and modern civilization and colonialism. modern civilization, it has been stressed repeatedly, has created the crisis of survival on earth and for human kind. The greatest 'achievement' of modern civilization has been to multiply weapons of mass destruction. Science has actively contributed to the creation of the present state of the world. As A. Huxley has pointed out, modern science has been destructive of liberty and peace. Gandhiji has argued that the boast about the wonderful discoveries and the marvellous inventions of science is an empty boast.

The Mahatma's critique of science emanates from his dissatisfaction with the divorce of science from morality. He argued that people's moral sense had no way improved as a result of scientific discoveries. The advance of science had added not an inch to the moral stature of nations or societies. It has not reduced hatred and injustice. Gandhiji was also opposed to certain existing practices/methods in science, *viz.*, the vivisection. The practice of inflicting pain and violence on live animals has been quite a normal way of carrying out experiments in modern science. This was ethically and epistemically unacceptable to him. In his own words, "I abhor vivisection with my whole soul. I detest the unpardonable slaughter of innocent life in the name of science and humanity so called ... Vivisection in my opinion is the blackest of all the blackest crimes that man is committing against God and his fair creation. We should be able to refuse to live if the price of living be the torture of sentient beings (Shambu Prasad, 2001).

5. *Hind Swaraj* on Education

The creation and smooth working year after year of such an ideal and philosophically deep society as *HS* would certainly require an appropriate and effective system of education. *HS* has devoted one chapter (No. 18) to discussing the various aspects of education. Gandhiji's views on education may not have generated as much controversy as his views on machinery, but they have not been less radical or less revolutionary, or less fundamental. Some people regard Gandhiji's views on education strange and crazy.

Gandhiji formulated his theory, philosophy, practice of education, and constantly conducted experiments in educational matters in Ashramas which he set up in South Africa and India. For example, he founded the Phoenix School at the Phoenix settlement outside Durban in South Africa in 1904. But this experiment failed due to the lack of funds. His second ashrama was set up in 1910, outside Johannesburg in South Africa, and it was known as Tolstoy Farm. After returning to India in January 1915 from South Africa, he set up Sabarmati Ashrama in 1915, at Ahmedabad, and Sevagram Ashrama near Wardha, in 1936.

In the Concise Oxford Dictionary, education means the act or process of educating or being educated, through systematic instruction, and the development of character and mental powers. It is obvious that this meaning of education is not of much help to know as to what really is education. Gandhiji and Vinobaji have helped us to understand the true meaning of education by stating both what education is not and what it is. They have infused the term with the deepest meaning as will be evident from the discussion which follows:

Education for Gandhiji and Vinobaji involved training of the mind, will, and desires. It involved the union of the individual with the universal soul or God (Yoga), industriousness (Udyoga), and co-operation (Sahayoga). Contrary to the conventional viewpoint, education should not mean the knowledge of only the 3-Rs; reading, writing, and arithmetic. Similarly, education must not mean only the knowledge of letters, because otherwise education would become only an instrument which can be abused or misused or used for exploitation. In practice, this is what education has become at present. It has come to mean only the accumulation of certificates on the demand side, and becoming "emperors in the field of education" (Shikshan-samrat) on the supply side.

Such education does more harm than good. Today's education makes one discontented. We study certain books without knowing why. It may add to anyone's information quotient, but not to his happiness, ethics, morals, knowledge, and wisdom.

Education must give us control over our senses. Education is that which gives us swaraj or liberation. Today's education does not give us the main thing namely, control over our senses, or the ceiling on our desires. Education ought not to show that there is no need for doing my own duty. Education must enable individuals to live as per the framework or ethical system of righteousness (*dharma*), money (*artha*), carnal desires (*kama*), and liberation (*moksha*). Education must inculcate a sense of duty and spirit of service in the minds of students. From this perspective, today's education in India is a false education, a rotten education.

As usual, Gandhiji's position on education is a balanced

position. His criticism of today's education did not make him recommend that teaching of the 3-Rs, teaching of certain sciences etc. should be completely excluded from the curricula. We should not make a fetish of those branches of knowledge. The good way out would be to teach these subjects only after the ethical, moral service, and dharmic sensibilities, of students are properly and firmly built up on the strongest foundation. Gandhiji has also advised that there is no point in making the present type of education with its many faults compulsory. Similarly, the present type of education need not be made a part of adult education. Instead, our ancient school system is a far better alternative (pp. 100-106).

Gandhiji has also insisted that the aim of education must be character-building. Primary education in particular, ought to work towards the building of character among the students who are at that time of an impressionable age.

Gandhiji has also presented the contours of language policy for the whole of India. The main points of this policy are:

(a) We have to improve all our languages.
(b) English education for obtaining Swaraj or Home Rule is not necessary.
(c) English books which are valuable should be translated into various Indian languages.
(d) Religious i.e. ethical education should occupy the first place in the educational scheme or plan.
(e) Every cultured Indian should know, in addition to his own provincial language, if a Hindu, Sanskrit, if a Mohamedan, Arabic; if a Parsee, Persian; and all should learn Hindi.
(f) A universal language for India should be Hindi with the option to use Persian or Nagari scripts (pp. 100-106).

In the Gandhian or *HS* perspective education can be strengthened by adding here Vinoba's views on education. According to Vinoba, there cannot be any system or institutionalization of education. If fails to promote excellence, it loses the quality of natural joy – experience, it then becomes a mere duty or punishment.

The policies for compulsory education, women's education, the spread of literacy in general and adult literacy in particular, are necessary but they should not prove to be red herrings in the sense that they should not come to be regarded as if educational reforms begin and end with them. After all, they are subsidiary concerns, and there is much more to education policy than making these aspects become of central importance.

The core area of educational reforms happens to be the spread of the idea of Basic Education or Nai Talim or New Education, or Jivanna Sikshna first propounded by Gandhiji in 1937. As per this idea there would be per day one-hour basic schools, family schools, and the ideal village universities in almost each village.

The basic idea, ideals, and method of Nai Talim are to promote a union between (a) Knowledge, Action, and Joy; or (b) Shruti, Smriti; or (b) Shruti, Smriti, and Kranti; or (c) union, industriousness, and co-operation, and (d) bread labour. Nai Talim is the philosophy and method of education in which education is imparted through the place of work rather than through formal schools. It involves the giving of the education of life through life in the immediate environment or surroundings. It is thus a *swadeshi* education. It is closely tied up with village life. It eliminates the rural-urban divide (See Vinoba, 1965). Nai Talim is education without examinations and it automatically solves most of our current educational problems regarding child labour; lack of school buildings and blackboards; suicides related to examinations; lack of textbooks; heavy school bags; too many holidays; large-scale absenteeism; bunking of schools, classes; high dropout rate; and the resources crunch (Vinoba, 1965).

Nai Talim is a learner-child centred, dynamic, co-operative, non-violent, system geared towards self-sufficiency, Swedeshi and self-reliance. In Nai Talim, education promotes independent critical thinking, spiritual development, social consciousness. It does not promote acquisitiveness and competitive spirit. In the basic education system, the school is organized on the model of a good family.

In Nai Talim, the teacher would be a village servant (*Gramasevaka*), and what he would be paid would not be a salary but a '*dakshina*'. Nai Talim is a means to bring about a total revolution; a thorough reconstruction of a society. Nai Talim would not be state-introduced, state-dependent, state-promoted, state-run (See Vinoba, 1965).

Gandhiji has reflected very briefly on a number of other

educational issues also in *HS, viz.*, on religious education, adult education, compulsory education, and so on.

The issue of religious education has always remained extremely sensitive and controversial. In the din caused by such a controversy, Gandhiji stood very firm and maintained that we cannot and should not do without religious education. India will never be Godless, rank atheism can never flourish in India. In order to restore India to its pristine glory we have to return to religious education. One would recall here Vivekananda who held exactly the same views about the religiosity of the Indian people and the Indian nation.

Explaining the nature of New or Basic Education, Gandhiji has said that this education is meant to transform village children into model villagers. The current primary education is a farce designed without regard to the wants of village India, and for that matter, even of the cities. Basic Education links the children to all that is best and lasting in India. It keeps the children rooted to the soil with a glorious vision of the future (Parel, 1997, p. 175).

At present, adult education has been either completely neglected or its scope has been extremely limited, it being confined to teaching only 2-Rs namely, reading and writing. Gandhiji has said that if he were in charge of the adult education campaign, he would begin with opening the minds of the adult pupils to the greatness and vastness of their country (Parel, 1997, p. 175).

Gandhiji had a vision of "a true system of education" which he has advocated in *Hind Swaraj*. According to him, the goals of education should be:

(i) To foster love which is the supreme knowledge and the greatest virtue.
(ii) To teach the 3-Rs (reading, writing, and arithmetic), and 3 Hs (hand, heart, and head).
(iii) To make students self-sufficient, sensitive, and confident.
(iv) To promote character development of students.
(v) To promote the highest development of students' minds and souls.
(vi) To draw out the best from the students.
(vii) To foster four virtues in students, *viz.*, vitality, courage, sensitivity, and intelligence.
(viii) To promote physical, mental and moral development of children.

(ix) To teach students the importance of 'bread labour' and self-dependence (Swaralamban).

Gandhiji believed that parents have a very significant role to play in transforming the character and destiny of students. Education is primarily the responsibility of parents. The Family should be the starting point of education. The most important tenet of Basic Education is education through work and work while engaged in education.

The Gandhian system of education would have the following elements:

(i) Boys and girls would have co-education.
(ii) The education for boys and girls would mainly consist of manual training under the supervision of an educationist.
(iii) Education would be divided in the following stages: Stage I, 1 to 8 years of age. Stage II, 9 to 16 years of age. Stage III, 16 to 25 years of age.
(iv) The sequence of introducing various subjects for teaching and learning would be: general knowledge, drawing simple geometric figures, reading, and writing.
(v) Nothing should be taught to a child by force.
(vi) Play is an essential part of education which should appear to the child like a play.
(vii) All education should be imparted in the mother tongue.
(viii) Religious education is indispensable.
(ix) The boys during the II stage (9 to 16 yrs.) should be taught their parents' vocation in such a way that they will by their own choice obtain livelihood by practising the hereditary craft. This does not apply to girls.
(x) During II stage, the child should acquire general knowledge, geography, world history, botany, astrology, arithmetic, geometry, and algebra. Similarly, each child should know how to sew and cook.
(xi) In the III stage (16-25 yrs.) every young person should have an education as per his or her wishes, and circumstances.
(xii) During the II stage (9-16 yrs.), education should become self-supporting i.e. the child, all the time that he is learning is working upon some industry the proceeds of which will meet the expenditure of the education.

(xiii) Teachers should be paid not very high salaries. They should be paid only a living wage. They should be inspired by the spirit of service, and they should be men of character.

(xiv) Big and expensive buildings are not necessary for educational institutions.

(xv) English should be taught as one of the languages, while Hindi as a national language should be taught to everyone.

(xvi) The children should live at home. They should not be separated from their parents, and they should not be sent to residential schools. The education that children imbibe naturally in well-ordered households is impossible to obtain in hostels. The intimate relationships of the home are the foundation of all social and rural education, and this is something of central importance. Gandhiji always gave the first place to culture of the heart and the building of character.

(xvii) Education ought to develop non-violent capabilities of the child. This would happen if education is creative.

(xviii) Mass education must be made free, universal and compulsory. It should not be perfunctory. It should be given through village crafts and not through books.

(xix) Children, while learning, should actually produce articles that are marketable which should be sold to make education self-supporting.

(xx) Gandhi's system of education is closely linked with his other concepts such as Swadeshi, Antyodaya, Sarvodaya, Swaraj etc.

Gandhi's basic aim was to develop a spiritual mind within a spiritual society and his idea and system of basic education was to help to achieve this aim. Gandhiji did not give predominance to the intellectual aspect in the curriculum. Modern India has discarded this education. In fact, it never really adopted the Gandhian system of education. Modern system of education in India has rejected, has forsaken almost, each of the elements (given above) of the Gandhian system of education. Gandhiji himself was confident about the validity of the basic Education system. He has said, "I have given many things to India but this system of education is, I feel, the best of them. I do not think I will have anything better to offer to the country" (quoted by Radhakrishnan, 2004, p. 14). The scholars in the field of education also have praised this system. For example, John Dewey has said, "Gandhi is one step ahead of all other systems and is full of immense potentialities" (Radhakrishnan, *op. cit.*, p. 15). Modern India has, however, remained unconvinced. As a result, what exists in India today is the monstrous, commercial, moneyed, unequal, highly expensive educational system. As said earlier, the present educational system has been built by the corrupt politicians, who run this system as private kingdoms whose educational emperors (shikshan Samrats) they are. As in other fields, in the field of education also, we have neglected, deserted Gandhiji at our own risk.

6. *Hind Swaraj* on Religion and Communalism in India

Gandhiji had dreamt of a 'dream-Bharat' which was to be a social order that was firmly and securely founded on non-violence, truth, and compassion. He had hoped that all inter-personal, inter-religious, inter-family, and international problems can be solved through developing a culture of non-violence and peace. He, more than once, demonstrated that this was actually possible in real life. It is widely accepted that Gandhiji won political freedom or political independence for India by using the principle and method of non-violence.

The authority no less than the first Governor-General of India (Lord Mountbatten) has testified that Gandhiji was the one-man army without any arms which succeeded in quenching communal fires which had erupted in Bihar, West Bengal, Naokhali, Calcutta, Delhi, etc. after the independence of the country was announced. However, the communal riots in India during the past century (20th century) go to show that Gandhiji's Herculean efforts to solve the problem of communal violence have not always met with success. They have not resulted in rooting out completely or fully the menance of communal disharmony in India. Those efforts have not been successful in wiping out the darkest blot on the whitest sari of Bharat Mata. Even his martyrdom has not proved enough in this context. The unsympathetic critics of Gandhiji have always pointed finger at these riots as the example of his failed principle and method of non-violence. The reality of communal violence before, during, and after the freedom movement is the heaviest cross Gandhiji had to carry in his life.

One of the appealing and endearing aspects of Gandhiji is his very candid, bold, courageous, and balanced position about the role, importance and relevance of religion and spirituality. The views of Gandhiji and Vivekananda are quite similar on this point. Because of the humbug and negative role of religion on many occasions, many people have adopted the stance of being irreligious, secular, atheist (or agnostic or nihilist), and they have undermined or downplayed the role of religion in individual, social, and national life. In *HS* Gandhiji has said, "Religion is dear to me, and my first complaint is that India is becoming irreligious. Here I am not thinking of the Hindu, or the Mahomedan, or the Christian or the Buddhist religion, but of that religion which underlies all religions. We are turning away from God" (p. 42).

Defending religion further, he has said that many of us bring unlawful charge(s) against religion. Humbug there undoubtedly is about all religions, but it is much less harmful than that of modern civilization. Religious superstition is harmless compared to that of modern civilization. Moreover, we can always fight religious superstition not by disregarding religion but by appreciating the other's religion (pp. 42-45).

Gandhiji did not subscribe to the doctrine of secularism which has been the dominant philosophy or doctrine under modern civilization. Secularism has been an anti-religious thought since Greek times itself. The combination of secularism, individualism, and nationalism is so deadly that it can cause disintegration and the absence of peace. Vinoba, therefore has asked for a synthesis of spirituality and science.

What has *HS* to say about the problem of violent communalism in India? Can there be one nation or can there be communal peace when there are multiple religions in the country? Has the coming of Muslims to India unmade the nation, and destroyed peace? What have been the causes of communal violence in India? Many people believe that the formation of one nation and communal peace in India are not possible now because two major religious communities in India namely, Hindus and Muslims are the old, sworn, and inborn enemies of each other.

As usual, Gandhiji's analysis of this point also is novel, unconventional, and original. According to him, it is the presence of railways, doctors, and lawyers in the country who have been the obstructing factors in the process of the creation of communal harmony, and the formation of the Indian nation. On the face of it, this is a curious explanation of communal strife in India. But what it means is that it is the modernization or coming of modern civilization which is at the root of communal riots. It is modern civilization which has given birth to the disease of communal violence. The railways, doctors, lawyers, and "such other maddening conveniences" have enabled man to violate the limits or restrictions imposed physically and intellectually by "Nature, God, and Maker". To convey this perspective effectively, Gandhiji has said "... man is so made by Nature as to require him to restrict his movements as far as his hands and feet will take him ... God set a limit to a man's locomotive ambition in the construction of his body.... I am so constructed that I can only serve my immediate neighbours, but, in my conceit, I pretend to have discovered that I must with my body serve every individual in the universe .... railways are a most dangerous institution. Man has gone further away from his maker" (p. 51).

According to *HS*, a major obstacle to Home Rule or self-government in India is the sectarianism or a sectarian nationalism fostered by certain sections of both the Muslim and Hindu communities. The solution to this evil lies in the development of a moderate, liberal nationalism. Gandhiji introduced a distinction between religion as organization, and religion as ethics and spirituality. Underlying all organized religions is a universal ethics and spirituality, which teaches the unconditional love for God and one's neighbour. At the same time, religion as organization or institution serves as a convenient means of a certain type of pre-political identity, and as a means of reacting, much yearned for, to gain certain spiritual ends. As such, every organized religion has legitimacy. It follows that organized religion ought to practise tolerance for each other (Parel, pp. liii).

In order to understand the above, let us note what is spirituality. Religion is of a specific name such as Hindu, Sikh, and there are both principles or values and rituals in it. If a person lead life with faith in the following, then we can say that he is a spiritual being or he is leading a spiritual life: (i) Faith in eternal values, (ii) Faith that life exists even after death, (iii) Unity of all life, (iv) Belief that God exists or belief that there is intelligence and organization in the universe. (This concept of spirituality is from Vinoba).

Has the coming of or introduction of Muslims unmade the nation and destroyed the social harmony in India? In *HS*, Gandhiji has rejected this theory. He believed that India cannot cease to be a nation because people of different religions have come to reside in it. The introduction of foreigners does not necessarily destroy a nation; foreigners merge in it; in fact, a country is one nation only when such a condition obtains in it. The country must have a faculty of assimilation. India has always been such a country (p. 52).

Gandhiji has rejected another theory in this context, the theory that Hindus and Muslims are inborn enemies, and they cannot live together peacefully. He held that such a thought is a legacy from the past when Hindus and Muslims fought with each other. But they have long since ceased to fight, and, therefore, the notion of inborn enmity is a false notion. It is to be remembered that Hindus and Muslims ceasing to fight was a pre-British phenomenon; it is not true that the fighting between Hindus and Muslims ceased only after the coming of Britishers to India. In fact, with the British advent, the quarrels recommenced. It is the "divide and rule" policy of the British Raj which incited the people of both the communities to fight with each other even for small things (pp. 53-54). There have been bitter quarrels between Hindus and Muslims, between Buddhists and Hindus but all these have not come in the way of formation of the Indian nation. We should also not forget that many Hindus and Muslims have the same ancestors, and the same blood runs through their veins.

Communalism is quite rampant in India because political parties/organizations are for gaining and retaining power through religionalism (*dharmavad*) and regionalism (*Prantavad*). The politics of power and elections have increased caste divide and communal divide. Their ideology is that power grows out of the barrel of a gun, and that a gun is the best tool for social transformation, that the country can enjoy peace only if it is fully armed. They obviously believe in building up a violent social order. Their goal is power and not the truth.

One of the causes of periodic communal conflicts in India has been over cow slaughter and cow protection. Gandhiji's stand on this issue was such as would result in the safety of both the cow and the man. In other words, his view would end the communal violence on this count. He held the cow in an affectionate reverence; he believed that the cow was a protector of India; it was the most useful animal in hundreds of ways. Thus, his belief in the principles of non-violence, love, compassion, etc., and the functional value of the cow made him a staunch opponent of cow slaughter. But, he said, "Because of this, I should not bring myself to kill some person to protect or save the cow. Just as I respect the cow, I respect my fellowmen also. Therefore, one should not kill a human being for protecting the cow. I should sacrifice my life to save her, but I should not take my brother's life. This is the law of our religion" (pp. 53-54).

In *HS* (pp. 54-58), Gandhiji has minutely examined the issue of cow slaughter at length. He can be seen at his persuasive best, and as a very sharp, minute examiner, while analyzing the issue of the cow. The major thrust of his argument was that Muslims alone should not be blamed for cow slaughter and related violence. Hindus also may sometimes become responsible for it. One of the solutions, therefore, is for Hindus to "turn the searchlight inward". According to him, Hindu-Muslim conflicts have remained intractable due to obstinacy, insistence, unreasonableness, sense of superiority, and rigidity in views and observances of rituals and rites. Hindus, and even Jains, have been trading in cow meat to make profits. It is also wrongly believed by many that while Hindus believe in *Ahimsa,* Muslims do not. Very often, the selfish and false religious teachers put many such misconcepts in the minds of people. The British used to join hands in this mischief. The Holy Koran contains hundreds of passages which are acceptable to Hindus. But if there are a few unacceptable passages, that is not sufficient reason for violent conflict. Would the British ever allow Hindus and Muslims to come together? If two brothers want to become brotherly, no one can stop them from doing so". Thus argued Gandhiji (pp. 54-58).

Communal unity is essential for communal harmony. But we should have a correct notion of unity and follow the correct path for achieving it. Gandhiji held that unity must not mean only political unity which may be imposed. It means an unbreakable unity of hearts. The first thing essential for achieving such a unity is for every man, whatever his religion may be, to represent in his own person Hindu, Muslim, Christian, Jew, etc. In short, every Hindu and non-Hindu has to feel his identity with everyone of the millions of the inhabitants of Hindustan. In order to realize this, every man should cultivate personal friendship with persons representing faiths other than his own. He should have the same regard for the other faiths as he has for his own (pp. 171-72). National unity or integration should be achieved through religion, spirituality and culture and not through nationalism and religionalism. The former is conducive to universalism, non-violence and peace, while the latter leads to violence, colonialism, imperialism, and racial religious fundamentalism.

The arguments presented in this context by C. Rajagopalachari, a great intellectual, a man with a very sharp and keen intellect are certainly worth noting here. He has said that it is true that there has been a nationwide decline in morality in India. Instead of becoming disappointed because of this, the important work that needs to be done is to revive or resurrect religion. Religion is the only entrenched area on which we can progress and become prosperous. We must realize that any politics without religion (dharma) cannot bring national welfare, progress, and plenty. Politics without religion corrupts everyone. Reforms in politics is not the way to deal with this problem because politics cannot be reformed. For such reforms, religion (dharma) is very much essential; we have to replace politics by religion. Religion (dharma), Dharma means to be scared of sin (*pap*). It means faith in God's grace and not religious rites. The words like secularism are meaningless.

The great thinker *Tolstoy* also was against institutionalization of the religion and the state. Yet he did not subscribe to the doctrine of secularism, nor did he adopt an anti-religious stand or the ideology of individualism. Instead he advocated adoption of true religion or spirituality. According to Tolstoy, the history of the Christian church has been the history of cruelty. Similarly, the government or the State has failed to bring peace in the country. The government has been the instrument of exploitation and violence. Therefore, ideal Christians should seek the Kingdom of God within themselves. Gandhiji would fully endorse this analysis and viewpoint.

7. *Hind Swaraj* on the System of Justice

The beliefs, sayings, proverbs (i.e. folklore) in wide currency or circulation in the ordinary life of the masses perfectly and accurately expresses the true nature or character of institutions, systems, professions, etc. About the lawyers, judges, pleaders, legal or judicial system, law courts, doctors, hospitals, it is widely believed that 'no wise man should climb the steps of the houses of the lawyers, law courts, and doctors', or 'that man is wise who never ever climbs the steps of the houses of lawyers and doctors'. It is further said that 'there is perhaps no difference between lawyers and liers', and that the lawyers' uniform is a black coat because it appropriately and correctly reflects or expresses their black deeds.

It must be more than a mere co-incidence that Gandhiji has devoted two chapters (Chapter XI and Chapter XII) in *HS* for discussing common and ancient wisdom regarding the merits, demerits, advantages, and dangers from lawyers and doctors, who are the products or progeny of modern civilization and whose stranglehold on the masses has increased significantly over a period of time. In the very opening of his discussion, Gandhiji has opined that the advice that people should normally not go to law courts and hospitals was a correct, sound, wise advice. Then comes from him the heaviest sledgehammer blow to the lawyers and doctors when he says that it was his firm view that the lawyers have enslaved India. They have accentuated Hindu-Mahomedan dissentions; have confirmed English authority, ... have never done a single good thing and the lawyer's profession teaches immorality. It is exposed to temptations from which few are saved; ... the lawyers will, as a rule, advance quarrels; their interest exists in multiplying disputes; ... they are glad when men have disputes. The petty pleaders actually manufacture disputes. Their touts, like so many leeches, suck the blood of poor people. Lawyers are men who have little to do. Lazy people, in order to indulge in luxuries, take up such a profession. Hindu-Mohamedan quarrels have been often due to the intervention of lawyers. ... the greatest injury they have done to the country is that they have tightened the English grip over India. Gandhi's most severe criticism of the modern legal system is that it had become a handmaid of colonial rule. Would it be possible for the English to carry on their government without law courts? It is wrong to consider that courts are established for the benefit of the people. Those who want to perpetuate their power do so through the law courts.

According to Gandhiji, men became more unmanly and cowardly when they resorted to courts of law. Without lawyers, courts could not have been established and conducted, and without the latter, the English could not have rule at India. If pleaders were to abandon their profession and consider it just as degrading as prostitution, English rule would break up in a day. We are wrongly charged that we love quarrels and courts, as fish love water. Gandhiji has said that what is true of pleaders is equally applicable to courts or judges; they are first cousins, and one gives strength to the other (pp. 58-61).

H.D. Thoreau was similarly highly critical of judges. According to him, we cannot leave important things to be decided by judges because they recognize no authority but the constitution. They are merely the inspectors of a pick-lock and murderer's tool. The judges merely pronounce the verdict of law. Their verdict is not touched by the love of truth. Thoreau believed that where there is judgement, there is falsehood. Judges are tools; little men. Certainly, they are not to be more respected because their master enslaves their understanding and conscience. They persist in being the servants of the worst of men, and not the servants of humanity.

Thus, in Gandhiji's assessment the above is the nature and character of the modern system of justice. It is a true characterization or a true statement because we have got it from the 'insider' or from the lawyer (Gandhiji) who was a successful lawyer himself, of course, the success defined in terms of standards laid down by Gandhiji, and not the conventional standards. How horrible, dark, dangerous our legal system is! Modern man has constructed a judicial system wherein everything except justice is available, and wherein the truth is the first and greatest casualty. It is a system wherein lies are told or lies are traded on an oath of truth. All the constituents of this system vie with each other to add to the negativities of the system. They have formed a mutually admiring narcissistic club wherein each one congratulates or compliments the other for having contributed to the creation of such a 'beautiful, well-organized, and well-functioning' system. But the chief reality or the greatest truth about this system is its venality, uselessness, and barrenness. No wonder Gandhiji had a very great abhorrence for it, and he likened it to a prostitute.

The lacunae of this system are legion; while the character-related ones have been indicated above, the examples of functional problems are given below: The system works without any qualms although the feature, Justice delayed is justice denied applies to it perfectly well. The system is extremely time-consuming. It is marked by intolerable delays and the backlog of cases is mind-blogging. It is a multi-tired, complicated, highly expensive system which is beyond the reach and means of the most people. The process of appointment of judges, their promotions needs to be improved urgently. The relative competence and economic status of judges and some practising lawyers is another problem needing attention. It is a centralized system which needs to be decentralized in order to make it more accessible, convenient, affordable for the rural, local, unlettered, simple people.

In fact, the implication of the above is that it would be better to dismantle the present rogue system, and to endeavour through appropriate education to minimize disharmony, conflicts and disputes by following the path of truth, ahimsa, compassion, mutual understanding, the principle of 'live and let live'. The remaining cases of conflicts can be sorted out by creating a functioning decentralized, rural, local system of justice.

8. *Hind Swaraj* on Medical or Health System

After having presented his assessment of the modern system of justice, Gandhiji turns to the examination of the modern system of medicine in *HS*. This clubbing together of doctors and lawyers may be surprising to many because the doctors are held by the public in far more esteem, honour, love and awe as compared to the pleaders. Some people regard doctors even as semi-gods. It is, his penetrating, discerning, revolutionary eye which enabled Gandhiji to know, to unravel the problems and afflictions of these systems. The views Gandhiji has expressed in *HS* without fear and favour are truly radical, unconventional, and revolutionary.

It was Gandhiji's view that the profession of doctors, like that of lawyers, was also harmful and hateful. The whole modern system or modern civilization was like the 'Upas' tree i.e. the Javanese tree so poisonous as to destroy life for many miles round. Its branches are represented by parasitical professions such as law and medicine. Immorality is the root of the 'Upas' tree (professions). Newer and newer diseases have come up as the modern civilization has progressed. As a student, Gandhiji had the intention and ambition to become a doctor to serve the country. But after he came to know the reality, he was disillusioned, and abandoned his ambition.

Gandhiji disliked the medical profession also because it served the interests of colonialism. The British have certainly used and effectively used this profession against Indians. English physicians used the profession for political gain (pp. 62-63).

Notwithstanding its immense prestige, and large-scale public dependence on it, the medical profession has hardly ever been in a position to give a true, sound health of body and mind to anyone. It hardly spends any time and other resources on the prevention of diseases. Its emphasis and attention have been on the curative side of the health system. But in this respect also, the medical system hardly ever helps to completely root out, or completely cure the disease forever or permanently or lasting for long. The spirit, the approach of modern medicine is to create an appearance-disappearance cycle of diseases which Gandhiji has explained well in *HS* as given below:

The task (business) before the doctor is really to rid the body of diseases of the patient. The diseases occur due to negligence and indulgence. There is a creation of the sequence of ill-pill-bill, and the 'pill culture' enables the sick person to go through the sequence/cycle of indulgence-affliction-pill use-cure-indulgence. The medical profession saves the sick from taking the punishment which is his due for his indulgence. The doctor's intervention in a sick case helps the sick to indulge more. A continuance of a course of medicine must, therefore, result in the loss of control over the mind, the loss of mastery over oneself, and it helps to repeat the indulgence in vice (pp. 62-63). Doctors induce us to indulge, and we become deprived of self-control, and become effeminate. Consequently, we become unfit to serve our country, and our slavery is deepened (p. 64). It may sound harsh and exaggerated but it is true that the modern hospitals kill rather than save.

Hospitals the world over are increasingly becoming like five-star hotels. In a way, Gandhiji had predicted this when he had said, "Hospitals are institutions for propagating sin" (p. 63). He has further said, "Doctors violate our religious instincts" (p. 64). How? By killing lakhs of animals every year for experimentation, by practising vivisection, by using animal fats and spirituous liquors in preparing medicines, and so on.

Currently, the motivation behind opting for the medical profession is not noble. It has suffered from a significant degradation. Earlier, 'the roots of honour' of different professions used to be service, sacrifice, compassion, love, sympathy, and so on. It is no longer so. The major motivation invariably is now to make more money, to amass wealth, to obtain honours and riches. There is no real service of humanity in the medical profession now (pp. 64-65).

One can easily observe that the medical/health system is becoming extremely machinery—oriented, and, therefore, it is becoming increasingly mechanical. In the treatment of patients, there are a heavy intervention or invasion of machines, gadgets, equipment, medical tests, bio-technology and bio-medical engineering. The role of affection, concern, care, service, love, humanness in the treatment and in taking care of patients is definitely going down. The relationship between the patients and doctors is also changing for the worst; it has become highly money-oriented and commercial. The very serious problem of severe side-effects of modern medicine has remained deliberately, purposefully unattended.

The modern medical system does not heal either the body or the mind or the soul. It neglects the soul i.e. the spiritual and moral foundations of bodily health. Thus, ignoring the soul, the medical profession puts men at its mercy and contributes to the diminution of human dignity and self-control. Modern medicine, taking a purely bodily view of health, ignores the need for the health of the soul, which is necessary for the maintenance of even bodily health (pp. 63-64). It is interesting that Gandhiji had already seen some of these things a century back itself. One of the highly worrisome dimensions of the modern health system is the collusion between the medical profession and the pharmaceutical industry – the collusion which is helping the said industry and doctors to make huge profits at the cost of consumers (patients). Capra, for example, has now criticized this aspect of the modern system. Gandhiji, however, had done so 100 years back itself. Gandhiji had exposed the hand-in-glove relationship between the medical profession and the pharmaceutical industry. Such an alliance has made the health system a profit-driven system. Gandhiji wanted it to remain an honour-driven and vocation-driven profession.

The implication of these stark realities is that the people, when they are ill, should not get admitted in the hospital, nor should they go to any doctor for treatment. Neither his body nor his mind, nor his soul will benefit by going to a doctor or to a hospital. Hospitals are a profit-driven five-star institutions, its doctors completely money-minded. This applies to every system of medicine (allopathy, Ayurved, Homoeopathy, Unani, etc.). This was true in the past and it is true now also. Such views of Gandhiji are well-expressed in the following Sanskrit verse which compares a doctor with the messenger of death (Yama) in Hindu philosophy. It conveys that perhaps Yama is better than a doctor or a physician.

> *Vaidyaraj Namostubhyam*
> *Yamaraj Sahodara* |
> *Yamaraj Harati Pranaha*
> *Vaidyaraj Pranaha Evam Dhanam cha* ||

Broadly, this verse means: He! Vaidyaraj, my salutation to you. You are the brother of Yamaraj. Yamaraj takes away Pranaha (life). Vaidyaraj takes away both pranaha and also wealth. Physician heal thyself!

What is Gandhiji's prescription for the cure? He would say, avoid, prevent, becoming sick by avoiding negligence and indulgence. Always have full self-control. Please remember that one who conquers others is strong, but one who conquers the self is mighty. So be mighty. If you do fall ill in spite of all efforts and precautions, there is no use going to a doctor or to a big hospital. Then what does one do? Chant the 'Ramanama' with full faith, and you will be completely rid of your illness. The 'Ramanama' is the ultimate, most potent, unfailing, most effective "Ramabana" or the remedy (as certain in its effect as the arrow released by Rama). The 'Ramanama' is the cure of all cures.

In short, Gandhiji's health model goes beyond allopathy, homoeopathy, Ayurveda, naturopathy, unani, etc. It can be called spirituopathy.

9. Gandhiji on Economic Development

In 20 chapters of *HS* there is no inclusion of a chapter (or a section) on economic development. Yet we have included in our book, a section on "Gandhiji and development" for two reasons. First, development today is one of the very important and controversial themes of global discourse, and second, Gandhiji has said a lot which is of fundamental importance on development. His views on development are quite in tune with the spirit and message of *HS*. The objective of this section, therefore, is to discuss some of Gandhian ideas on economics and economic development based on his write-up titled "Economic development and moral development", included in Hind-Swaraj by its editor, Parel (pp. 156-164).

We have heard about different ages or "*yugas*" or time periods such as Satyayuga, Stone Age, Iron Age, Atomic Age, etc. In the past 150-200 years, mankind is said to be living in the Development Age. In this age, development is supreme value, a dominant theme, an objective *par excellence*, the super ideal, widespread obsession, a value which has shaped the entire value system, which, in turn, has determined the mind sets of the people.

Gandhiji has presented a picture of 'Alternative Development'. In one of his speeches, he addressed to himself a question as to whether economic progress clashes with real progress? In this speech, his basic ideas on economic development are explained. He had a radically different understanding of the meaning, nature, and scope of the concept and process of development. The intellectual culture of Gandhiji was all-encompassing in the sense that his understanding was inspired by such diverse sources as the New Testament, Shakespeare, and A.R. Wallace (co-discoverer of the principle of natural selection), and the Indian scriptures.

What is the meaning of progress or development? For Gandhiji there are three related terms in this context namely, economic progress, moral progress, and real progress. Economic progress means material advancement without limit. Moral progress means advancement in the observation of morality. Real progress occurs when moral progress occurs along with material progress. Moral progress and real progress are mostly the same. Thus, real progress occurs when progress of the 'permanent element' in us occurs. According to Gandhiji, the relationship between development, progress, riches, affluence, on the one hand, and moral development, or real development, on the other, is negative. The material affluence has, in all times, been a hindrance to moral or real progress. This is illustrated by the rise and fall of Roman Empire, Egyptian Empire, the empire of the Yadavas, and by the lives of the greatest teachers of the world such as Jesus, Buddha, Muhammad, Krishna, and so on. The negative relationship mentioned above has been vividly illustrated in a Biblical story in which a very rich man comes to Jesus and asks him what he should do to inherit eternal life. Jesus tells him "Go thy way, sell whatever you have and give to the poor, follow me and then shall have a treasure in heaven". The rich man becomes sad to hear that and goes away. Jesus tells his disciples that in this way, "It is easier for a camel to go through the eye of the needle than for a rich man to enter the Kingdom of God."

Thus, according to Gandhiji, in so far as we have made the modern materialistic craze our goal, in so far are we going downhill in the path of progress. Economic progress without limit is antagonistic to real progress. We cannot serve both God and Mammon at one and the same time is an economic truth of the highest value. The western nations are groaning under the heel of the monster-God of materialism, and moral growth has become stunted.

Gandhiji's development economics is clearly different from mainstream or conventional development economics. The former is based on, again, a biblical advice: "Take no thought for the morrow" or the promise given by Him in the Gita that "Yogakshemam Vahamyaham" i.e. it is my duty to provide for the daily basic needs of all living beings. Two or three implications of this advice and promise are: In economic progress, people's daily wants should first be satisfied. The security of one's livelihood should not be a problem in a well-ordered society. The test of the progress of a society is whether there is absence of starvation among the masses, and not how many millionaires there are in that society. How contemporaneous is this perspective! In spite of such a sane advice a century back itself, the mad mad modern civilization is regularly publishing the number of millionaires in different countries, and indicating the level of richness of different countries on that basis. Second, pauperism leads to nothing but moral degradation. (Budhikshtaha Kim na Karoti Papam" means which sin, what kind of sin will the hungry not perpetrate?) The advice in conventional economics is exactly opposite. Since it favours capital-intensive technology, accumulation of more and more capital presumably to accelerate the growth rate requires higher and higher rate of saving. Gandhiji values scriptural advice rather than that of mainstream economics. He, accordingly argued that people should not hoard (save) money for selfish ends, but if they wished to hoard money as a trustee for millions of people, they should have as much riches and hoardings as they want. It may be noted that trusteeship is an integral part of Gandhian development economics.

In his speech on 'Does economic progress clash with real progress', Gandhiji has given such an advice to India and had we followed it, by now, Indian society would have been a sane society of the highest order. Gandhiji has said, "… we must keep our civilization and morals … we need not be afraid of ideals. Our nation will only then be a truly spiritual nation. We shall then show more truth than gold, greater fearlessness than pomp of power and wealth, greater charity than the love of self. If we will but clean our houses, palaces, and temples of the attributes of wealth and show in them attributes of morality, we would be able to offer battle to any combination of hostile forces without having to carry the burden of a heavy militia. Let us first seek the Kingdom of God and his righteousness and the irrevocable promise is that everything shall be added upto us. This is real economics" (p. 156-164).

Gandhiji's basic ideas on economics, development, growth, progress can be summarized as follows:

i) The scriptures of the world are far safer and sounder treatises on the laws of economics.
ii) Jesus was the greatest economist of his time.
iii) We cannot serve both God and Mammon at the same time.
iv) Economic progress and moral development are inversely related.
v) The possession of riches has been a hindrance to real progress or real growth. The real growth (progress) is moral growth.
vi) Take no thought for the morrow.
vii) The economist has a place in society if he interprets, investigates laws of God, and shows how to distribute wealth so that there might not be poverty.
viii) Economists mostly formulate and prescribe laws for the rich. Such economists are an unwelcome intrusion in our society.

ix) Man should rest content with what are his real needs and become self-sufficient.
x) Human beings are an integral part of Nature, not outside nature.
xi) We need to respect, worship nature.
xii) The goal should be production by masses and not mass production.
xiii) There is enough for everybody's needs but not everybody's greed.
xiv) Simple living and high thinking.
xv) The Means should justify ends.
xvi) Yogakshemam vahamyaham. Everything shall be added unto to us.

Gandhiji's insistence that development must (should) mean spiritual development is clearly reflected in the following definition of development given by him:

"I want development, self-determination, and freedom, but all these I want for the soul. I do not think that steel age is an advance over flint age. I am indifferent. The intellect and all faculties of man must be harnessed to spiritual development. Development must mean human development, spiritualization, and progress towards the destiny of man". Thus development must mean soul-development, development must result in the creation of a spiritual nation.

Gandhiji has visualized a system of government and a system (method or mode) of production in *HS*. He was opposed to both the range and scale of high, large technology-based modes of production. This is because mechanized or capitalistic production methods had a number of vices. (i) They lead to centralization and concentration of production, economic, and political systems. (ii) They economise (save) and substitute capital for labour and thereby create mass unemployment of labour. (iii) The philosophy and approaches and goals (such as profit maximization) of industrialists result in exploitation of labour. (iv) They create and entrench inequalities of income, wealth, assets, consumption, and regional development. (v) They are anti-village development or anti-ruralization or anti-Arcadian civilization. They promote, nurture towns and cities which, by their nature, tend to resort to violence and untruth. (vi) They increase dependence, they are not conducive to self-reliance and Swadeshi. (vii) Because of mass production, they have to become compulsive demand generators which they do by creating, nurturing unnecessary wants, unnecessary necessities, and for doing so, they spread untruth, falsity, through advertising and other sales promotion techniques which waste valuable resources. It is amazing that modern man talks of resources are limited or scarce and yet waste valuable resources on advertising. (viii) They are anti-Awadeshi and anti-self-reliance. (ix) Because of these features, capitalistic production modes are anti-Swaraj.

Instead of tackling these problems through appropriate measures, socialists, communists, etc. have sought to solve them by changing the ownership of means of production from the private-ownership to state ownership. But this has not helped anywhere. With the concentration of ownership of the means of production in the hands of the Government or the State, the problem of centralization has become all the more intractable and serious, and urgent. The states which tended to become dictatorial used their political power to usurp more and more economic power.

The real, correct solution to the problems of using capitalistic modes of production lies in decentralization of everything, giving the topmost priority to agriculture, promoting small agro-industries, promoting human-scaled, human-faced technology, economy, and polity. Such systems of production and government are what *HS* had advocated.

Another aspect of economic development which has received attention in *HS* is consumption or consumer behaviour. In *HS* consumption is not simply a matter of economics, but has a civilizational dimension. Consumer behaviour at present (and its discussion in conventional economics) has been discussed from the point of view of utility maximization. According to *HS*, this is not enough. It is necessary that we discuss how demand is generated, and what are the environmental consequences of increase in consumption. There are certain features of consumption in modern civilization. First, maximization of consumption (and production), exalting the notion of consumer's sovereignty, and the promise that more is always more welfare-increasing than less of it. The goal is maximization of production and consumption, or the promotion of consumerism. The use of more goods and a variety of goods is taken to be a mark of being civilized, advanced, progressive. As J.D. Sethi has effectively put it, the new consumption problem is that of insatiability of contrived wants and boosting of consumption through the credit card revolution. Second, utility, or satisfaction from consumption is regarded as amoral. The body, the physical and not the ethical or moral considerations, have become the focus of consumption activity. There has been the emergence of a new kind of slavery. People are being enslaved now by the temptation of money and the luxuries money can buy. There has been a fall in moral standards due to greed. The solution, according to Gandhiji, for such a problem is to bury modern civilization and replace it by true civilization.

In the area of consumption, the terms commonly used are, *inter alia*, preference, utility, and welfare. Certain points which occur implicitly or explicitly in *HS* about these concepts may be mentioned here. (i) For Gandhiji, man is the ultimate measuring rod and he tended to take individualistic rather than collectivistic viewpoints of welfare (i.e. he focused on man rather than caste, class, tribe, etc.). (ii) At the same time, unlike mainstream economists, he also believed that one's behaviour as an economic agent cannot be isolated from one's behaviour as a moral agent. Preference, therefore means ethical preference. Gandhiji had a normative concept of preference.

The main arguments in the Gandhian perspective on consumption can broadly be summarized as follows:

(i) Wants ought to be limited; resources are enough. (wants may be unlimited, but needs are limited.) There is enough for everybody's needs but not for every body's greed.

(ii) The goal in consumption ought to be
- Minimization of wants = peace and happiness
- Voluntary simplicity
- Voluntary austerity
- Voluntary poverty
- Ceiling on desires

(iii) The principle of minimization of wants serves the individual (health, peace), social (distributional) and environmental (ecological) good. This economic principle is extremely important because it has a spiritual dimension. The practitioner of this prime principle is said to undertake *'Tapas'* or *'Tapaha'* which means purificatory action, ascetic self-denial and mortification.

(iv) The Gandhian consumption theory is founded on Swaraj i.e. self-control.

(v) This does not mean he glorified or celebrated poverty. For him, for the poor and hungry, God appears in the form of a bread.

(vi) Pleasure without conscience is one of the seven deadly sins.

Gandhiji is well supported by (he is in very good company of) various saints and poets in India in this regard. For example, Santa Kabir has spread this ideal in his beautiful, simple *doha* (a poetic construction) in Hindi:

Sai itana dijiye jame kutumba samaye
Maya bhi bhukha na rahu sadhu na bhukha jaye.

It means, Lord! Give me only that much which will enable me to feed my family. Any visitor or guest (atithi) should not be required to go hungry from my house, and I should not also be needed to suffer from hunger. The ideal of voluntary simplicity or voluntary poverty has been taught again by Kabir when he describes his mental frame or mental state by saying 'mana laga fakiri me' i.e. now my mind is attracted towards poverty.

Similarly, an Urdu poet has said in Urdu,

Tangadasti buri aur mal ki kasarat bhi buri,
Inhi do chijose aadmika imaan badal jata hai ।

It means, extreme scarcity and extreme plenty are both bad. They change man's morality and ethics.

One comes across the approval of this consumption ethics in various popular sayings such as

Thoda hai thodeki jarurat hai
(a little is available, a little more is needed);
Hum us deshke vasi hai janha thodeme gujara hota hai
(We belong to that nation where we can live with little).

The Gandhian consumption ethics is founded on, *inter alia*, the teachings of the Bible which John Ruskin has highlighted in his book *Unto This Last*. The Bible says, Till the light of the eye can only be through tears, and the light of the body through sack cloth, till Christ's gift of bread and bequest of peace shall be Unto this Last as unto thee, the enjoyment of luxuries is a cruel thing to do.

Things, conveniences, commodities, goods, wealth are different from happiness (sukha). They do not give joy and happiness. One gets happiness from or through peace, purification of emotions and sentiments, and mind transcendence. By giving the doctrine of minimization of wants, Gandhiji brought about a confluence of the material and spiritual, and thereby created a path of peace and happiness.

10. Hind Swaraj and Pandit Jawaharlal Nehru

Gandhiji's book *Hind Swaraj* edited by A.J. Parel includes certain supplementary writings of Gandhiji which are related to the theme of *HS*. Apart from letters between Gandhiji on the one hand, and Polak, Ampthil, Tolstoy, Wybergh on the other, the book contains three letters between Pandit Jawaharlal Nehru (P.J.N. or just Nehru hereafter) and Gandhiji. Specifically, there are two letters dated 5-10-1945 and 13-11-1945, from Gandhiji to PJN, and one letter dated 9-10-1945, from Nehru to Gandhiji.

The *HS* revolution did not actually occur in India because most of the political leaders, political parties, scientists and technologists, and other elites could not afford to implement or work for the revolutionary ideas and vision of *HS*. As the heir or successor to Gandhiji, as the most powerful leader during the freedom movement and immediately thereafter, as the leader who, barring the Mahatma, had the largest mass following, and the leader who could have taken India on the Gandhian path shown in *HS* but did not do so, PJN has to take most of the blame for why *HS* remained in the book and did not see the light of the day. It is the irony of history that Nehru saw the revolution in Fabian socialism and in communism of the then Soviet Union but could not see it in the life and thought of his own Bapu.

Gandhiji and Nehru agreed with each other on certain matters but they also differed on some other matters and many of their differences were very deep, basic and fundamental. At the heart of their disagreement was the basic thesis of *HS*. Nehru found *HS* impracticable. He could not see the originality and the revolutionary potential of *HS*. He could not show the respect to the ideas in *HS* which they deserved. In a study like the present book on *HS* it is but appropriate to discuss at least briefly the relative positions or relative viewpoints of Nehru and *HS* on the alternative world-view.

When Gandhiji died, Nehru gave a highly emotion-charged speech which reflected the attachment and love of Nehru for Gandhiji. If Nehru had a similar attachment or devotion or fervour for Gandhiji's ideas, programmes, and methods, the contemporary history of India (and of the world through India) would have been very much different today. But he chose not to be guided by the 'light' he so highly eulogized in his above-mentioned speech. Nehru said, "Friends, ... the light has gone out of our lives and there is darkness everywhere ... our beloved leader, Bapu, as we called him, the father of Nation is no more.... The light has gone out, and yet I was wrong. For the light that shown in this country was no ordinary light. The light that has illumined this country for these many years, will illumine this country for many more years, and a thousand years later that light will still be seen in this country and the world will see it and it will give solace to innumerable hearts. For that light presented the living truth and the eternal man was with us with his eternal truth reminding us of the right path, drawing us from error, taking his ancient country to freedom". *HS* is at the centre of this light. It is unfortunate that Pandit Jawahar Lal Nehru refused to be guided by this light, and took the country on the path which was very much different from the Gandhian path.

The three letters exchanged between Gandhiji and Nehru enable us to have a peep into their relationship and viewpoints. One of these letters from Gandhiji to Nehru reveals that Gandhiji had a desire to live upto 125 years of age. Gandhiji might have hoped that if both of them (Nehru and Gandhiji) come to agree on the path or model for the development and reconstruction of India, she can be made economically, socially and morally a strong country which can contribute to the development of a peaceful, non-violent Indian social order and the world social order. Gandhiji was keen that both of them should understand each other clearly and without confusion, that there should not be a misunderstanding and doubts between them. He also wanted that every one and all the political parties should fully and clearly know the points of agreement and disagreement between them.

On the basis of Nehru's letter to him dated 9-10-1945, Gandhiji himself has listed in his letter to Nehru dated 13-11-1945, the points of agreement between them. These points are as follows (Parel, p. 155):

(1) Gandhiji said to Nehru that the real question, according to him (Nehru), is how to bring about man's highest intellectual, economic, political and moral development and he (Gandhiji) agreed entirely.

(2) In this there should be an equal right and opportunity for all.

(3) In other words, there should be equality between the town dwellers and the villagers in the standard of food and drink, clothing, and other living conditions. In order to achieve this equality today people should be able to produce for themselves the necessities of life, i.e., clothing, foodstuffs, dwellings, lighting and water.

(4) Man is not born to live in isolation but is essentially a social animal independent and interdependent. No one can and should ride on another's back. If we try to work out the necessary conditions for such a life, we are forced to the conclusion that the unit of society should be a village, or call it a small and manageable group of people who would, in the ideal, be self-sufficient (in the matter of their vital requirements) as a unit and bound together in the bonds of mutual co-operation and interdependence.

Prior to presenting the gist of their talks with each other, Gandhiji told Nehru that there is not much difference in their outlooks. This can be said to be the understatement of the millennium because the outlooks of Nehru and Gandhiji differed vastly on many big and small matters. Some of these matters are mentioned below:

(i) In respect of the alternative paradigms, while Gandhiji offered a civilizational alternative, Nehru's vision remained confined to the relative nitty-gritty of socio-economic and political matters. The depth and breadth of Nehru's vision was quite limited compared to that of the Mahatma's. Gandhiji challenged modern civilization. The wanted to root it out and replace it by ancient Indian civilization. Nehru tried to reconstruct the social order on the basis of borrowed ideas from the Western world-view. Nehru, unlike Gandhiji, was wedded to modernization, and although he did see the strengths of ancient Indian civilization, he did not think of building the future in terms of ancient Indian civilization's principles, tenets, and philosophy.

(ii) While Gandhiji dreamt of creating an Arcadian civilization, Nehru regarded villages to be dung-hills or dung-heaps. While Gandhiji was essentially a 'farmer', Nehru was an urban and urbane individual.

(iii) In Nehru's scheme of things ethics and morals were not as crucial as they were in Gandhiji's world-view.

(iv) Unlike Nehru, Gandhiji believed in the need, importance, and uses of decentralization.

(v) Gandhiji wanted ultimately the withering away of the state, and minimization of the state in the intervening period. A believer in socialism, central planning, gigantic industries as Nehru was, he thought that the State has a more than marginal role to play in the life of society.

(vi) Nehru regarded *HS* to be old fashioned, outdated, impractical, and Utopian. In 1940s, Nehru used to highlight that while Gandhiji had written *HS* about 35 years back, he (Nehru) had read it 20 years back. The point of his argument was that many changes, developments had occurred during the years after *HS* was written, and therefore, the ideas in *HS* had tended to become outdated and irrelevant. On the other hand, *HS* was the seed of the whole Gandhian thought which flowered subsequently. The truth and validity of *HS* were the same for Gandhiji in 1910, and during the 1940s. He has said that barring some stylistic changes, he would not change any part of the core of *HS* even in 1940s.

(vii) The Western imperialistic discourse had a complete hold on Nehru's thinking, and he could not believe in the viability of any other alternative discourse. While Gandhiji swore by *HS*, Nehru regarded it as old-fashioned thinking. It may not be wrong to say that Nehru was not impressed by *HS*. He was skeptical about it. He was anti-*HS*. As said elsewhere also, Nehru was a believer in Western socialism. He was a great admirer of the progress made in the Soviet Union under communism (after a visit to Soviet Union in 1929, he said that he has left half of his heart in Russia), and he was the believer in mixed or central economic planning. All these were an anathema to Gandhiji. Nehru did take pride in India and her civilization but he never thought that modern civilization was a curse and ancient Indian civilization and the only best alternative to modern civilization.

(viii) Nehru's concept of Swaraj was quite narrow in comparison to the meaning of Swaraj which Gandhiji discussed in *HS*. It is very unlikely that Nehru would have believed in the necessity of self-control, abstinence, etc. for Swaraj.

(ix) The views on science, technology, religion in *HS* are very much different from those held by Nehru. Nehru was a believer in the need for huge, gigantic, complex, highly sophisticated, capital-intensive and labour-saving technology. He was a technology-enthusiast and a technology-optimist. He regarded big projects as the temples of modern India. It may be noted that many of these modern temples have turned out to be tombs. As it is well known, *HS* has advocated simple, small-scale, human-faced, labour-intensive, capital-saving, human-scaled 'appropriate' or 'intermediate' technology. Between science and religion while *HS* valued both and recognized the role and importance of religion, Nehru was a secularist and propogated secularism in India, and he was an agnostic.

(x) Gandhiji was convinced "that if India is to attain true freedom and through India the world also, then sooner or later the fact must be recognized that people will have to live in villages, not in towns, in huts, not in palaces. Crores of people will never be able to live at peace with each other in towns and palaces. They will then have no recourse but to resort to violence and untruth. I hold that without truth and non-violence, there can be nothing but destruction of humanity. We can realize truth and non-violence only in the simplicity of village life" (Parel, p. 150).

Nehru differed. He said, "I do not understand why a village should necessarily embody truth and non-violence. A village is backward intellectually and culturally and no progress can be made from backward environment. Narrow-minded people are much more likely to be untruthful and violent.... The modern means of transport as well as many other modern developments must continue and be developed.... We should encourage the village to approximate more to the culture of the town (Parel, pp. 152-153).

(xi) While the *HS* paradigm is original and revolutionary in material and spiritual matters, the Nehruvian paradigm is a borrowed, imitated, commonplace paradigm. There is not much in it which can be called revolutionary.

(xii) One thing which *HS* paradigm does not have and the Nehruvian paradigm has is the public acceptance, public adoption, public embrace. The people in India and the world have ensured self-extinction by adopting the so called scientific paradigm and by discarding a spiritual paradigm. The desertion of the Guru by the disciple has resulted in the defeat of the Gandhian Path.

IX

"Swaraj Sutre" or the Gist of Hind Swaraj

The book *HS* has many unique features. It is small but beautiful; it is revolutionary; it has certain stylistic novelties. Further, Gandhiji has summarized the discussion in the form of points at different stages of discussion in the book. He has, for example, given a set of 19 points on pp. 116-118; a set of 4 points on p. 118; a set of another 4 points on p. 155; and another set of 16 points on pp. 130-131. All these 43 points can be called the basic tenets or elements of HS. They can also be called 'Swaraj Sutre'. 'Sutra' means thread, string, an aphorism with minimum words and maximum sense. 'Sutra' is a terse sentence which is suggestive and which gives vast scope for interpretation, unfolding the meaning. There has been a strong tradition in India of constructing '*Sutre*' on different themes. It may not be impertinent to say that 'Swaraj Sutre' belongs to the august line of '*Bhakti Sutre*' of Narada, '*Yoga Sutre*' of Patanjali, '*Brahmsutre*' of Shankaracharya, and '*Saamya sutre*' of Vinoba. In recent times, Vinoba has enriched this tradition by giving us '*Saamya Sutre*', which help one to meditate on the '*Saamya Yoga*' of the Bhagavad Gita. The gist of *HS* which Gandhiji has given can be said to constitute '*Swaraj Sutre*'. '*Saamya Sutre*' and '*Swaraj Sutre*' which together define and explain completely the alternative world-view.

After merging/clubbing together some of these 43 'Sutre', we present 32 'Sutre' below:

(1) The English language will be used in India only on rare occasions.
(2) The real Home-Rule is self-rule or self-control.

(3) The way to Home-Rule is passive resistance or love-force or soul-force or satyagraha.
(4) In order to exert this force, Swadeshi in every sense is necessary.
(5) The lawyers and doctors should give up their professional practice, take up hand-looms, teach Indian and English people so as to enlighten them, give up the courts, and refuse to be judges.
(6) Doctors need to realize that they should mend souls rather than bodies; that it is better that bodies remain diseased rather than that they are cured through diabolical vivisection. They will advise rather than pamper them by giving useless drugs.
(7) Wealthy persons should speak out their minds, fear no one, devote their money to establish handlooms, and always use hand-made goods and ask others also to do so.
(8) It is useless to blame the English for our slavery. They came, and they still remain here because we invited them.
(9) Action is much better than speech.
(10) India can become free only through suffering. No nation has risen without suffering.
(11) It is an idle excuse to say that we will do a thing only when the others also do it.
(12) We shall certainly not use the machine-made goods. They are harmful in their nature.
(13) We should not bear enmity towards the English, but we can do so against their civilization.
(14) The real question is how to bring about man's highest intellectual, economic, political, and moral development.
(15) In this there should be equal rights and equal opportunities for all.
(16) There should be equality between town-dwellers and villagers in the standard of food and drink, clothing, etc. In order to achieve this, people should be able to produce for themselves the necessities of life.
(17) Man is essentially a social animal—independent and interdependent.
(18) The unit of society should be a village i.e. a small and manageable group of people who would be self-sufficient

in the matter of their vital requirements as a unit, and bound together in bonds of mutual co-operation and interdependence.

(19) There is no impossible barrier between the East and West.

(20) There is no such thing as Western or European civilization, but there is a modern civilization, which is purely material.

(21) It is not the British people who are ruling in India, but it is modern civilization, through its railways, telegraphs, telephones, etc.

(22) Bombay, Calcutta and other chief cities in India are the real plague-spots.

(23) If the British rule was replaced by Indian rule tomorrow by Indian rule-based modern methods, India would be no better. Indians would only become a second or fifth edition of Europe or America.

(24) East and West can really meet when the West throws overboard modern civilization almost entirely. They can also seemingly meet if the East adopts modern civilization. But that meeting would be like an arms-truce in which both nations live in the Hall of Death in order to avoid being devoured, the one by the other.

(25) No man can bring about reform of the whole world. To attempt to do so by means of highly artificial and speedy locomotion is to attempt the impossible.

(26) Increase of material comforts does not in any way whatsoever because condusive to moral growth.

(27) Medical science is the concentrated essence of Black Magic. Quack treatment is infinitely preferable to what passes for high medical skill.

(28) Hospitals are the instruments that the devil has been using to keep his hold on his Kingdom. They perpetuate vice, misery, degradation, and real slavery.

(29) It would be sinful for anyone in any way whatsoever to take part in the abominations that go on in hospitals. If there were no hospitals for venereal diseases or for consumptives, there would be less consumption and less sexual vice among us.

(30) India's salvation consists in unlearning what she has learnt during the past 150 years. The railways, telegraphs, hospital, lawyers, doctors, etc. have all to go. The simple

peasant life is the life giving true happiness, and all, particularly the wealthy, will have to live such a life consciously, religiously, and deliberately.

(31) There was true wisdom in the sages of old having so regulated society as to limit the material condition of the people. The crude plough of perhaps five thousand years ago is the plough of the husbandsman today. Therein lies salvation. Long live the people !

(32) *HS* has envisaged a different system of Government.

These distilled-principals of *Swaraj-Sutre* or tenets of *HS* can be said to be the extended, elaborate exposition of the new vision of life that had dawned on Gandhiji after reading the book by John Ruskin namely, *Unto This Last*. Gandhiji has distilled the following three principal tenets of *Unto This Last*. In *HS*, the three tenets of *Unto This Last* become more than thirty. The book *Unto This Last* is the seed of *Hind Swaraj*, and *HS* is the seed of Gandhiji's whole vision.

(a) The good of the individual is contained in the good of all.
(b) Everyone's work is equally precious because everyone has an equal right to exist.
(c) A life of labour i.e. the life of the tiller of the soil and the handicraftsman is the life worth living.

X

Hind Swaraj: Utopia, Relevance and Action Programme?

If we are determined to condemn some idea or ideal or value or thought, we can do so easily by designating or calling it as "uneconomical", or as "Utopian", or as "irrelevant".

Is the *HS* world-view Utopian and irrelevant? What were Gandhiji's own views in this regard?

According to the Concise Oxford Dictionary, Utopia means an imagined perfect place or State of things. Utopia is also the title of a book (1516) by Thomas More. Utopian means idealistic. Similarly, relevant means applicability and usefulness of the ideas or matter in different times and/or places.

Sometimes, Utopia is said to have two meanings, positive and negative. The former can be said to mean desirable ideal. In a negative sense, Utopia means something impractical. As far as Gandhiji's position is concerned, there is no question of anything being non-implementable in actual or real life. The goal may take more time or less time to be achieved, or it may be more difficult or less difficult, but it is not impossible at anytime, anywhere. There is no unrealism of any sort about swaraj because what was visualized was the transformation of institutions rather than their liquidation. In order that swaraj should not be an unattainable goal, Gandhiji conceived 'soft' and 'hard' versions of that goal. As he has said, "I do not ask India to follow today the methods prescribed in my booklet namely, Hind Swaraj". If they do that, they would have Swaraj not in a year but in a day. Through the booklet, I am giving the country a pardonable programme for the attainment of Parliamentary Swaraj. The change is seen as a process and *HS* is a final stage preceded by parliamentary swaraj.

Gandhiji has further stated "It would be a mistake to think that I am aiming at the swaraj today itself. India is not yet ripe for it. I am for myself working for the self-rule, but today my corporate activity is undoubtedly devoted to the attainment of parliamentary swaraj. Hind Swaraj is an ideal condition. Immediately, I do not dream of no railways, no machinery, no army, no hospitals, and no law-courts. They will be there but as 'necessary evil'; they will be minimal; some of them will be transformed in nature and shape and in objectives or goals. For example, machinery will be there as spinning wheel, the factories will grow for the benefit of the people and not for draining the masses dry. The army will be cut down, and it would consist largely of volunteers. The '*shanti-sena*' will replace the usual military or army".

In 1909 itself, Gandhiji had developed a realistic view of the implementability of the *HS* paradigm. He was conscious, aware of the difficulties in the path of *HS*. However, at no stage he had felt that it was impossible to create a new society. He was hopeful that since "only fringe of the ocean has been polluted (by the modern civilization) it is those who are within the fringe alone need cleansing. He felt that millions of Indians were not touched by the modernization disease. If social workers went into the interior, and worked with the masses to retain, maintain purity of Indian civilization, it is not altogether beyond the realms of possibility to create a new civilization. Alas! Between 1909 and today, 'polluted fringe' or 'polluted minority' has swelled and has now become quite large and strong. The creation of the India of Gandhiji's dream has become 100-fold difficult now.

The *HS* was a severe condemnation of the Western Modern industrial civilization, and it asked the people to discard this destructive civilization and live in the light of Indian civilization, culture, and spirituality. Since today India is much more enamoured by Western, modern civilization and she has adopted modern civilization much more wholeheartedly than what was the situation in 19th and 20th centuries, the creation of *HS* has become far more difficult, but the relevance of the Book has increased many-fold.

Has *HS* become irrelevant after India gained political independence? The answer has to be 'no' because *HS* is not only about the political freedom of India: it has universal objectives. It is about the emancipation of the soul. Gandhiji did not want only the replacement of 'brown sahibs' in the place of "white sahibs".

Further, since colonialism continues to exist, and since Indians are becoming more and more neo-colonised now than before, the *HS* retains its relevance even today. In about 1909, *HS* was ahead of its time by more than a century. What Gandhiji said about education, medical model, technology, etc. 100 years back, scholars like A. Huxley, F. Capra, Ivan Illich, and others are saying today. The manner in which the Central Parliament and State Legislatures are functioning in India today constitutes the most solid evidence in favour of the relevance of *HS* even today. The themes, ideas, programmes, advice, suggestions contained in *HS* are all alive today. The world is in greater need of *HS* today than ever before.

The perspicacity and prescience of *HS* has been validated by the history. Even if we take only 100 years after the publication of *HS*, we are confronted by two World Wars and hundreds of small and big wars, the communist, fascist, Nazi and other dictatorships wrongly called revolutions, racial holocausts, communal violence, the emergence of the 20th century as the most violent century in which more than 20 to 25 crore people have been killed in wars, civil wars, state violence, terrorism, spending many billions of dollars on weapons and advertisements, 'pathology of normalcy', degradation of environment and ecology, death of forests, rivers and seas, continuation of the threat of nuclear war, etc. support the picture of modern civilization drawn in *HS*. Gandhiji did not feel the need for revising *HS* even after many (40) years after its publication. The efforts of some scholars to take a 'Fresh Look' or try to 'revisioning' of *HS* shows that diagnosis, prognosis, and prescription in *HS* are quite valid and relevant even today.

Since *Hind Swaraj* has been validated, and it is not Utopian and irrelevant, what is our duty so that the vision of *HS* can be put to use for increasing the welfare, peace, and happiness of all the people i.e. to create world-Sarvodaya or global swaraj.

Instead of harping that *HS* is a dream, it is necessary to realize that it is the call, demand of our time (*Yuga-dharma*) that we should adopt a '*Karmayogic*' approach, and attitude to invest all our physical, mental, and spiritual strength and resources to implement *HS*. We give below the steps, measures, action-programme required to make *HS* a reality.

- The first thing we should do is to accord *HS* the enormous intellectual or theoretical respect even if we do not agree with its contents. We need to work our programmatic implications of this classic work. We also need to undertake services of research works, investigations into the issues raised in various foras. The illustrative list of steps which we should commit to undertake is given below:

- Undertake relevant research but do not imprison *HS* in research rooms. In particular, the search must go on to know whether the force of love and non-violence can become the guiding force in the affairs of the society.
- India has to become a 'world leader', but today she is a blind follower of the west. Revive the ancient Indian civilization.
- Study, understand, and implement constructive works programme.
- Raise a 'shanti sena' of at least 7 lakh village servants (gram sevaks), and activate the '*Acharyakul*'.
- Work with the guiding principles like 'one step at a time is enough', 'adding zero before one, and after one give two vastly different results', and 'the beginning has to be done though odds are heavy'.
- Educate the masses in the real sense of that term.
- Clear rejection, clear denial and not ambivalence in respect of modern civilization are necessary.
- Gandhian thought is eternal and there is quite a good following of it in all sections of society in all the countries. What is lacking is the practice. Mankind will have to try to strengthen the practice or action; the thought ought to be transformed into appropriate behaviour of people.
- There is a need to create, practice, and evolve the technique of 'moral persuasion' which would involve persons in power, and non-governmental respected, wise individuals explaining, educating, persuading, advising, reprimanding the people to act whenever crucial, life-and-death issues crop up in the life of the nation.
- Society should establish one Ashram each at the distance of every 25 miles which would act as a power house behind the development of that area in all aspects.
- At least one person per village needs to be trained as a 'grama sevak' who will sit ('bury' himself) in that village and help the villagers in all matters so that 'dung heaps'

or 'dung hills' will be transformed into things of beauty which would live as families. 'Grama sevakas' would be trained in the above-mentioned Ashramas.

- The villagers in each village should meet together at least once a week; they should discuss various developments, problems at such meetings which may end after a common prayer. All efforts should be made to create village republics with the Gramasabha, village panchayat, and other bodies, and to ensure that they function effectively.
- Both Gandhiji and Vivekananda have emphasized the need for spiritual youth with iron will, muscles of iron, and nerves of steel for national reconstruction. Such youth would teach, preach, and practise nation-building.
- The basic action programme (Satyagraha, constructive works, and collective prayer) has been separately and elaborately discussed in Chapter XI.
- Some specific programmes, projects, policies which would be required to make living happy and sustainable are as follows: (i) To promote organic farming to achieve self-reliance and security in food availability to all the families and villages. (ii) To achieve self-sufficiency in cloth through charakha or spinning wheel. (iii) To achieve self-reliance in health through exercise, yoga, nature cure, and herbs. (iv) To promote self-reliance in education through Nai Talim. (v) To undertake water management, constructing lavatories, and village cleanliness. (vi) To oppose communalism and its accompanying dictatorship, and to promote communal harmony and equal respect for all religions. In short, the programmatic implications of *HS* are people's education, people's organization, people's agitation and CWP.

A serious scholar of *HS* has given a fairly long list of suggestions about what we can do to transform Gandhiji's dream into a reality albeit over a long period of time (Kanti Shah, 2009, pp. 215-225). We present a summary of his ideas below:

(1) The materialist philosophy founded on the principles of competition, avarice, self-interest is wholly erroneous, and spurious. It is a totally perverted view of human nature.

(2) Consumerism or myopic hedonism brings no joy or peace or happiness; they are not the raison d'etre of human existence.
(3) The relationship of human beings with Nature cannot be defined in terms of conflict or the former conquering the latter. Human beings have to live in harmony (and not disharmony) with Nature.
(4) Science that is bereft of morality and human values can invite only destruction. Science + violence = Total destruction, while Science + Non-violence = Sarvodaya.
(5) There is a dire need for a new humanistic, ethical, moral, normative economics. There will have to be a fundamental change in the definition of development and progress. The present widely used perverse model of development needs to be discarded. The developmentalism shatters ecological balance.
(6) The self-indulgent, wasteful, and extravagant and resource-intensive lifestyles created under the delusion of modernity have to be discarded.
(7) Human beings ought to be freed from the stranglehold of the market and commercialization.
(8) It is a superstition to hold that only the massive, expensive, complex technologies are scientific and efficient.
(9) The faith in urbanization and centralized order must be eliminated.
(10) Education has to be related to work, social needs, and life. The current educational factories are to be overhauled.
(11) The idea of the nation-state is unlikely to last long.
(12) It is a warped perception which equates happiness with mammon worship and the pursuit of wealth, as well as the selfish rate-race and cut-throat competition.

Something is said to be relevant if it helps mankind to understand the state of the world and to tackle the host of problems mankind is facing in its day-to-day business. An umpteen number and types of changes have taken place during the period after the book *HS* was published. The most serious problem humanity is facing today is that of survival. The thoughts in *HS*, if followed sincerely, honestly, have the capacity to save human civilization from extinction. Therefore, *HS* is as relevant today (if not more) as it was in the earlier years.

XI

A Three-Stringed (*Tri-Sutri*) Programme for Swaraj

A way out of the current civilizational crisis and the way to Swaraj requires sincere, honest implementation of a comprehensive action-programme, the outline of which has been presented towards the end of previous Chapter X. In this Chapter (XI), we discuss at some length the three-legged or three-part programme comprising satyagraha or passive resistance (PR), constructive works Programme (CWP), and all-religion collective daily prayers (ARCDP) inspired by equal tolerance and acceptance and respect for all religions or Sarva Dharma Samabhava which comprises four things. (i) Loyalty towards one's own religion. (ii) Respect for all other religions. (iii) Reforms in all religions. (iv) Opposition to '*Adharma*'.

The last component of the action programme mentioned above is as important as the other two. This programme has the sanction of practice; there is a Mass every Sunday for the Christians, and Muslims gather together for a collective prayer on certain days. In practice, the effectiveness of this measure has been well demonstrated. The daily practice of morning and evening collective mass prayers help to calm down people, and to return to their normal activities. The effectiveness of mass prayers has been amply demonstrated in quenching communal conflagration in India in the 1930s and 1940s.

The Collective all-religions prayer is a very important gift from Gandhiji to mankind. This gift can be said to be as effective as his gift of Satyagraha. Gandhiji's collective, all-religious prayers became unprecedented, miraculous and magical events; lakhs of people used to attend them, and they became symbols and expressions of communal harmony in India. These prayers helped to break the walls of all differences such as castes, languages, religions, and sex; they helped to resolve communal conflicts, and they helped to make satyagraha and the freedom struggle successful.

In a country like India, where spirituality alone lives, religion alone lives, the religion is the nation's life, to discover and to make a wide, successful use of the practice of prayer was a *stroke* of *genius* on Gandhiji's part. He held that the present generation in India is sitting on the summit of faithlessness, and, consequently, it is afflicted by spiritual atrophy. The people in India must learn to counter violence by non-violence, and to acquire and nurture the requisite strength. To be able to do so, prayer is the first and the last means. To create an ideal social order, there is a need for co-operation, consent, collective efforts, which can be nurtured by collective all-religions prayer. It can help to promote harmonious relations among people belonging to different religions, castes, races, languages, and nations. Prayer has the power with which even the most destructive atomic device can be successfully countered. This power of prayer has remained neglected so far. However, the programme for the development of this power would have to be given top priority in the coming years.

The second constituent of the action programme for creating a Swarajist social order is Satyagraha. Although, there have been some satyagrahis in India during the Ancient and Middle Ages (For example, Saint Tukaram; Prahlad), the most unique example of a satyagrahi is Gandhiji in recent times. Gandhiji has been a Satyagrahi *par excellence*. Gandhiji has explained the art, science and spirit of Satyagrah on the basis of continuous contemplation, and ongoing actual experience gained. He has explained the nature, prerequisites, and so on of Satyagraha in the two books, *Hind Swaraj*, and *Satyagraha*. In South Africa, Satyagraha is the greatest, and the most valuable of Gandhiji's gifts to the people. Once Gandhiji himself has said, "I have rendered a great service to India and to England by showing them the way to come out of their unnatural situations by using non-co-operation approach".

What is Satyagraha and Passive Resistance (PR)?

PR is a method of securing rights by personal suffering; it is the reverse of resistance by arms. When I refuse to do a thing that is repugnant to my conscience, I use soul-force. If I do not obey the law that is applicable to me, and accept the penalty for its breach, I use soul-force; it involves sacrifice of self. Man-made laws are not necessarily binding on man. If man will only realize that it is unmanly to obey laws that are unjust, no man can enslave him. This is the key to self-rule or home-rule. PR (soul-force) is matchless, it is superior to the force of arms. Even a man weak in body is capable of offering PR; control over the mind alone necessary; PR is an all-sided sword. It blesses all parties to a dispute (Parel, 1997, pp. 88-98; Gandhi, M.K., 1928; and Bhole, (6).

Gandhiji has clarified three very important points, the understanding of which is essential for deciding whether to be a passive resister or not, and for the success of Satyagraha. These three things are: (a) What is the sanctity and sacrosanctness of the existing man-made laws of the land? (b) How far does the majority-view or majority-decision need to be accepted and honoured? (c) What qualities does the passive resister need to possess?

Soul-force is certainly superior to body-force. The use of soul-force takes place when I do not obey the law, and accept the penalty for its breach. On the other hand, there is a law which is applicable to me. I do not like it, and by using violence, I force the repeal of the law. This is the use of body-force. Soul-force involves sacrifice of the self. In our daily lives, citizens are required to be law-abiding and law-obeying. To be law-obeying is regarded as a duty and virtue of citizens. The people are alarmed if someone talks of disregarding or breaking the law under any situation or circumstances.

Gandhiji did not subscribe to this viewpoint. His stand, position in this regard, as in many other matters, was clear, forthright and revolutionary. According to him, "...that we should obey laws whether good or bad is a new fangled notion. It is contrary to our manhood, if we obey laws repugnant to our conscience. The teaching to the contrary is opposed to religion, and means slavery. Man-made laws are not necessarily binding on him. We are sunk so low that we fancy that it is our duty and religion to do what the laws lay down. If man will only realize that it is unmanly to obey laws that are unjust, no man's tyranny will enslave him. This is the key to self-rule or home rule" (pp. 92-93).

Further, he believed that "... It is superstition and ungodly thing to believe that an act of a majority binds a minority. As to the question who can be a passive resister, his answer was that resister has to observe perfect chastity, adopt poverty, follow truth, and cultivate fearlessness, and be courageous" (p. 96). Another requirement is the faith, belief in God. This requirement is best put by Swami Ramadas, a 17th century Maharashtrian saint who stated that agitations, "movements are important but they should be founded on God (*Saamarthya aahe chalwalinche, jo je karil tayanche, parantu yeth Bhagawantache adhistan pahije*)". Gandhiji's Satyagrahis were, therefore, always imbued with religious, spiritual, godly considerations.

Satyagraha is variously known as (i) passive resistance, (ii) non-co-operation, (iii) civil disobedience, (iv) non-violent non-co-operation, (v) direct action, and (vi) aggressive pacifism. However, among these terms the term Satyagraha has been the most widely used across time and space. It is only in his book, *Hind Swaraj,* that Gandhiji has used the term passive resistance far more often than Satyagraha. Even then, Satyagraha and passive resistance were synonyms in Gandhiji's view.

The two very important features of Satyagraha are: non-violence is its heart and soul, and that in spite of being non-violent, it is very much a revolutionary idea. A large number of conflicts, disputes, wars, skirmishes, civil wars, the state vs. people conflicts, discontent and unrest, etc. are daily crying for resolution or settlement. Two types of forces are pitted against each other in this task. Satyagraha, or soul-force, or compassion-force, or suffering-force, or justice-force, or love-force, or truth-force, or spiritual-force on the one hand, and brute-force, or gun-force, or fear-force, or arms-force, or body-force on the other. There is an ethical difference between the two types of forces; the soul-force is ethically superior to brute force.

The need to resort to Satyagraha may arise for (a) getting political freedom from alien rule, (b) dealing with one's own Government, (c) dealing with issues and problems arising among the people in the same country. Now, in the recent past in India, two schools of thought have emerged; the first school tends to argue that Satyagraha was a necessary and appropriate technique or measure to fight with the alien Government, but once the country became free, Satyagraha vis-à-vis the own-Government may not be justifiable. The second school argues that Satyagraha remains justifiable, relevant appropriate as long as there is injustice, corruption, repression by the State or by any group. In other words, the former school of thought has created a new divide between 'they' and 'us'. According to this school, Satyagraha is relevant against 'they' but not against 'us'. This has created considerable confusion about the nature, appropriateness, and utility of Satyagraha. In his book, *Gandhian Utopia,* Richard Fox has opined that after Gandhiji's death, the position that Satyagraha is a revolutionary technique has been undermined.

Gandhiji believed that civil disobedience is the birth right of every citizen, and the day he renounces this right, he ceases to exist as a man. Just as it is a duty of man to co-operate with the good, so also it is his duty to non-co-operate with the bad. To suppress civil disobedience is to imprison the conscience of man. The strength and power of satyagraha is derived from the values of Truth, love, and compassion. Both the individual and the society can use it in both political and family spheres, and at the level of the family, village, country and the world.

Gandhiji used to say that Satyagraha is as old as the mountains; it is a moral equivalent of war, it is a complete alternative to violence, it is useful wherever quarrels exist. It is a multi-stage process, in which first an appeal is made to the power of discrimination and thinking of the opponent. Gandhiji also used to say that "he was getting increasingly convinced that many times it is not possible to obtain results merely by appealing to the goodness of the powers that be. In such a situation, there remains no alternative but to use Satyagraha".

According to Stephen Hobhouse, "at present the Western nations are not ready to share equitably the wealth and resources of the planet with poor nations, and the West is squandering the wealth and resources of this planet to produce highly destructive weapons of war". The Cut-throat competition rules the roost. Similarly, many countries are coming under dictatorships. If the countries go to war against each other, and if people oppose dictatorship with armed revolution, the problems of fear, insecurity, repression, violence, greed, and poverty in the world will become all the more serious. All this can be avoided by using the technique of Satyagraha.

In the opinion of C.E.M. Joad also, Satyagraha based on moral strength is an important technique and a path which can save human civilization from annihilation. Reverend J.C. Winslow also has said that to keep on fighting with the help of soul-force till the injustice is eliminated is an inseparable part of Satyagraha. *Today, Satyagraha is the only key by using which we can free the mankind from the world which has become like a mental asylum, and lead it on to the path of justice, wisdom, and peace.* Similarly, Michael Saunlither has argued that Satyagraha can stop even nuclear war. The 'destructive trinity' (fear, hatred, and power) can be countered by using Satyagraha i.e. by using the 'constructive trinity' (truth, love, penance). Tolstoy also has said that the question of passive resistance is a question of the greatest importance not only for India but for the whole of humanity (For details of arguments, see Bhole).

To sum up: The foregoing discussion and reasoning on Satyagraha has established the need, importance, relevance of Satyagraha; it shows that the humanity's birthright of Swaraj can undoubtedly be secured by its other birth-right, Satyagraha. As seen above, Gandhiji's perception, vision on Satyagraha is corroborated by the views of intellectuals like Richard Fox, Stephen Hobhouse, C.E.M. Joad, Reverend J.C. Winslow, Michael Saunlither, Tolstoy, and others.

The third constituent of the action programme for Hind Swaraj is the Constructive Works Programme (CWP). The actualization of the Gandhian world-view would require implementation of CWP. Gandhiji had firmly believed that Swaraj or Grama-Swaraj can definitely be established if the people implement CWP on their own strength and with mutual co-operation. CWP may be defined as a programme of daily work to be done through mutual co-operation at the local level. This programme consists of more than 30 items or activities and if implemented sincerely and honestly in body and spirit, it has the potential to affect revolutionary changes in economic, social, political, educational, ethical, cultural, spiritual dimensions of the people and institutions. Gandhiji used to say that non-violence, communal harmony, eradication of untouchability, and Khadi are the four pillars of CWP. Satyagraha and CWP are like the Siamese twins. They depend on each other for effectiveness, as CWP can make the foundation of Satyagraha deep, wide, and strong.

CWP is a symbol of non-violence or '*ahimsa*'; Gandhiji believed that CWP is the only means for creating a phenomenal or miraculous awakening in Indian villages. It can also give appropriate shape, form, and turn to the national politics. CWP is not a programme of merely social service or social work; it is not meant to give only some education to children; it does not aim at creating just a little more employment; and it is not satisfied with lifting just a few people above the poverty line. Behind its mild, soft appearance, CWP is very much a revolutionary idea. The specific activities which make the CWP are listed below:

(1) Communal unity, (2) removal of untouchability, (3) prohibition, (4) khadi, (5) other village industries, (6) village sanitation, (7) basic education, (8) adult education, (9) service of women, (10) education in health and hygiene, (11) development of provincial, regional languages, (12) promotion of Hindi as a national language, (13) working for economic equality, (14) organizing peasants and industrial labour, (15) working with adivasis, (16) leprosy eradication and service of the lepers, (17) eschewing party politics, particularly by the students and youth, (18) satyagraha, (19) afforestation, (20) protection, preservation, and service of the cow and its progeny, (21) promotion of vegetarianism, (22) holding collective all-religious prayers, (23) study of religious and spiritual books, (24) payment of taxes, wages in kind, (25) spread of Sanskrit language and devanagari script, (26) development and maintenance of village gardens specially with medicinal herbs and plants, and (27) revival of villages and rural technology.

The CWP was designed and introduced by Gandhiji in the year 1941. The programme initially included only 13 items, the list was subsequently extended by Gandhiji and his colleagues. CWP is a blueprint for social resurgence. It has been rightly said that while Hind Swaraj gives a general outline of Gandhiji's political philosophy, CWP presents the concrete steps or programme by which that philosophy may be actually implemented. CWP can be called construction of poorna swaraj or complete independence by truthful and non-violent means. Gandhiji was confident that if CWP could be successfully worked out, the end of it would be independence or *swaraj* we want. It was the outcome of conversations Gandhiji had with co-workers at Sevagrama Ashrama. It had a connection with the Civil Disobedience Movement, it is not exhaustive but it is sufficiently comprehensive and indicative.

Gandhiji was quite often laughed at, and even criticized by the people for giving importance to, in their view, small, trivial, insignificant things or matters. Recall, for example, how Gandhiji once left a meeting of very high order congressmen to attend to the injured foot of a goat. Or recall how they wondered as to how making a salt would bring independence. He was called a mentally unbalanced or faddist by many. But Gandhiji knew well the relative importance of different things, issues, matters, and so on. He had the ability to make revolutions out of 'small' things. He was also generally confident about his views and decisions. Accordingly, he had anticipated the negative response from the skeptics to his CWP and had warned them that they would be committing a grave error if they oppose such a programme. In this connection he has said, "Let not the reader (of *HS*) make the mistake of laughing at any of the items as being part of the movement for independence. It is the office assigned to the constructive programme which gives it an irresistible prestige and power. Such at least is my view. It may be that of a mad man. For my handling of civil disobedience without the constructive programme will be like a paralysed hand attempting to lift a spoon" (Parel, 1997, pp. 170-181).

CWP has been called, by Gandhiji himself, the construction of 'Poorna Swaraj' by truthful and non-violent means. The Independence will be complete only to the extent of our approach in practice to truth and non-violence. In other words, CWP is the means to obviate the necessity of violence and falsity in efforts to achieve *Poorna Swaraj*. Gandhiji was completely confident that if the CWP was planned well, and if it was successfully worked out, the end of it would the independence we want. Just as a flag of any nation is only some cloth tied to a stick if seen outwardly, but as a symbol, it inspires sacrifice of anything including life, similarly, if we do not see the symbolic content and multipurpose usefulness of CWP, we would continue to belittle the revolutionary character of the CWP.

In view of its crucial importance, it would be worthwhile to restate the philosophy or principles and goals of CWP.

The case for CWP is based on the need for synthesis of the material and moral development of society. CWP offers the means of survival of mankind during not only 21st the century but also for all centuries to come. In other words CWPs help to create an economy and society of permanence. To the present strife-torn world it would help to establish a qualitatively better, sustainable social order. CWP constitutes the heart of the Gandhian revolution in centuries to come. In Gandhiji's own view, CWP is the truthful and non-violent way of winning 'Poorna Swaraj'. It has been said that this programme is the best instrument of creative economic, political, educational, and moral revolution. CWP is the only testament of hope for our village masses. It is central to the understanding of the concept of swaraj. Decentralization, co-operation, mutual aid or help, voluntariness, sharing, self-reliance, self-help, and building or development from below are the important principles of CWP. It is a concrete expression of Ahimsa.

For creating a new social order, both the means namely, agitations and constructive activities, are necessary. Constructive work is a must for Swaraj and Ahimsa. Gandhiji has gone to the extent of saying that it is not absolutely necessary to win freedom if the co-operation of the whole nation is secured for CWP. Of course, for all this, there is a need for a dedicated and huge band of young and 'yati dharmi' social workers. There is also a need for creating facilities to train the constructive workers. Gandhiji had given a quick estimate of about seven lakh workers who were needed to conduct CWP in the whole of India (one worker per village).

XII
Post-Gandhi *Hind Swaraj*

The thinking on and the efforts towards perfecting *HS* did not come to an end with the death of Gandhiji. A significant extension and restatement of the theory, philosophy, and action-programme of *HS* took place for a number of years after the demise of Gandhiji. This chapter explores and presents these developments.

Romain Rolland, French litterateur whom Gandhiji called the wise man of Europe and a sage, had a premonition that Gandhi's end also will be Christ-like. He had expected that one day Gandhi might be killed. Gandhi himself used to say that life is a preparation for suffering, martyrdom, and death. A total of about eight attempts did take place on Gandhiji's life during the years of his public service in South Africa and India, but he survived in seven of those attempts. But on January 30, 1948, the killer succeeded in his brief and mankind witnessed another martyrdom, another crucifixion.

Just before he was killed, Gandhiji was busy giving concrete shape to some of his ideas in *Hind Swaraj* by devising different schemes, plans, and programmes many of which were radical or revolutionary. For example, he was formulating his last will which was to transform or convert the Congress Party into a Lok Sevak Sangh, earlier band of social workers who would serve but not assume power. He was also having discussions with social and political workers for implementing honestly the CWP. Further, he was showing the light as to how to deal with crises, calamities by working for quenching communal fires by walking unprotected, and barefoot in the worst affected, dangerous, violent areas, while being on fast, and by holding all-religious, collective, open, mass prayers twice a day every day.

It has to be confessed that towards the close of his life, Gandhiji appears to have partially failed in his mission clouding the usefulness and relevance of his thought and techniques, at least on the face of it. The partition or vivisection of the country did occur notwithstanding his stand. The partition was accompanied by the movement of population across the new borders on a mass scale, and the communal frenzy and violence erupted on an unprecedented scale, killing millions of people. Gandhiji's mission of love, non-violence, composition, peace appeared to be forsaken everywhere, and people appeared to be unprepared to grasp his message. In the terminology of *HS*, India in the late nineteen forties appeared to be at the stage of 'parliamentary swaraj' only; she was far far away from the goal of Hind Swaraj or 'poorna swaraj' or 'global swaraj'.

What is the story of Hind Swaraj after the assassination of Gandhiji? Were any efforts made to keep alive and extend the paradigm of *Hind Swaraj*? Did any leadership emerge to take the place of Gandhiji to guide and lead the nation towards reaching the goal of HS? Yes, India witnessed an exciting period of a quarter century of generation of '*mantras*' and '*tantras*' to create *HS* or 'poorna swaraj' after 1948. Vinoba led these developments.

Kanti Shah has discussed *HS* in (a) Gandhiji's time, (b) Vinoba's period, (c) a century later, and our time (2009). It appears to us that this kind of periodization is not meaningful; the periods overlap in this scheme. A more meaningful period distribution can be (i) the entire post-Gandhi period of 1948-2011, (ii) 1948-1978, the golden or epoch-making period of '*Aarohana*' or ascent of HS, and (iii) 1978-2011 – the period of stagnation, decline, descent.

The entire post-Gandhi period of 1948-2011 was an extremely eventful period, the examples of some events being (i) there occurred transfer of power and India became independent nation, (ii) India was divided into two parts or the country suffered from vivisection, (iii) communal riots on an unprecedented scale took place, (iv) mass-movement of population between the two countries took place, (v) the country adopted a new Constitution and became a Republic of India, (vi) Five-Year economic planning, Community Development Programme (CDP), and Panchayat Raj (PR) were introduced, (vii) In the 1990s, the New Economic Policy of privatization, Liberalization, deregulation, globalization were introduced.

These and other events which were introduced, promoted,

supported by the state and other government bodies were not inspired, influenced, guided by the spirit, vision, mission of *HS*. While formulating policies and programmes for national development, The *HS* paradigm was neglected or rejected, while the conventional approaches were chosen by most of the country. Thus, immediately after independence and throughout the years thereafter the attitude towards *HS* was one of neglect and antagonism.

In spite of hostile attitude of the state towards *HS* there were some wise persons, scholars, social workers, political leaders who worked quietly and with faith in their heart towards building up India in the light of *HS*. Vinoba Bhave (just Vinoba hereafter) led the group of Sarvodaya workers for establishing HS. Who was Vinoba, and what and how did he extend, strengthen, and enrich the vision and mission of HS?

Vinoba was a spiritual heir of Gandhiji. India has produced a galaxy of spiritual men and women who have enriched the Indian world-view. The resplendent flowering of this indigenous world-view has occurred in the thinking and life of Gandhiji and Vinobaji (G-V). Both of them, through their constant contemplation, experimentation, and self-practice, have conceived and enunciated all the major core ethical principles and value systems and the organizational-institutional superstructure and programmes for sustainable, stable, peaceful social order.

There has been a perfect harmony in the perspectives of G-V. Vinobaji's own attitude vis-s-vis Gandhiji's has been one of self-effacement, and accepting Gandhiji as the final authority. Yet, it is necessary to discuss specifically Vinobaji's views because he has significantly extended and enriched Gandhian thought, including HS, and he has added many ideas, ideals, and programmes to the Gandhian movement after Gandhiji's martyrdom. In Vinobaji's hands, the vision of *Hind Swaraj* has become more fully and subtly developed and stated. Vinobaji has quietly effected a remarkable ascent or ascension (Aarohana) in Gandhiji's vision.

The work which Vinoba did was Gandhiji's work. As Vinoba has said, "Thoughts that resided in Gandhi's heart the propagation of which was circumscribed by the body now enter our hearts unhindered. My conscience bears witness to my unstinting effort to follow Gandhiji's ideals of love and non-violence. I do not remember a moment when I acted unmindful of these principles.

There is not an iota of doubt in my mind that after Gandhi's departure I have been working to fulfill his mission" (Shah Kanti, pp. 117-118).

Vinobaji was a *'samnvayacharya' par excellence* i.e. a master preceptor of synthesis, integration of diverse, conflicting viewpoints, traditions, schools of thought. He was also a master *'sutrakar'* i.e. a formulator or composer of *'sutras'* i.e. short, concise, technical sentences or precepts or aphorisms. A very subtle thinking many nuances of meaning was his *'forte'*. He was a very very well-read man; in his own words, he had read literally "thousands of books" in 21 languages which he knew (a great polyglot). Contrary to the belief in intellectual circles, both G-V were very well-read persons. In spite of his excellent command over English, Vinobaji has written hardly anything in English. His writings and speeches have mostly been in Hindi and Marathi. His idiom has been heavily Sanskritised, religious, spiritual, and following the tradition of Indian *rishis, munis, sages, yogis, seers*. He has explained his ideas by making profuse references to Indian mythology, history, legends, parables.

Vinobaji has made a huge contribution to literature pertaining to a vast range of themes. These contributions have been published in *Vinoba Sahitya*, Vol. 1 to Vol. 20 (Hindi). Out of these, a few more directly relevant books for the discussion of *HS* are: (a) *Ahimsa Ki Talash* (Hindi), (b) *Democratic values*, (c) *Sarvodaya Vichar Aani Swaraj Shastra (Marathi)*. (d) *Saamyayoga Samaj Darshan (Hindi)*; (e) *Sarvodaya Aur Samyavad (Hindi)*, (f) *Lokniti (Hindi)*.

Through these books, innumerable speeches, and across the country *'Padayatra'*, Vinobaji gave a big push to *HS* so much so that the period 1948-78 may be regarded as a golden period or epoch-making period for *HS*. In quick succession he engendered a number of *'Mantras'* and *'Tantras'* to make *HS* replete with meaning. Vinoba was at his best, gave idea after idea, goal after goal, programme after programme to make *HS* a concrete reality. The advancement in terms of *'tantra'* took place in the form of Bhoodan and Gramadan, etc. due to which this period can also be called a 'period of sacrifice'. Instead of regarding *HS* utopian, he gave humanity the hope that it can forever be rescued from the maelstrom of violence. Some of these *'Mantras'* which gained widespread circulation or currency among the people of India are as follows:

- Our *mantra* is Jai Jagat, our *tantra* is Gramaswaraj (while our sacred words) are victory to the world, our technique or path is Gramaswaraj).
- Jai Grama, Jai Jagat (Victory to the world! Victory to the village).
- Sabai Bhoomi Gopalki. (All the land belongs to the Lord).
- Abhidheyam Param Samyam (We should desire and work for perfect equality).
- Sarvesham Avirodhen. (No opposition to anyone).
- Sarva bhoot hite rataha (devoted to the welfare of all).

In the period under discussion, (1948-1978), the *HS* world-view came to be known by other terms, and by more than one term. One may say that *HS* appeared in its new *'Avatar'* or incarnation. Of course, the goals, content of *HS* remained the same in its new and old *'avataras'*. The new names of *HS* were, for example, *Gramaswaraj*, *Sarvodaya*, and *Saamyayoga*, and all these names stood for the same paradigm or world-view. Thus, *Hind Swaraj = Gramaswaraj = Sarvodaya = Saamyayoga*.

While guiding the Indian society towards Swaraj, Vinobaji revived the ancient tradition and practice of *'padayatra'*, (travelling on foot) and *'charaivati'* (walk and walk). At one stage, Gandhiji decided to use only minimum clothes to reflect the poverty in India, and to identify with the poor in the country. Vinobaji also decided to use only the minimal clothes, and, in addition, he decided not to use modern means of transport and communication, *viz.*, railways, buses, cars, aeroplanes, ships unless circumstances demanded. He achieved four things through such a decision: (a) To reflect Indian poverty. (b) To identify with the poor. (c) To protest against or reject the modern, high, complex, large-scale technology. (d) To help achieve integration, harmony between different groups of people. Thus, the protest against railways which occurs in Hind Swaraj, was made live by living according to it.

It was stated above that *HS* and Saamyayoga (SY) are different names for the same world-view. This would be clear from the following brief discussion on different aspects of Saamyayoga (SY).

The word *Saamyayoga* is a new word which has been coined by Vinoba by joining two Sanskrit words namely, *saamyam* and yoga, both of which have a number of meanings. *Saamyam* means equality, equanimity, equability, balance of mind, sameness, evenness, harmony. It encompasses economic, political, social equality (justice), equanimity of mind through its complete control (*manoyoga*), and the attainment of Supreme Equality (*Param Saamyam*) i.e. the realization of the Supreme Being or *Brahma Nirvan*. In a state of *Param Saamyam*, the difference, division, separation, distinction, dualism of any nature whatsoever (*viz.*, between man and man, man and God, animate beings and inanimate things) completely vanishes. In other words, *Param Samyam* denotes unity (*ekatvam*) or monism (*advait*). In *Saamyayoga*, *saamyam* is not an ordinary objective or goal, it is the subject of total devotion, engrossment and constant, unbroken contemplation, meditation and action (*abhidheyam*). In fact, while other types of equalities are to be established, *Param Saamyam* is to be realized as it is the only Reality.

The philosophy of *Saamyayoga* does not belittle equality in economic, political and social spheres, but it impresses upon man that all such types of equalities are the means to achieve the Supreme Equality, and that they cannot be achieved, that they are meaningless without equality of mind and without constant efforts to attain *Param Saamyam*. Social equality and mental equanimity are necessary not only because they help in day-to-day living and ensures the stability of a social order, but also because they are a means of climbing upwards towards *Param Saamyam*. Thus, Vinoba has emphasized, highlighted the material as well as the spiritual value of equality; he has stressed the spiritual dimension behind material equality.

Yoga also means many things; one dictionary gives about 32 meanings of that word. In the present context, it means joining, uniting, union. By combining it with *Samyam* to define the social ideal, Vinoba wishes to stress that while reconstructing an alternative social order and running it, any ism or conflict, or controversy or disputation or antagonism (or *vad*) is of little use. Class, caste, religious, linguistic, racial, communal, gender and any other type of interest conflicts (wars) are unnatural and suicidal. What is natural and life-sustaining is brotherhood, co-existence, cooperation, togetherness, interdependence, and mutual or social affection. The differences in views, stands, opinions (*matbhed*), and interests need not, should not, must not result in anger, hatred, antagonism, enmity, difference of minds (*manbhed*).

The reconstruction, social revolution must aim at uniting one heart with another, binding all hearts the bonds of affection and love, and generating or letting loose the power of natural and positive love. The opposition to and from none (*sarvesham avirodhen*) should be the cardinal principle of social transformation. The word *Yoga* thus indicates that the equality should be established through persuasion, compassion, love and peaceful or non-violent means.

The purport and import of uniting the word *yoga* with *samyam* can well be illustrated with the help of the following verse:

Samano mantraha
Samiti samani
Samanam manha
Saha chittameshaam
Samani va aakuti
Samana hridayani vah
Samanamastu vo manha
Yatha vah susahasati

Saman means one, uniform, same, equal, similar. Broadly speaking, these lines convey that in order to make our organization, collectivity, society strong and best, let our consultations, deliberations, resolutions, plans, counsel, be one; our meetings, associations, assemblies be one; our *chittas* be together; our intentions, purposes, wishes, feelings, emotions, be one; and our hearts be one.

It is because of his stress on *yoga* and *sarvesham avirodhen* that Vinoba has redefined the role of *Satyagraha* (non-violent non-cooperation or passive resistance) in *Sarvodaya* Movement. He has emphasized that a *satyagrahi* ought to be *satyagrahi* also. He discouraged the use of this weapon as far as possible, he invented the new concept of gentle or mild (*saumya*), gentler or milder (*saumyatar*), and gentlest or mildest (*saumyatam*) *satyagrah*, and argued that its effectiveness progressively increases as one moves from the mild to the mildest form. This technique in its new version gives more emphasis on ever increasing patience, tolerance, persuasion, self-introspection and self-purification (freedom from malice, ill-will, hatred).

A crucial aspect of any social system is its underlying conception of the nature of man, his attitudes, motivations, and behaviour. Vinoba has often pointed out the great importance of *Prakriti shodhyaha* i.e. the need for correctly understanding the nature of man, his mind, his chitta, and the nature of whole creation. As explained in Chapter 5, the conventional, modern perspective in this regard (under both communism and capitalism) is that man is homoeconomicus, an economic man, economic being.

In *Saamyayoga,* there is a total, fundamental change in this perception. It holds that man is different, separate from body, mind, and *chitta;* that he is the soul or *atman*. This is called *atmavad or atmanatmavivek*. It is also believed that the same *atman* lives in man and in literally everything in this creation (*atmaupamya vritti*), and that there is no difference between his being and the Supreme Being (*manushaha saumyam or advait*). In *Saamyayoga* man becomes well aware of his true nature and power (*atmashakter bhanat*), but he is also constantly taught to transcend the self, to become ego-free, to eliminate egoism and egotism, and to merge his self with the society and the Supreme Being (*aham mukti shabdat*). Thus *atmashakter bhanat* is balanced with *aham mukti shabdat*. It is further believed that the whole creation belongs to God; that He alone exists in and pervades each and every atom and particle in it; and that the only power (*satta*) which exists is that of God (*ishavasyam idam sarvam*). Similarly, it is believed that the quality of goodness or purity (*sattva*), passion or cause or any activity (*rajas*), and darkness or ignorance (*tamas*) are the three essential constituent qualities, attributes, properties of man, society, nature, and the whole creation.

As said earlier, all this reasoning, causation, explanation about the nature of the Creation is fundamentally, vastly different from the one given by Darwin's theory of evolution, Einstein's theory of relativity, Marxian theory of dialectical materialism, and Smith's theory of laissez-faire. According to Vinoba, the theory of Saamyayoga is spiritual, unique, wonderful; it is neither possible to disprove it nor to replace it.

The implications of this reasoning for the working of the social order are vastly beneficial. As Vinoba has pointed out, a *proper balance in the above-mentioned three attributes is very much necessary for balanced, healthy life of the individual and society*, and, therefore, society must be organized by taking this fact into account. For keeping *tamas* in balance, the bodily or manual or physical labour (*sharirshram*) or 'bread labour' (earn thy bread by sweat of thy brow) is necessary. For keeping *'rajas'* in balance, doing one's own duty and serving the society through it is necessary. In other words, *rajas* has to be kept in balance by *karmayoga* i.e. by doing one's own duty not with a motive of profit but with the motivation of service. It is important to note that the G-V alternative of a new social order is not merely economic, social, political order but requires a homoestatis or balance in *'Satva'*, *'Rajas'*, and *'Tamas'*.

In short, the motivational foundation of *Saamyayoga* is constituted by bread-labour, doing one's own duty, service, *karmayoga*, giving up or renouncing or generosity (*tyaga*), pious or devotional acts or sacrifice (*yajna*), austerity or self-denial or voluntary poverty or minimization of wants (*tapaha*), and granting or giving or offering gifts (*danam*). In order to remove the common misunderstanding or misconception that *danam* undermines, compromises the self-respect or the honour of the receiver. It may be pointed out that *danam* in Indian culture has always meant a different thing from charity, alms, philanthropy. It has been a regular religious duty enjoined on the individual for expressing gratitude to society, for repaying at least partially the debt they owed to society. As Vinoba, the *rishi of Saamyayoga,* has revealed, *danam* in Indian culture has also meant proper division and equitable or fair or just distribution and sharing of tangible and intangible possessions (*danam sanvibhagaha*). It is interesting to note that in many verses in the *Sama veda,* while indisposition to give (*adansheelata*), niggardliness or miserliness (*anudarta*), and selfishness have been strongly condemned, disposition to give (*dansheelata*), generosity (*udarata*), service (*paropkar*), and kindness (*daya*) have been highly eulogized.

Unlike capitalism and communism, this motivational, behavioural, attitudinal, value foundation can enable the *Saamyayogic* social order to solve conundrums such as (a) the ownership of wealth, property, and the use of their fruits, (b) class conflicts or class wars, (c) conflict of interest between the individual and society, and (d) conflict between man, other beings, and nature. It can help eliminate exploitation, injustices, inequalities, and violence which are engendered by the pursuit of self-interest. *Saamyayoga* rejects individualism without sacrificing the freedom, liberty, dignity of the individual; it also rejects the lopsided paramountcy or dominance of society. Dualistic thinking which regards society and individual to be separate parts does not exist in *Saamyayoga.*

The ethical principles and the value system underlying *Saamyayoga* and its action programmes are presented below in a rather long list:

Truth, non-violence, compassion, love, non-accumulation and non-possession, fearlessness, trusteeship, decentralization, withering away of the State and the freedom from any system (framework) of controls and rules (*Shasan-mukti and tantra-mukti*), freedom from exploitation (*Shoshan-mukti*), physical or manual labour or 'bread-labour' for literally everyone, and the equal value and status of all types of labour, co-existence and co-operation with friendship, affection (*Snehen Sahajivanam*); social workers' freedom from accumulated funds (*nidhi-mukti or kanchan-mukti*), all land (everything) belongs to God (*Sabai bhoomi Gopal ki*); individual is his own leader and guide (*ganasevakatva* or *atmadipobhava*); collective (*samuhik*) *Sadhana; Samuhik Samadhi; Samuhik mukti*; renouncing untouchability; Swadeshi; and equal tolerance (acceptance) of all religions.

The programmes for *Sarvodaya* are:

Bhoodan (land-gift), *gramdan* (village-gift), *sampattidan* (wealth-gift), *shramdan* (labour-gift), '*Sarvodaya patras' sammatidan* (consent-gift), *jivandan* (life-gift), *acharyakul* (association of teachers), *nai-talim* (basic education), *khadi, shanti sena* (peace brigade), *gram nirman* (village building or reconstruction), *go-seva* and *go-raksha* (service and protection of the cow), *ashram-sthapana* (setting up of ashrams), *samuhik sarvadharma* or *maun prarthana* (collective all-religions or silent prayers), and *satyagraha*.

What are the sources of '*Saamyayoga*'?

The *Bhagvad Gita* (Gita hereafter) is one of the major sources of *Saamyayoga*; it puts forth the ideal of *Saamyayoga* before humanity and teaches the art and philosophy of achieving it. The whole of the *Gita* is a hymn to *Saamyayoga* and, therefore, Vinoba has named the *Gita* itself as *Saamyayoga* as Tilak has called it '*Karmayoga*', and Gandhiji has called it '*Anasaktiyoga*'. One can show that there are about 30 verses in the *Gita* which directly and specifically refer to the ideal of equality (*samyam*). Apart from the *Gita, the Vedas, Upanisads,* other Sanskrit texts and classics, (*Vedanta*) and the whole of the literature of Indian saints have been the basis and inspiration of Vinoba's views, position, discussion of *Saamyayoga*.

Vinoba has explained, expounded his vision of *Saamyayoga* in his writings and literally thousands of talks or discourses, many of which have been published in the form of books. The books such as *Talks* on *Gita, Samyasutre, Ahimsa Ki Talash, Sarvodaya aur Samyavad, Swarajyashastra* are directly relevant in his context. In his famous essay on Gandhi and Marx also, he has presented a profound analysis of the meaning, similarities, and differences of Communism and *Saamyayoga.*

The nature and extent of the State (Government) in 'Saamyayoga' is an important aspect of '*Saamyayoga*' which we ought to understand well. Compared to the other systems, the thinking in *Saamyayoga* regarding the role of the State is highly profound and remarkably subtle. It aims at the end or withering away of the State i.e. at statelessness (*tataha shasan mukti*), and at substituting self-governance in the sense of own-self-control or own-self-restraint (*swa-shasan or atmanushasan*) in its place. It also seeks the end of authority or power of the mind over the self, and the end of one's own desire for power over others. Similarly, according to Vinoba, a subtle and important point is that statelessness (*shasan-mukti*) is more important than the complete elimination of exploitation (*shoshan-mukti*) in *Saamyayoga* because it is impossible to eliminate exploitation altogether; even in family relations, some exploitation tends to always exist. It is important to note that the *Saamyayogic* social order will be free from external governance (*shasan mukt*), but it will not be without any governance (*shasanheen*). As just stated above, there will be a governance in it by the self or soul (*atmashasan or atmanushasan*) accompanied by the steadfast, unswerving faith that God is the only one and ultimate ruler in this world (*Ishavasya Vritti*).

Man can achieve real freedom only when he becomes free from wants, desires. Further, freedom for oneself is impossible as long as the explicit and dormant desire for power is not rooted out from one's own self. Therefore, renouncing the desire or ambition for power (*sattakanksha tyaga* or *na tvam kamaye rajyam*) is an inseparable dimension of the goal of statelessness in *Saamyayoga.* Every individual in *Saamyayoga* would say, "I would not submit to the will of any external authority or to the power of my mind, and I will not make anyone submit to my authority". As Lincoln has said, *"Just as I will not be a slave, so also I will not be a master."*

Statelessness in *Saamyayoga* does not mean freedom from only the Nation-State. It means freedom from the external imposition of all types of systems or frameworks or rules or injunctions or prescriptions (*sarva-tantra swatantrata*). Moreover, in *Saamyayoga,* the realization of the power of the self or soul (*atmashakter bhanat*) renders any external authority redundant and ineffective.

After having discussed the role of the State, we now discuss the role of the market and related matters in '*Saamyayoga*'.

It should be clear by now that *Saamyayoga* is basically a vitally different paradigm from the paradigms of the market and the state, and their numerous variants. In fact, as explained in Chapter 5, although the Market and State have been conventionally posed as alternatives to each other, they are a little different from each other in fundamentals; there is a basic unity in them. It is the *Saamyayoga* which really can be posed as an alternative paradigm.

It is true that the conventional paradigms also have given some thought to the issues of equality, justice, elimination of exploitation, etc. However, equality has primarily meant economic equality, and the State is expected to play an important role in ensuring economic justice in them. They try to achieve equitable distribution of income and wealth through some combination of taxation, public expenditure, nationalization, confiscation or expropriation, and growth. Obsessed with growth, development, modernization, industrialism as they are, they first allow inequality to increase, and then feign to struggle towards achieving equality. They profess the ideals of peace and equality, but promote and celebrate competition, productivity, efficiency, individualism, money-making, materialism, and the pursuit of power which are bound to engender hatred, enmity, conflicts, inequality, and violence. They are thus riddled with basic contradictions. Empirically, none of the countries which had tried one or the other of these models has been successful in achieving even a semblance of equality. The value foundation, and the means, methods, programmes of Saamyayoga, on the other hand, are internally, mutually consistent, and they are bound to be successful in creating an equitable, just, peaceful social order.

Saamyayoga is a theory of justice but it is not a theory of merely economic or distributive justice, and it goes far beyond the utilitarian, social contract, and Rawls' theories of justice. It is a complete conception of justice; it is a theory of Social Ideal; it puts forth a new conception of society and a grand vision of the way in which the aims, purposes and methods of social co-operation are to be understood.

Generally, all the numerous types of systems can be grouped into three basic categories namely, individualistic, hierarchical, and altruistic. *Saamyayoga* is much more than an altruistic social order. It simultaneously achieves self-interest (swartha), interests of the others or society (*parartha*), and the spiritual interest (*paramartha*). It is worth highlighting that it does not sacrifice the economic, material interests of the individual while serving the other interests just mentioned. It simply redefines self-interest more widely so as to include social interests and spiritual goal in it.

The differences between the *Saamyayoga* and communism are so basic that even Vinoba, a great synthesizer (*samanvayacharya*) as he was, had ruled out the possibility of their convergence or synthesis. He had said that *Saamyayoga* and *Saamyavad* (communism) were in a state of confrontation in order to swallow, devour each other, and that only one of them was going to survive in the near future.

To summarize, *Saamyayoga* is a new term which has been specifically coined by Vinoba, and he has enriched the Sanskrit vocabulary and Indian philosophy by adding it to the line of concepts of *bhakti-yoga, jnana-yoga, and karma-yoga*. Its synonyms are *Sarvodaya, Gram-Swaraj*, and *Hind-Swaraj-Saamya Yoga* is at once both the philosophy and programme of both the personal and social life. Its objective is to attain the highest or supreme equality (*Param Samyam*), the supreme peace (*Param Shanti*), and the supreme happiness (*Param Sukham*) at both of these levels. *Saamyayoga* is to be achieved through *karmayoga, jnana-yoga, and bhakti-yoga*. In one sense, the two parts signify the same thing namely, oneness or unity of life; *Saamyam* means one and yoga also means one. *Saamyayoga* is thus a new word for stating the Vedantic philosophy of oneness or unity (*ekatvam*), or the end of duality of any nature whatsoever (*advait*).

On a social plane, *Saamyayoga* is about creating a spiritual social order in a scientific way. It is about the Total Revolution or aamoolagra parivartan i.e. it seeks to revolutionalize not only social organization, social structure, and social institutions but also the value system underlying them. It teaches that social transformation involves a change in mind, a change in thinking and views, a change of heart, and a change in institutions. In other words, *Saamyayoga* is a holistic alternative to the conventional social paradigms in more than one sense. For example, it emphasizes (a) a change in the core as well as superstructure of the social system; (b) its economic or material as well as meta-economic and spiritual dimensions; (c) its scientific as well as spiritual dimensions; and (d) its individual as well as social dimensions.

The conceptual development and enrichment (as discussed above) of *HS* during 1948-1978 was accompanied by a similar advancement in the methods and programmes for implementing *HS* vision. The movements, '*Aandolans*', and '*Yajnas*' emerged to make the goals and ideals of *HS* practicable. The values and programmes of *Saamyayoga* listed earlier give us an idea about developments in this regard. Among these programmes, *Bhoodana* and *Gramadana* (B-G) are widely known in India as well as abroad. They are also novel, revolutionary, inspired measures which have a great potential for transforming the societies in keeping with the goals of HS. Louis Fisher has said that "Gramadana is the most creative thought coming from the East in recent times". We present below some maxims, aphorisms, and programmes about Bhoodana and Gramadana.

- *Danam Sanvibhagh* (*dana* means equitable distribution).
- *Sabai Bhoomi Gopalki, Na Kisike Malkiki* (All land belongs to Gopal, i.e., God; it is not owned by anyone).
- *Mumbai, Delhi me hamari Sarkar, hamare gaonme ham hi Sarkar* (There will be our government in Mumbai and Delhi, and in our village, we ourselves are the government).
- *Gramaswaraj* is our birthright and we must get it.
- *Hamara mantra Jai Jagat, Hamara tantra Gramaswaraj* (Our sacred words are Hail the world, our path or method is *gramaswaraj*).
- Think globally, act locally.
- *Vishvam pushtham grame aasmin anaturam* (Let there be a view of prosperous universe in our village).
- *Yatha grame tatha Vishve* (As in the village, so in the universe).
- *Mata Bhoomi, putro aham pruthivyam*. (Land is our mother, I am the son of planet Earth).

What is *Bhoodana*? *Bhoo* means land and '*dana*' means giving or donation or gift by someone to another. *Bhoodana* thus means gift or donation or giving of land with love to those who are landless by those who possess at least some land. There are some interesting points to be remembered about *dana*. (a) The psychology of the giver and taker. In *dana*, giving comes from the heart and of love, and very elevated sense of duty and the desire to be truthful. In *dana* nobody demands and yet the giver gives. The secrecy is an important aspect of *dana*. This is conveyed by the practice or saying in India that "the left hand shall not know what the right hand gives." (b) *Dana* has been regarded as a very great virtue, and Indian culture and tradition have been rich with the scintillating and legendary line of great givers known as 'danashoor' (brave giver) person such as Karna, Harischandra, King Harsha, King Shibi and so on. (c) Adi Shankaracharya has defined *dana* as 'danamsanvibhagh' i.e. dana is equitable distribution. (d) The critics of B-G have queried that why should the landless depend upon the favour and mercy of the land giver to get land? In *Bhoodan*, the receiver may think that his honour, self-respect, is compromised, he may be burdened with obligation. But the spirit of bhoodana in particular and '*dana*' in general is such that there is no question of the receiver losing his self-respect. (e) If we stick to the donation 'right' aspect of dana there would not be a place for, for example, eye donation. (f) The motivation behind dana at temples, and that too the mind boggling quantities is difficult to understand. Certain temples in festivals receive 'gifts' in hundreds of crores of rupees. The first *bhoodana* took place on April 18, 1951, at Pochampalli in Andhra Pradesh (AP) in India when Ramachandra Reddy gave 100 acres of his land to the landless people in that village.

The goal of *Bhoodana* was to get land and to redistribute it as equitably as possible. The work of *Bhoodana*, according to *Bhoodana* leaders, was the work of revolution, sacrifice, and worship. It was the work of changing life and joining hearts. It was to reduce the deluded attachment to land. *Bhoodana* and other daily donations or 'givings' would keep the balance and harmony in the society. The work of *bhoodana* was the work of 'turning the wheel of *Dharma*' (*dharma chakra parivartan*). The intent of *bhoodana* was not to avoid revolution; it was to save the country from violent revolution, or to bring about non-violent revolution in India. The peace and happiness in the country vitally depended on solving the land problem, and it was certain that this problem could not have been solved through legal means or violent killing of the rich. The best way to solve this problem was through love and compassion. Bhoodana provided this path. Bhoodana movement includes the industrial labour movement also; ultimately, the practice of Bhoodana in all earnest will result in breaking of the shackles or removing the slavery of industrial labour also.

Thus, the long-term aim of Bhoodana was to enhance the qualities (Gun Vikas) of everyone and to bring about the spiritual growth or progress or development of everyone, along with the short-term material aim of tackling land and other problems. An important lesson of Bhoodana is that if we appeal to the goodness of people, all types of spiritual and material issues of mankind can be solved.

Bhoodana demonstrated that it is not poetic imagination to think that it is possible to get land from the people in a peaceful manner. Bhoodana is not only a movement; it is a 'Yajna'. It was an experiment in Ahimsa; it was a peace-Yajna. It contained the seeds of world revolution. Vinoba has said that "he realized God through Bhoodana, and he saw that there is a goodness in every heart, and it can be appealed to". Bhoodana was the 'Yajna' of non-violent revolution. Bhoodana was not an ordinary or simple event; it axed the existing order deeply; it was a demand of 'yuga-purusha'. "The work of Bhoodana gave me, Vinoba said, the feeling that I had become the mouthpiece of the poor; that '*rajchintamani*' (The king of the philosopher's stone) had come in my hands; that I had experienced God's love."

The Bhoodana Movement has been called 'Bhoodana Yajna' because the donation of the land is regarded similar to a 'voluntary sacrificial act' or offering ablutions. It was also called as 'diksha' i.e., an initiation into the life of sacrifice and social responsibility. Bhoodana was never a mere movement or charity or bhiksha (alms) or a reformist activity. It always had a revolutionary, spiritual purpose par excellence towards creating a socio-economic-political-spiritual-moral order that is marked by love, compassion, Ahimsa, equality, justice and absence of exploitation. It aimed at creating a new man. There was no place for hatred towards anyone, including those who did not donate any land.

What is *Gramadana*? Grama means a revenue village or a 'pada' or a 'tola'. Gramadana does not mean gift of the village to some entity, some individual, some institution, or some organization inside or outside the village. Gramadana means the gift to, or sacrifice of the village by the villagers. It involves the solemn resolve or vow undertaken by the villagers, entirely on their own volition, to give their land and other wealth or valuables (partially or entirely) to the village. A gift of the village(s), for example, by the King to someone in appreciation of his service to the King cannot be called gramadana. The Gramadana is a fully developed or advanced (or wider and broader) vision of the Bhoodana. In Bhoodana and Gramadana (B-G), 'dana' may not be a one-time act; it may be a continued and a repeated act, and, therefore, there is a continuous *'bhagadana'* (gift of a part) or *'dandahara'* i.e., stream of 'dana'. This idea of a possibility of a repeated 'dana' is reflected in the term namely, *'Bhoodan Ganga'*, widely used in this context.

The first Gramadana took place on May 24, 1952, in the village Mangroth in Uttar Pradesh in India, when all the village landlords from Mangroth attending Vinoba's meeting unanimously announced that they had decided to donate their entire land to bhoodana. The decision heralded the voluntary abolition of private individual ownership of property, and vesting it in the community or village as a whole.

During the years which followed the Mangroth event, the revolutionary ideas of *Bhoodana-Gramadana* (B-G) flowered into many related ideas and ideals such as *Sampattidana* (gift of wealth), *Sammatidana* (gift of consent), *Shramadana* (gift of labour), *Buddhidana* (gift of intellect), *Prakhandadhana* (gift of tehsil), *Zilladana* (gift of district) and so on.

Gramasabha, panchayat, gramakosha, the village as one family, absence of political parties in the village, the abolition of the right to private property, *satyagraha*, absence of majority rule, constructive works programme, are some of the important components or aspects of Gramadana.

The synonyms of Gramadana are: *Gramaswaraj, Sarvodaya, Ramraja, Lokniti* (people's politics), *Lokshakti* (people's power or strength), *Loksatta* (people's power), village republics, Hind Swaraj, and Saamyayoga.

The aim of Gramadana is equitable resources sharing and spiritual or transcendental development. The initial aim of Gramadana was that there should not be anyone in the village who is landless. Its second aim was that no one in the village should have ownership right to land individually or collectively. The land in the village belongs to everyone in the spirit of *'sabai bhoomi*

Gopalki' (All the land belongs to Gopal or God). It would establish a non-violent revolutionary social order, build the inner strength of the people and empower the people. It is a divine vision and mission; it is not merely a programme or a movement, its goal is ascension.

Gramadana is a unique approach to revolution because it recognizes all dimensions such as religious, spiritual, moral, social, political, cultural and economic of the society. In the last analysis, it seeks to revive the teachings of Gautam Buddha. It is an alternative body of thought, and an alternative social arrangement for the daily worldly activities and business of human collectivities. Gramadana is a Buddhist Revolution.

Gramadana gives great importance to the family and abolition of ownership rights. It envisages that eventually every village in the country would be transformed into one family or '*gramakutumbakam*' without compromising or sacrificing the spirit of universalism. Gramadana has given a greater sense of realism and practicability to the ideal of universalism by choosing the ideal '*gramakutumbakam*' over the ideal of '*vasudhaiva kutumbakam*' (i.e., the whole earth is a family). Vinoba has given the mantra of '*Jai Jagat*' (hail the world) while simultaneously choosing the ideal of 'gramakutumbakam' over the ideal of earth-family. Therefore, Gramadana is very much today's '*Yugadharma*' or Zeitgeist or the spirit of the time. All this is very much consistent with Vinoba-enunciated advice of "think globally but act locally". This approach is promotive of the ideal of *Swadeshi* also.

It is worth reiterating that this enlightenment by Vinoba on universalism is the best way to reconcile the interests of the individual and those of the whole world. The idea of a village-family is the middle path between a nuclear family and the world-family. It may become practical or attainable in due course.

In gramadana, nobody, including the sovereign king, has the right to own the land. There is no private or public ownership of land and other assets in this social order. The entire land in the village belongs to that village. As per the ancient wisdom, land is our mother and no one can own a mother. To end the private ownership of the land (and other assets) is itself a great revolution, which gramadana brings about.

Whom does the land really belong to? Some people would say, it belongs to the tiller. Some others would say it belongs to the whole village, i.e., to all the people in that village. Some would say that it belongs to God (sabai bhoomi Gopalki) in principle, but in practice, it belongs to the Gramasabha on behalf of God, and on behalf of all the people in the village.

Gramadana also seeks to ensure that the land in any village must always remain with that village. There cannot be any buying and selling of land between a given village and any outside party. To sell the land to any outsider is regarded as disloyalty to the village (i.e., *gramadroha*).

The continuous thinking by Vinoba and his co-workers on gramadana has resulted in modifying from time to time the conditions to be fulfilled by the villagers in order that their villages are designated or registered as '*gramadani*' villages. This has given rise to different 'types' of gramadana which are: Simple (saral) gramadana, quite new (*abhinava*) gramadana, attainable or easy (*sulabha*) gramadana, and total (*samagra*) gramadana. These are not different types of gramadanas. They reflect the desire and thinking in favour of relaxing or softening the conditions so that more and more villages come in the fold of gramadani villages.

Thus, the issue of practicability has not been ignored in the gramadana model. The philosophy of gramadana has been made more and more acceptable by making the conditions of gramadana more and more easy. In 'sulabha' gramadana, for example, efforts were made to balance the two opposing motivations, *viz.*, 'social responsibility' or 'social commitment' (*samaja prerana*) on the one hand, and self-interest (*swartha prerana*) on the other. We may talk about '*saral*' or '*abhinava*' or '*sulabha*' or '*samagra*' gramadana, but the meaning of gramadana remains the same in all these cases.

Gramadana is the foundation of *gramaswaraj* or *Hind Swaraj*. As explained by Vinoba, gramadana means the land belongs to all, it belongs to Gopal or God. Just as air and water belong to God and they are for everybody, land also belongs to God and it is for everybody. Gramadana means all land and all wealth in a given village belong to that village or they belong to all the people in that village. To put it differently, gramadana means all the land and wealth in a village belongs to the gramasabha on behalf of God and all the people in the village. In gramadana, everybody must give to the village a part of whatever he possesses (land, skills, mental and intellectual capabilities, physical strength etc.).

Is there a difference between bhoodana and gramadana?

According to Vinoba, there are certain subtle differences between the two. As said earlier, gramadana is a wider and broader vision than that of bhoodana. While gramadana is an ocean, bhoodana is a river. While love and compassion inspired bhoodana, compassion and pursuit of justice or equality (saamyayoga) inspired gramadana. Intelligence, splendour of knowledge, and intuition (pratibha) have been the forces in gramadana. The philosophy of bhoodana when advanced further would, progress in the form of a total comprehensive programme of gramadana or gramaswarajya or sarvodaya. Bhoodana was individual 'dana', while gramadana was a collective experiment for creating a new social organization or social order which would serve as an alternative to the current social order.

Gramadana is a 'new-age harbinger' *mantra* and *tantra*. It is not regressive. It is a complete life-philosophy, a complete people's democracy, the newest of thoughts, and mightest unconquerable (*ajeya*) universal thought. The gramadana movement helped to spread the message of social, economic and moral revolutions. Gramadana showed for the first time the possibility of rural development as envisaged by Gandhiji. It advanced Gandhiji's idea of non-violent total revolution. Gramadana showed the possibility and practicability of a non-violent world revolution; it also brought forth the total outline of non-violent social order.

Gramadana is not only compassion-induced '*danadhara*'; it is compassion-induced total village planning. It has tremendous potential for peace. The gramadana programme is more powerful than the atom, and it is a path of redistribution for wealth and land through love. It has been rightly claimed that gramadana is the purest of pure religious, economic and scientific thought. It has the potential of solving all our issues and problems such as untouchability, casteism, land management, economic planning, social planning etc. It would not be wrong to say that gramadana is an ancient as well as post-modern thought at one and the same time.

The gramadana programme is 'trusteeship in action'; it is a practical form of trusteeship; and the Gramasabha is the best instrument of continuous revolution. Vinoba has made wonderful efforts to inculcate spiritual values in collective and social life through gramadana. It has been a great experiment to 'create a new man', to bring about a human revolution, and to effect progress in human qualities (*gun-vikas*).

Gramadana is the best path for fulfilling mankind's quest for democracy. It is *'poorna prajatantra* or *lokatantra'*. It has presented before us a picture of the future social order. Gramadana is a total revolution; it is not a revolution for any one class or value or caste or religion. This revolution would result in social order which will work on the basis of decision by all, strength of all, and interests of all. In this total revolution of all, there is no scope for war and antagonism between labour and capital. Today's villages, towns and cities, are mere collectivities of residences. There is no unity, brotherhood, and village spirit (*gramabhavana*) among them. This picture will be altered and there will be a stateless, self-dependent village system, and party-less governing system through the gramadana social order.

There is fundamental unity among human beings, and gramadana makes the use of this unity for revolutionary social transformation or social change. Gramadana is a perfect non-violent revolution.

In a gramadani social order, what would be the political, social, economic superstructure in India? It is envisaged that for quite some time to come, the present geographical, political, economic governing entities will continue till they are transformed into the gramadana mode. Ultimately, the world-structure or world arrangements will be such that there will be a world panchayat (i.e., world samiti) on the one hand and village panchayats on the other. Between these two units, there will be nations, provinces, zillas, etc. which will primarily do the coordination work; they would serve as connecting links for some time to come, but ultimately they would wither away.

To repeat, ultimately, there will be only the world and the village after gramadana. For convenience, there may be different nations, but the ultimate reality will be marked by the existence of only the world and the village. All the powers related to the material aspects of life will vest and rest in the village. The states, districts, etc. will be only the representatives and co-ordinators of village societies. The whole structure or system will thus be founded on the village. There will neither be private nor the state ownership of money, capital, wealth, property. There will be village ownership of all these. The goal of the system will be to replace the current power politics, party politics, party representatives by village representatives, and people's politics of service and sacrifice. The individuals, organizations, institutions, different functioning units would be connected in the form of oceanic circles.

At present when the strong centralized nation-states rule in all the countries, they will have to summon the necessary political will and pass suitable legislation to help the villages transform themselves from their present status to the status of 'gramadani' villages. Ultimately it is the will of the people which will initiate the transformation process. At present it appears that both the people's will and the political will of the government determine the success of all transformation processes.

After gramadana, in the Government's land records, only the names of villages will appear; the names of any individuals will not appear in those records. Further, although the ownership of land in the gramadani village will vest in the gramasabha, gramasabha cannot sell the land of the village to anyone, particularly to outsiders.

The leftists (Communists, Socialists) believe that every society is divided into two classes namely, the 'haves' and the 'have-nots'. Gramadana roots out this notion of class division of society. It believes that everyone in the society is a 'have' or everyone in the society is a 'have not' depending on how you look at the matter. It is the fundamental belief of sarvodayists that the greater truth than the class conflict is that nobody has been sent to this earth without absolutely any strength.

Gramadana is not a formal co-operative organization, although the principle and value of co-operation is very much needed in it. In gramadana, every individual can cultivate his land separately or independently, while in co-operative farming the farming takes place or is done collectively in a group. There is also a danger of bureaucratic interference, corruption, apathy, red tapism, inflexibility in co-operative farming, while such ills would be absent in gramadana because there are only '*sevaks*' and not bureaucrats or masters in the gramadana order.

How does gramadana deal with issues such as absentee landlords and the hereditary rights of the people? The landlords staying outside the village will have to surrender their whole land to the gramasabha. Since the final goal the gramadana is to establish gramaswaraj, this goal cannot be achieved if part of the land in a village is owned by the landlords staying outside the village.

The land which remains with the farmers after they have given a part of their land to the gramadana will not be owned by those farmers, but they will have the right to cultivate that land, and to pass on that land to their heirs for the purpose of tilling. In case of any dispute on this matter, the decision of the Gramasabha will be final.

When is a given village said to be a gramadani village? When does a village get designated or registered as a gramadani village?

At the outset it should be noted that a given village becomes a *gramadani* village only of its sweet will; no one (no government, no other body) can force any village to participate in gramadana. It is entirely a voluntary act. Subject to this, any given village comes to be called a gramadani village when it satisfies or meets certain conditions formulated by the state governments and the *Sarva Seva Sangh*. The State Governments have passed the Gramadana Act and the village which fulfills the provisions of this Act, becomes a gramadani village legally also. For making gramadana, the villagers of a given village have to fill the Declaration Form as per the legal provisions of the Gramadana Act. These forms have to be submitted to the revenue officer who needs to scrutinize them, and accept or reject them after the scrutiny. The villages whose forms are accepted and approved are declared as gramadani villages.

The process or steps involved in this connection are given below. There is nothing rigid about these conditions. There are some regional (state) variations in them.

1) The landlords or owners of land in a village would declare to the collector in writing that at least 60 per cent of the land privately owned by them in that village would be donated by them to the village. They would do so through a gift document and by their free will and without taking or expecting any compensation whatsoever.
2) The number of land owners whose gift documents (danpatras) are approved should be at least 75 per cent of land owners living in that village.
3) The number of adult landless who have accepted to be members of the gramadana society (gramadana samaj) should be at least 75 per cent of the total population in the village.
4) When the collector calls a meeting for declaring a given

village as gramudani village, at least 51 per cent of the adult population of the village must be present in that meeting and at least 51 per cent of those present in the meeting should vote in the favour of gramadana.

If and when these 4 conditions are fulfilled, the collector would announce through gazette that the said village has become a gramadani village.

5) The villagers will surrender to the village all their ownership rights.
6) They will have (donate) one-twentieth part of their cultivable land to the landless in that village.
7) After donating the land to the landless, the land owners may keep the remaining land with themselves for cultivation; and they may be entitled to the income from that land, generation after generation.
8) The villagers every year will have to give one-fortieth part (or the part decided by gramasabha) of their annual income to the '*gramanidhi*' or '*gramakosh*' of the village for public purposes.
9) This will form a gramasabha of one adult from each family in the village, which will monitor the work of '*gramamandal*' or '*panchayat samiti*'.
10) The Gramasabha will perform all work in the village unanimously, or by consensus.

In revolution through gramadana, three institutions namely, *Gramasabha*, *Gramasamiti* or *Sevaksamiti*, and *Gramakosh* or *Gramanidhi* play an important role. Before we proceed to discuss their work it is essential to make some terminological clarification. Sometimes, Gandhiji has referred to gramaswaraj as Panchayat Raj. But this Gandhian Panchayat Raj is different from the state panchayat raj. And yet, many people tend to use Gandhian Panchayat Raj and the state panchayat raj synonymously. The mixing up of the two panchayat rajes has enabled the authorities to make claims for the state panchayat raj which really belong to the Gandhian Panchayat Raj. To use somewhat harsh language, the similarity of terminology to describe two diverse ideas or concepts has enabled the government to hijack the terminology. We should guard against such misuse of terminology.

Similarly, there is a gramasabha in both the government

Panchayat Raj and Gandhian Panchayat Raj but, as we shall show soon, scope, authority, of these two gramasabhas are quite different from each other. The same is true of gramapanchayat and panchayat samiti also. It is feared by some that the word gramadana or gramaswaraj may help to establish stateless ideal sarvodaya raj only for the villages. If so, what would happen to the towns and cities? In order to avoid such a dilemma, some people have suggested that we should use terms like *lokswaraj* or *nagarswaraj* instead of *gramaswaraj*. In our view, in a country that is overwhelmingly agricultural and rural, gramaswaraj is an apt term. The only thing that would need to be done is to work for revolutionary changes of the mind, heart, thinking, lifestyles, etc. in urban areas also.

Gramadana's Gramasabha would be constituted by all the people in the village who are 21 years old or older. Sometimes it is said that all adults in the village will be the members of the Gramasabha. We think that the specification of the exact age is better than saying that every adult would be a member of the Gramasabha. It may be noted that there would not be any election, or there would not be any need to be a member of a political party in order to become a member of the Gramasabha. The Gramasabha will be the owner of all land and other assets in the village. The process of decision making would be as follows: the gramasamiti will decide something unanimously; this decision will be put before the gramasabha, which, in turn, will decide about it unanimously; the gramasabha's decision will be final.

In Vinoba's words, the Gramasabha would be the '*gramamata*' or '*gramadurga*', and its strength will be derived from the strength of each individual in a village. The Gramasabha will deal with the government and other institutions on behalf of the villages.

Another important organization in gramaswaraj would be the '*gramasamiti*' or '*sevak samiti*' or '*grama mandal*'. Every year, a panchayat (i.e., gramasamiti) consisting of about 5 to 8 persons will be selected unanimously by the Gramasabha for running the day-to-day administration, planning and policy of the village. The gramasamiti will enact laws, dispense justice, and manage the village affairs unanimously, but it would not have the right or authority to punish anyone. Similarly, the gramasamiti will not have any right or authority to own anything belonging to the village.

The third important organization in gramaswaraj is the 'gramakosha' or 'gramanidhi'. This fund will be built out of the gifts or donations or danas of the 40th part of everybody's yearly income. This fund will be utilized for the development and welfare requirements of the village. This contribution to gramakosh is not a tax, it is a 'dana', and if someone does not pay this contribution, the Gramasabha cannot punish him because the gramasabha does not have punitive powers. But such a situation can be handled by resorting to satyagraha by the villagers.

We have attempted to explain so far the need, meaning, philosophy of gramadana. Before turning to the discussion of its performance, let us briefly present below the main features or characteristics of the gramadani social order. This picture is mostly in the words of Mahatma Gandhi and Vinobaji.

The elimination of the right to own private property is the foundation of gramaswaraj or gramadana. It will have the walls of village industries, and the windows of *Nai Talim* (or basic education). The village would be the basic unit for thinking, policy-making and planning in gramaswaraj. The primacy for the village and the people is the *sine qua non* of *gramaswaraj*. There will be a sovereign government in each village in this social order, or there will be a republic or kingdom in each village; all the powers will vest in the hands of the village. The provincial governments will not exercise authority or power over the villages; they will only create and maintain cordial relations among the villages, if needed. Gramapanchayats will form zilla panchayats which will form provincial panchayats, which will form the national panchayat. There will be a federation of villages. Every village will function as per its own intelligence, and the governments at higher echelons will provide only advice or consultation to the villages. The gramasabha at the village level will have the right to elect representatives for the provinces.

The power of the government and the level of government will be inversely related to each other: the higher the level of government, the lesser will be its powers. Every village will be a powerful and free republic; it will also be independent vis-à-vis other villages. Such a sarvodaya samaj will not be organized like a pyramid, it will be organized like an oceanic circle. The individual will be at the centre of such a circle, who will be ever ready or ever willing to make sacrifices for the villages. In such a society, there will be an improvement in the quality of the individual (Gunvikas). The outer or bigger circles will never try to destroy the inner circles. In fact, they will strengthen the inner circles, and while doing so, they themselves will become progressively stronger and stronger.

The priorities of such a samaj or republic will be (in a descending order) to increase the output of foodgrains (annam bahu kurvit), to increase the production of cotton, to maintain grazing grounds for cows and other animals, to maintain sports grounds, to grow commercial crops, etc.

There will be compulsory education through Nai Talim. Ahimsa, Satyagraha and non-cooperation will constitute the support system. Rearing livestock and increasing milk output would be given high priority. In other words, the efforts will be made to ensure that the rivers of milk, curd, etc. will start flowing once again in this blessed land. The society would also take all steps to protect and maintain the quality of land. There would be hardly any need for a complex judicial system, a huge police department, and a vast army in such a society.

Agriculture would continue to be the main or central economic activity in India during the gramaswaraj era. Khadi and gramodyoga will become an inseparable part of the economic activity. The village government will regulate the role and size of modern industry, business, commerce, and trade, and it will actively encourage the development of village, cottage, and tiny, small-scale industries. The villages will prepare their own plans, and they will regulate imports and exports. Today, the land has become fragmented and inequitably distributed.

In the gramadani ideal social order, everyone, irrespective of his or her status, position, and riches, will do work on farms at least for a few hours daily. Everyone would be in touch with nature. There will be a withering away of the cities over the period of time and every village will become a family, every village will become a '*gokul*'.

Gramadana is visualized to eliminate the global crisis of survival. It would help to transform our endangered, dying, modern civilization into a civilization of permanance. Gramadana will improve social, political, economic, cultural, moral, and spiritual development of villages.

According to Vinoba, every village will be transformed into one family. The end of the right to private property also would help to increase the wealth and economic freedom of the villages. It will also stop the internal as well as external drain of resources from the villages to the urban and metropolitan centres. It will also enable the villagers to determine the prices of their produce in the villages. All such changes will increase production, prosperity, and wealth in the villages.

The Justice pertaining to all matters concerning the village will be done in the village itself. All the necessities and vital goods will be produced in the villages themselves. All the villages will follow the ideals of swadeshi, self-sufficiency, and self-reliance. The importance of money will go down drastically; there will be a significant increase in barter exchange.

Gramadana will result in a true economic, political, social, cultural freedom for all the people. The increase in love among the people will resolve conflicts such as majority-minority, rich-poor, and high caste-low caste. The culture of peace will be established in villages in due course.

Gramadana will promote face-to-face, direct, partyless democracy through economic, political, administrative, technological decentralization. As said elsewhere also, Gramadana will establish self-sufficient, self-reliant, self-dependent, self-governing '*sarvodaya villages republics*' or '*sarvodaya village kingdoms*'. The gramadana will revive and redevelop '*grama sanskriti*' (i.e., village culture) or the arcadian civilization. In such a civilization, every village will be a 'gramaswaraj mandir'.

It will be the responsibility of the village to meet or fulfill all the educational and cultural needs of the village. In every village, the '*Acharyakul*' will be established which will deal with all the educational and cultural needs of the village.

The security or protection or defence of the village will be the responsibility of the whole village; there will not be a separate or special 'varna' (such as Kshatriya varna in the past) for this purpose. But each village will create or establish '*shanti sena*' which will look after security needs of the village(s).

Disputes or conflicts in the village will be resolved or settled by using the means of ahimsa, satyagraha, adopted at the local village courts.

The Bhoodan-Gramadan Movements were launched in 1951 and 1952, respectively. They had short-term, long-term, qualitative and quantitative aims which have been discussed so far in this book. It is but natural that there have been differences of opinion as to whether B-G movements have succeeded or not.

A serious difficulty in the way of arriving at any firm conclusion in this context is the non-availability of reliable, detailed data. Some information on this matter that is available to us is presented below in Table 1. It tells us about (a) the number of acres of land donated by the people in bhoodana. (b) the number of acres of land distributed to the landless through bhoodana. (c) The number of donors of land. (d) The number of gramadani villages. (e) The number of gramadanas that are registered with the authorities. (f) The state-wise distribution of the information on bhoodana and gramadana. The information pertains to the period of 1951-1984. The total bhoodana of about 53 lakh acres that took place between 1951-1984. A part of this donated land was disputed land, another part was taken back by the donors, and still another part of donated land was non-cultivable or barren land. If we deduct such 'useless' land of 11 lakh acres from the total donated land, we still have to accept that bhoodan resulted in the donation of 42 lakh acres of good, cultivated, undisputed land. About 25 lakh acres of this (42 lakh acres) land has been actually distributed to the landless people in India through bhoodana. In comparison with this achievement, the Land Ceiling Acts in different states could make only 9.93 lakh acres of land available for redistribution, of which amere 7.5 lakh acres of land was actually distributed to the landless people in India. Table 1 also shows that about 5.83 lakh people received land through the Bhoodana movement.

One of the aims of the Bhoodana Movement was that there should not be any one landless person in India. If this was to materialize, it was estimated that about five crore acres of land should become available for redistribution. But bhoodana was able to redistribute only 0.25 crore acres of land as compared to the required 5.0 crore acres of land. To put it differently, bhoodana obtained only 10 per cent (50 lakh acres) of required land for redistribution, and actually redistributed only 5 per cent (25 lakh acres) of the required land.

Similarly, Table 1 shows that 38,464 villages declared gramadana, of which only 3,103 gramadanas were registered with the government. If we assume that there were about 6 lakh villages in India around 1985, only 6.33 per cent of these villages had become gramadani villages by 1984.

Table 1: The State of Bhoodana Gramadana in 1984: (Land in acres)

State	*Land received*	*Land distributed*	*Number of receivers*	*Number of Gramadana received*	*Number of Gramadana registered*
Andhra Pradesh	195,510	99,530	32,312	4181	1
Assam	877	877	851	2200	285
Orissa	13,53,440	778,238	-	-	1309
Karnataka	20,000	8000	-	-	-
Kerala	-	-	-	-	-
Gujarat	103,530	50,984	10,270	1119	-
Jammu-Kashmir	121	121	-	-	-
Tamilnadu	24,375	22,837	16,000	1962	243
Punjab	5138	1026	233	-	-
Haryana	2074	2043	553	-	-
Bihar	21,17,756	590,496	433,754	2581	1046
West Bengal	16,000	9000	-	-	-
Himachal	4000	2400	-	-	-
Madhya Pradesh	410,151	238,629	59,805	-	-
Maharashtra	110,000	79,990	15,546	500	19
Rajasthan	546,965	142,699	14,124	195	195
Uttar Pradesh	436,054	417,621	-	25,726	5
Total	**53,46,021**	**24,44,491**	**583,448**	**38,464**	**3103**

Source: *Samyayoga Sadhana,* 16 April, 2001.

Thus, did the bhoodana-Gramadana Movements succeed or fail? The answer to this question would depend on which part of the proverbial glass we look at. On the face of it, B-G movements have failed to achieve both their long-term and short-term goals. They have failed in solving the land problem; they could redistribute only a very limited acreage of land when compared to the total size of the land in the country, and compared to the acreage of land required to achieve zero landlessness in the country. It is a matter of little comfort that the extent of land redistribution through B-G was much greater than what was achieved through the legal approach. The persistence of violence perpetrated by the so called revolutionaries, and its spread in many areas or states also can be taken to indicate the failure of these movements.

But this perhaps is a harsh judgement. The enthusiasm exhibited by the vast population, the willingness of lakhs of people to part with land voluntarily (though in small measure, do show the huge possibilities and potential of what can be achieved through peaceful means. Bhoodana-Gramadana Movements have not failed, they have remained incomplete, but they ought to be completed. If there appears to be a failure, it is of the movements and not of the thought, ideals, and philosophy.

In this context, some scholars and social workers have argued, in our view correctly, that the success or failure of a new revolutionary thought such as bhoodana and gramadana must be assessed by applying certain qualitative standards, and if we do so, we will have to come to the conclusion that B-G movements have been successful. These standards are: (a) whether mankind got a new or elevated or generous aim or goal through such a thought? (b) whether mankind got a path to reach that goal? (c) whether that path progressively became more and more easy and commendable? (d) whether the aim came near at least to some extent? Since we get a positive answer to these questions in the case of B-G, it has to be clearly and undoubtedly adjudged to have been successful.

Although we do not have any qualms in following this way of thinking, we cannot, at the same time, ignore the fact that the impact of B-G lasted only for a short time, say till 1965, after which it petered out. Similarly, the success must not remain confined all the time to qualitative standards. It must be seen concretely in terms of economic, political and social quantitative indicators. The revolution must not only occur, it must also be seen to have occurred. Just as the success (or failure) of the new model should not be judged only in quantitative measures, similarly it cannot be judged only in terms of certain abstract standards. Sooner or later tangible standards should become a part of the repertoire of assessment standards.

Gandhiji has sometimes called gramaswaraj as Panchayat Raj (PR). As a result we have two notions of Panchayat Rajs in India; one the Gandhian Panchayat Raj (GPR) and two, the Panchayat Raj introduced by the Government or the State around the year 1958, for democratic decentralization, which can be called 'Government or State Panchayat Raj' (SPR).

Now, many people think that these two PRs are very similar to each other or they are the same. The authorities have gone on implementing SPR claiming that they are following the Gandhian path of gramaswaraj. The government has been misleading the public in this context, as SPR has hijacked gramadana or gramaswaraj. Actually, there is a vast difference between these two PRs. In Vinoba's manner of speaking, they are different from each other as much as Rama and Ravana were different from each other. The politicians do not part with power; there is no genuine political will to decentralize power, and yet they are feigning, pretending that they are working for the empowerment of the people by implementing SPR.

Although the SPR was meant to bring about democratic decentralization, it has actually brought about only the deconcentration, delegation, and devolution. At present, the administrative, political, and economic power is concentrated in the hands of the Central Government. Some small parts of this power have been deconcentrated in the hands of the SPR. The SPR has not helped to decentralize the centre's and the state's power. Instead, according to Vinoba, there has been a 'nationalization of jealousy'. The present grama panchayat represents jealousy, and not service. The SPR is a 'decentralized plan for exploitation'. Since present panchayats are characterized by jealousy, power-seeking, power pursuit, lack of love and compassion, the consequences of their existence and working have been to make the body-politics of India thoroughly sick. The panchayats have become the centres, hotbeds, and gymkhanas of conflicts.

Another defect of the SPR is that it functions on the principle of the 'rule of the majority'. The SPR is afflicted by party-politics, election-politics, vote bank-politics and it is incapable of preserving the individual or unique personality of each village. The Government PR institutions are 'institutions of power' and not 'institutions of services'. Therefore, they have not been able to arouse the people's power.

The SPR set-up has created 'welfare villages' and it has promoted the 'culture of theyism' i.e., the attitude or the mind-set that the authorities would do all (small to big) things for the people and people need not do anything for themselves. In such a welfare state, people are made dependent on the government, making them idle and expectant of the share in largesse, compromising their self-respect, self-esteem, and self-dignity. Gramadana, on the other hand, frowns on the welfare schemes of the welfare state. It teaches the public the virtues and values of self-sufficiency, self-reliance, etc. Gramadana would end the welfare state, welfare villages, welfare schemes, and welfare programmes. It would create, promote, nourish the culture of true independence and freedom which Tagore has asked for in *Gitanjali,* and which we have called Swaraj.

The nature and features of institutions of the gramadana and government PR are very different from each other, *viz.* Gramasabhas of the two models, grama panchayat of the government PR, and panchayat samiti of the gramadana. The existence of grama panchayat does not require that the village should have done gramadana. The number of members of a grama panchayat is limited; it depends on the population of the village; it can vary from 10 to 30.

The members of the grama panchayat can be (are) members of political parties, and they are elected through periodic elections. The decisions of the grama panchayat and Gramasabha of the government PR are taken on the basis of the majority principle, while those of the gramasabha are taken unanimously, or on the basis of consent of all members.

The formation of the grama panchayat is based on population; generally, the a population of 2,000 to 5,000 makes one unit for the grama panchayat. It means that grama panchayat is not a natural unit; it is an artificial unit carved out for the purpose of administrative convenience. The quorum for the meeting of the gramasabha of the SPR is mostly kept at a low level. For example, in Maharashtra state, the quorum has been kept at 15 per cent or more of the total number of members of the gramasabha. It has also been prescribed that the Gramasabha should meet at least twice in a year, which again is of quite a low frequency. A very serious matter is that the Gramasabha can discuss only less important issues, and it can give only some suggestions to the grama panchayat which has the power to accept or reject those suggestions.

It short, the Gramasabha of the SPR is a powerless and meaningless institution. It is an artificial entity which has been conceived by the centralized state. On the other hand, the Gramasabha of gramadana is a natural, self-born, and sovereign institution. It takes decisions unanimously or by the consent of all. It is not born of state laws. Between the Gramasabha and panchayat, while the panchayat is more powerful than the Gramasabha in the SPR, it is the gramasabha which is more powerful than panchayat or grama samiti in the GPR or gramadana.

In SPR, the role of people is mostly ineffective. While the birth of the gramadana is from the womb of the collective decision of the people in the village, which is subsequently approved by the

Government, the birth of the SPR is from the womb of state decision which is then approved by the people only technically. The gramadana works on the basis of strength, consent, authority, and co-operation of the people. The SPR is merely an extension of the representative parliamentary democracy, and since the latter also is a type of the state, the SPR is also a part of the State. The people are supreme in the GPR while parliament is supreme in the SPR.

SPR has helped to disintegrate villages or rural areas. Its working has led to the penetration of the power of the state into the innermost parts of the hinterland. The elected representatives of the SPR have become the instruments and agents of the State for exploitation of local areas. In other words, the SPR system has tended to increase exploitation and State intervention. Gramadana would reduce exploitation and State intervention.

The SPR is a part of the modern nation-state and the modern industrial civilization which Gandhiji has aptly called satanic civilization. Gandhiji has also said that the SPR is the progeny of modern western civilization, and it is un-Indian, even anti-Indian. Gramadana or GPR, on the other hand, is an alternative to modern civilization and its aim is to wither away the nation-state.

The manner and process of introducing the SPR in India amply reveal how it is a state-engendered and not people-engendered system. The failure to even mention villages in the Draft Constitution, taking their cognizance subsequently but only in the Directive Principles and not the main body of the Indian Constitution, giving states powers to create PR institutions, making the State governments responsible for the passing of necessary PR laws, the empowerment of the State governments to supersede, abolish, intervene, and interfere with them, show that the SPR system is not born from the womb of the people's will, but has been installed or thrust upon the people by the government, and the people's approval has been taken only technically. SPR institutions in India are not independent, powerful institutions. They have come into existence and they somehow live as a result of delegation and devolution of powers and resources by the Central and State Government in India. These institutions function at the sweet will of politicians and bureaucrats. Across the states, PR institutions have not done much important, meaningful development work. This whole picture is miles away from what gramaswaraj would have been.

After introducing the SPR also, only the big landowners, wealthy, powerful, criminals get elected. All the inequalities, all the injustices, all the power games continue to persist, and greater and greater concentration of economic and political power in the hands of those who are already rich and powerful, is taking place. On the other hand, it is worth noting in all seriousness that gramadana or grama swaraj is against not only authoritarian or dictatorial systems but also it is a social order which is beyond the current type of representative parliamentary democracy. Decentralized modern democracy is not the aim of sarvodaya; it is the aim of the government PR. The aim of sarvodaya is to create a face-to-face, direct, participatory peoples' democracy.

To sum up, so far we have studied the meaning, nature, philosophy, and merits of Bhoodana-Gramadana. B-G is indeed the manifestation of the principles of Hind Swaraj in flesh and blood. Gramadana is one of the names of Sarvodaya and it is a body of thought on a civilizational paradigm which is an alternative to the modern industrial civilization, which is a dying civilization. The crisis which India is facing today is essentially the problem of the development of 6 to 7 lakh villages. Gramadana is the best paradigm to successfully deal with this problem. In gramadani civilization, the village would be the basic, natural unit which would get primacy in everything. Each village would be a family and the interrelationship among the people would be founded upon truth, love, ahimsa, compassion and so on. Similarly, there would not be a right to private individual ownership of land and other wealth. The gramadana paradigm goes beyond paradigms such as the state, the market, Marxism, Socialism, Capitalism, and even the decentralized modern democracy. Gramadana would spread the message of harmony and upliftment of all.

Before the arrival of the Mughals in India, we were a free country or nation with free and independent villages. In the Mughal period, there was a foreign-ruled or a slave nation, with free villages. During the British raj we were a slave nation with slave villages. We have to work now towards rebuilding India so that we again become a free nation with free villages. We need to work now towards creating self-sufficient, self-reliant, self-dependent, and self-governing village republics or village kingdoms and a federation of those village republics (kingdoms).

The sincere, serious, wholehearted implementation of the gramadana philosophy is the best way to achieve this very desirable goal. The powers that be, however, discarded the gramadana approach and, instead, embraced central planning, the Community Development Programme, Panchayat Raj, co-operativism and capitalism. The adverse consequences of this are galore, which have brought the country to the brink of disaster.

The idea of gramadana is only at the thought level today. Gramadana is yet to begin in India. Gramadana has so far been a non-starter in India, but it must be completed sooner than later. Gramadana has perhaps failed but it must succeed.

The golden age epoch-making developments, leap of faith, leap froging with respect to *HS*, did not last much after 1978. By the end of the 1970s, the popular enthusiasm and popular upsurge, and popular participation in Bhoodan-Gramadana Movement (B-G) had waned and these movements had become moribund. As time passed, B-G experienced a continuous decline and fall and reached stage of stagnation. These '*Aandolans*' remained merely on paper. One witnessed a decline, fall, and stagnation of something grand and redeeming. The retrogression was reflected in various indicators, such as: (i) simplicity came to be replaced by stiltedness in many spheres. (ii) poverty, hunger, unemployment, inequality, became aggravated. (iii) the culture of non-violence, peace suffered a setback and the people, once again came to repose faith in violence as a means of solving issues. The task of perfecting the application of 'soul-force' remained incomplete. (iv) Communal, linguistic, riparian conflicts continued to take place. (v) Conditions became so bad that Gandhiji cried out, 'I have no place in new India'. (vi) Five-Year Plans did not perform well. (vii) Khadi was wounded and allowed to die. (viii) Political emergency was declared which brought an end to the already defective democratic system. Dictatorship replaced 'democracy'. (ix) The performance of economic planning was poor. (x) India began dreaming about being a super power. (xi) The country suffered from the worst kind of ethical and moral degradation. (xii) The imposition of the Emergency on 25 June 1975, resulted in '*Matbhed*' (differences of opinion), and '*manbhed*' (differences in mind) in Sarvodaya circles. Accordingly, there was a split in the body of Sarvodaya workers. J.P. expired on 8-10-1979, while Vinoba expired on 15-11-1982 which meant that the

Sarvodaya Movement became leaderless and impactless. During the Emergency, many political leaders, social workers were arrested and put in jail.

In 1991, under the pressures of the World Bank, the International Monetary Fund (IMF), the Washington Consensus, the American Think Tank, and the 'Complex', India introduced the New Economic Policy of Structural Adjustment Programme (SAP) and the Stabilization Programme (SP) of deregulation, privatization, liberalization, and globalization. Through this policy India resurrected, accepted and adopted the paradigm of the market or private capitalism. India wedded herself to Modern Civilization with manifold enthusiasm, rejecting for the second time (the first rejection was when centralized planning was adopted in 1951), the world-view of Hind Swaraj. It is extremely pathetic that inspite of significant empirical evidence which has shown the failure of the state and market. Indian policy makers should have chosen the same failed paradigm of capitalism. The future generations in India will certainly blame the leadership for taking the country twice towards the precipice, thus endangering its survival.

Does it mean that there is no hope now for India and the world? If there is hope, which way lies that hope? The answer to these questions is that there is certainly a hope still, and it consists of adopting and implementing the *HS* way. There is a hope as yet because of the promises from Him and Gandhiji. Their promises are:

> *Yada Yada he dharmasya glanirbhavati bharat*
> *Abhyutthanamdharmasya tadatmanam srujamyaham* ||
> (It means whenever there is decay of dharma and rise of adharma, then I embody myself, O Bharat).

The second promise is from Gandhiji in the form of HS. Some people think that Gandhiji's voice has been silenced by burying him and his ideas deep. But it is not so because he himself has promised that he will speak from his grave. There is no doubt that Hind Swaraj or Gramaswaraj or Sarvodaya, or Saamyayoga will be his medium for speaking to us from his grave.

XIII
Summary and Conclusions

We have discussed in the preceding 12 chapters the main themes in Mahatma Gandhi's book namely, *Hind Swaraj* (HS). We have also discussed questions such as why was *HS* written? How has it been evaluated? What is the alternative world view *HS* has put forth in front of human kind? In Chapter 13 we present a rather long summary and conclusions of the discussion so far.

The book *HS* is quite slim in its size, but it is as high as a mountain and as deep as the ocean. It is a powerful spiritual and revolutionary manifesto. Gandhiji had hoped to use the British race for transmitting his mighty message of Ahimsa to the rest of the world through this book (Parel, p. xiii). Gandhiji has said that *HS* was written in order to demonstrate the sublimity of Satyagraha, and that book is a true measure of his faith in its efficacy. The greatest motive behind writing *HS* was to serve the country, to find out the truth, and to follow it. The deeper we dive, the more precious gems of wisdom we get from it.

Gandhiji announced his life mission first in HS, and this mission was to show the world the way for moral regeneration, the emancipation of India, and to save our endangered civilization.

The central concern of *Hind Swaraj* is to convey that civilization is a disease, but it is a curable disease, and it seeks to uproot modern western civilization. It further seeks to impress upon the people of India that they would be following a suicidal path if they adopt Modern Civilization (MC), and that they should revert, return to their own glorious civilization. Gandhi wanted to drive home the point that colonialism is inconsistent with the teachings of Christianity. Although Gandhiji mounted a scathing attack on modern civilization through HS, he recognized that both Western and Eastern civilizations had traditional and modern parts. He upheld the traditional part and denounced the modern part.

HS scrutinizes long-held notions about many central aspects of human civilizations, both old and new, both traditional and modern, and both Indian and Western and it challenges all inherited knowledge-systems. *HS* is a revolt against the British rule and modern civilization; it has political and civilizational message.

HS rejects the Western representative parliamentary political system and advocates grassroot direct face-to-face people's democracy. It offers a superior and different health or medical model, a different system of justice, different technology, different development model, which is also a sustainable moral civilization. *HS* was ahead of its time by more than 100 years in rejecting state and market paradigms.

HS has posed a counter-civilization, counter-culture, counter-world-view before us through its counter-revolution. *HS* is a practical and moral alternative to modern civilization. It shows a path for survival of civilization, our planet, nature, all living beings, and life itself. The theme and analysis of *HS* is basically spiritual i.e. it upholds that the goal of life is self-realization through self-control, and the best way to deal with social, national, international problems is through self-mastery. *HS* teaches the way to swaraj for India and other countries; its applicability and validity are universal.

HS is a youthful opposition to modern civilization which was written by a 40-year-old youth. The second youthful opposition to modern civilization occurred about 60-70 years after *HS* was published. But, while the first youthful opposition was by a visionary youth, the second one was from the alienated western youth.

In the recent past, various schools of thought have emerged to debate various national and global issues. For example, post-modernism, post-colonialism, neo-colonialism, post-nationalism, and so on. The reach and goal(s) of *HS* are wider and deeper than the reach of these debating schools. The goals of *HS* is to bring on earth *'Satyayuga'* (Age of Truth) and not *'swarna yuga'* (the age of gold). It has occurred in *'Ishavasyopanishad'* that gold covers, hides Truth; gold makes human beings to forget truth. There is a conflicting relationship between truth and gold. This thought occurs in Christian philosophy also when it is clearly said that one cannot serve both God and Mammon at the same time. Gandhiji who had studied the Upanishadic or Vedantic literature quite seriously appears to have used his knowledge of spiritual or religious philosophy to favour truth over gold. The alternative civilization to modern civilization is thus was founded on truth rather than gold; its gold is truth. The world view of *Hind Swaraj* is essentially the Vedantic or Upanishadic world-View.

Two cultures or civilizations have been in conflict with each other since ages. On the one hand, there has been '*Bhoga sanskriti*' or (hedonistic culture), or '*Ravana Sanskriti*', while on the other hand, there has been '*Tyaga sanskriti*' or the culture of sacrifice, or *Rama sanskriti* or *Ramaraj*. The '*bhoga sanskriti*' encourages people to indulge in liquor-taking, meat-eating, fish eating, and sex. It is said that the '*tyaga sanskriti*' teaches us to honour Ganges, the Cow, Govinda, Bhagavad Gita, and the Gayatri Mantra. It is obvious that the survival of civilization and life depends on the choice of *Rama sanskriti* as against *Ravana sanskriti*. Ancient Indian civilization or Rama-sanskriti is also known by some other expressive, interesting, educative terms *viz.*, ashrama sanskriti, rishi sanskriti, krishi sanskriti, go (cow) sanskriti, grama-sanskriti, and dharma sanskriti.

Gandhiji has used different expressive terms to sum up his vision, *viz., Ramaraj, Swaraj, Hind-swaraj, Sarvodaya, Swadeshi, Gramswaraj.* All these expressions stand for nearly one and the same thing. For example, in both *Hind Swaraj* and *Ramaraj*, moral authority and power are the basic foundations of the sovereignty of the people. *Ramaraj* is a kingdom of righteousness; it is not a Hindu raj; it is a divine raj, the Kingdom of God. *Rama* in *Ramaraj* is not the epic hero Rama, but he is '*atmaram*', which implies that sovereignty resides within. *HS* has been written for the illiterate masses, and by using an ideal being or a traditional symbol from Indian mythology, he wanted to explain in a concise manner his ideas to the masses. By using traditional symbols, he wanted to emphasize the need for a return to ancient Indian civilization. *Ramaraj* is founded on the idea of *trusteeship*. *Ramaraj* is a social order which need not resort to even *Satyagraha*. Where life is organized on the basis of trusteeship, there exists *Ramaraj*. Ramaraj is one where, if needed, the king renounces the kingdom and goes to the forest, or where the ruler leaves the capital and rules from the forest as a trustee. Ramaraj is one where the king and rulers are prepared, if needed, to renounce the most dear thing to themselves. The use of this idiom can be said to be one more unique gift by Gandhiji. He led India away from Western terminology. Along with Hind Swaraj, Ramaraj is a powerful term to pose an alternative to Western civilization. He replaced concepts of socialism, communism, and the welfare state by Ramaraj.

HS rejects the validity of colonial power, all schools of violence, and all relationships which employ brute force, and exploitation by the State, society, group, and a person. *HS* addresses itself not only to the Indian problem but also to issues in any period anywhere. *HS* should not be pinned down to any specific brute force. *HS* cannot be pinned down to any of clothes. *HS* is a *declaration of non-violent civilization* and culture; it does not merely point out the need for an alternative development model or alternative socio-economic-political institutions and systems; it specifies an alternative civilization and culture. *HS* is a text for survival of human civilization, nay, for the survival of life itself. *HS* is a critique and condemnation of the existing political system, development models, violent means, modern western industrial, technocratic, materialistic civilization and culture, and it offers an alternative to each of them.

Usually, liberalism, neo-liberalism, capitalism, socialism, communism, welfare state, and their many variants are taken to be alternative or contesting paradigms. *HS* does not view the issue in this manner; it talks of civilizational alternatives and not about models with limited scope. It recognizes an important point that capitalism and socialism (communism) may be different in certain respects, but they are similar in many more aspects. Civilizationally, both of them belong to one civilization namely, modern civilization.

HS is devoted to the task of restoring man to his true state; it deals with the question of what kind of world and what kind of men we want to create, and not what kind of system to produce greater wealth is to be created. The disaster and collapse of the 20th century was clearly foreseen by Gandhiji and he had alerted and forewarned mankind about the impending extinction of all beings and the planet on which they live. *HS* teaches the goals and gospel of love, peace, non-violence, self-sacrifice, soul-force, the art of loving, and the art of living, etc. to be practised in individual, family, community, social, national, and international life.

The social order in *HS* is based or founded on four '*purusharthas*' namely, dharma, artha, kama, and moksha. The problems and interests of the poorest and the weakest are the reference or referentials in the light of which the decisions would be taken in such a social order. Gandhiji has put this referential in very touching, heart-moving words. He has said, "I will give you a talisman. Whenever you are in doubt, or the self becomes too much with you, apply the following test: Recall the face of the poorest or the weakest man you have seen, and ask yourself if the step you are contemplating is going to be of any use to him? Will he gain anything from it? Will it restore his control over his life and destiny. In other words, will it lead to swaraj for anyone or Swaraj for hungry and spiritually starving millions. Then you will find yourself melting away".

HS has achieved multiple tasks: It has (a) identified the roots of all evils in the existence of modern civilization, (b) provided a fundamental critique of the modern civilization, (c) identified in general terms what is true civilization and civilizational alternative, and (d) defined a path for liberating ourselves and the whole world from the clutches of modern civilization.

As said above, *HS* does not only criticize, it offers an alternative to modern civilization – the alternative (i) which teaches that the worldly pursuits should give way to ethical living, (ii) which would create a high and pure civilization; (iii) which has a high moral stature, (iv) which teaches one to appreciate beauty in voluntary simplicity, poverty, and slowness, (v) which would restore man to his true state, (vi) which makes a plea that ancient Indian civilization be accepted as a starting point for the next phase of India's growth and reconstruction, (vii) which puts forth a concept of a 'normal society' having its roots in India's past, (viii) it makes a case for ancient Indian civilization.

We learn through Gandhiji's number of statements that he had no doubt about the suitability and superiority of the ancient Indian civilization (AIC) as the alternative to modern civilization. For example, he has said, (a) India has nothing to learn from anybody else. (b) The tendency of the ancient Indian civilization is to elevate moral being. (c) Indian civilization (IC) is undoubtedly the best, and that European civilization is a nine days' wonder. (d) It behoves every lover of India to cling to ancient Indian civilization. (e) In order to restore India to her pristine glory, one effort, among others, that is required is to drive out Western civilization. All else will follow. (f) The world view that is implicit in ancient Indian civilization is universally valid. (g) To bring on a New Age, Be Indian, feel Indian, live Indian, Return to India's civilization.

The *HS* world-view has been called a 'dream', or a 'radical utopia', or a 'true civilization', or an 'Arcadian civilization'. The basic elements, philosophy, doctrines of *HS* are listed below:

(i) The foundation of the *HS* paradigm is the multi-religious ancestral wisdom of Indian civilization and the essence of Indian culture.

(ii) HS presents a critique of modern civilization, and it offers an alternative to it.

(iii) HS is Gandhiji's vision of true civilization, and his teaching about non-violence.

(iv) HS is Gandhiji's adaptation and generalization of the Bhagavad Gita. It is interesting to learn that the Gita is the source of Hind Swaraj and *Saamyayoga*, both of which are the same or one.

(v) HS is a complete model of political independence, social reforms, self-purification, and spiritual realization.

(vi) HS teaches the gospel of love in place of that of hate; it replaces violence by self-sacrifice; it pits soul-force against brute force.

(vii) HS offers a glimpse of *dharma* or *Ramaraj*.

(viii) The goal of *HS* is not to maximize wants, consumption, and production, or to maximize GNP growth rate, or to pursue mass affluence or to make any country an economic, imperial, nuclear, colonial super power. The goal of *HS* is to end the rule of desires, greed, and myopic hedonism. The *HS* economics is based on Biblical advice namely, "Take no thought for tomorrow", and the Gita's promise that "Yogakshemam vahamyaham" i.e. I take care of your livelihood (thus spoke Krishna).

(ix) Unlike any other paradigm, the *HS* paradigm has stressed language as a crucial development factor. India cannot be said to have gained freedom till English is (remains) the primary medium of instruction, education, inter-personal communication, and administration in India. To be really independent, the mother tongue must become the primary medium of communication. To continue to use English as the primary language is to continue to be colonized. The aim of *HS* is to make the mother tongue the most important and the most used language for all purposes.

(x) The goal of Sarvodaya (in *HS*) refers to not only progress of everyone but also the progress in every aspect of life (material, ethical, spiritual).

(xi) The National Symbol of *HS* would be the spinning wheel and cow. National festivals to be celebrated would be such as 'Charkha Jayanti', 'Satyagraha Jayanti' etc.

(xii) In *HS*, development involves national reconstruction and nation building.

(xiii) The Centre of *HS* is man, and Gandhiji's political vision is expressed through an oceanic circle and not the pyramid. Socio-economic-political organization would be based on the idea of the oceanic circle.

(xiv) The backbone of the republics of villages should be natural, organic, non-commercial, self-consumptive agriculture. If Khadi is the sun of Indian industries, Agriculture is the sun of all activities.

(xv) *HS* would involve a return to Indian civilization and culture (*Satyayugaki vapasi*).

(xvi) *HS* offers a very high food, water, housing, and security and a peace potential. It is impossible even for the greatest tyrant to destroy 6 lakh strong village republics.

(xvii) In *HS*, changes occur very slowly, after long-testing. There would be no 'future shock' in *HS*.

(xviii) The *HS* society would function on the basis of moral duty rather than rights and self-interest.

(xix) Based on the principle of 'limited wants' and contentment, the *HS* model is non-competitive in both production and consumption; it is co-operative and co-existential. Its ideal is to 'Live and let live', and not, 'let live and live'. In short, *HS* rejects free market system.

(xx) The *HS* model gives top priority to poverty removal, employment generation based on the virtue of "bread labour, and minimization of mechanization."

(xxi) In *HS*, there would be a prevalence of grassroot, face to face, direct, all-inclusive democracy.

(xxii) In *HS*, society will have brought about economic, political, administrative, social decentralization. The economy, polity, technology, administration would be on a human scale. *HS* is characterized by the minimization of the state and market. In HS, the society or community will overshadow the state.

(xxiii) In *HS*, urbanization, urbanism, the evil, ugly, satanic cities will be replaced by self-sufficient, self-dependent, self-governing republics of villages or village kingdoms located in green rural expanses; urban civilization and culture would be replaced by a rural, Arcadian civilization.

(xxiv) In HS, the acid test for judging anything is whether it is consistent with *dharma*.

Ruskin's book *Unto This Last* is the seed of HS, and *HS* is the seed of the totality of Gandhian thought. While *HS* states the core philosophy, bhoodana and gramadana give the means for implementation. *HS* can be said to be the constitution of village republics. *HS* is founded on Vedanta.

To continue the explanation of various aspects of *HS*, let it be recalled that Swaraj is when we rule and control ourselves. The key to swaraj is satyagraha. The ends and means must always be fair and not foul. Violence must be eschewed always and everywhere. A mere end of alien rule does not mean Swaraj. There is much to be done before we reach Swaraj, starting from political independence. India is a good example of this viewpoint. After independence in 1947, many villages in all States show stark picture of extreme poverty, and dispossession among the people. The State is absent for providing livelihood and basic rights to these people. Then there have been events like the imposition of the Emergency in the 1970s. 'Suraj' and 'Swaraj' are yet to arrive in India. Modern civilization ought not to be ever desired or wanted by anyone. Modern civilization is like a terrible, ferocious wolf, which is, satanic, monstrous, cursed, wretched, devilish, self-destructive, suicidal, illusion, marks the arrival of *Kaliyuga*. It has led to mass dehumanization and alienation. Its sole aim is to pursue creature comforts.

HS is against thoughtless industrialization and the craze for machinery. *HS* puts forth new ends, new paths, new means, and the right means. The collective non-violence, love-force or soul-force for resolving social problems is a great contribution of Gandhiji.

The theme of *HS* is the moral inadequacy, extravagance, and treacherously deceptive and self-destructive tendency of modern civilization. *HS* came on the scene when modernism and western civilization as such were at their peak. The revolutionary character of *HS* should be obvious from the fact that it was in such unfavourable times that Gandhiji mounted a frontal attack on modern civilization. He questioned the alleged superiority of modern civilization, argued that a truly modern civilization is yet to be born, and gave the outline of a 'true civilization'. Most of the 20 chapters (each of which is quite small) are uncompromisingly critical of the modern civilization.

In his letter to Mr. Ampthill, Member House of Lords, England, Gandhiji given a preview of HS. Gandhiji wrote: the repression in India by British rulers is not the fault of men but of the system and the system is represented by the present civilization. The true remedy lies in England discarding modern civilization which is 'unsouled' by the spirit of selfishness and materialism. Railways, machinery are the true badges of slavery of any man anywhere. To me the rise of cities like Calcutta and Bombay is a matter of sorrow. India has lost in having broken her village system. The use of violent methods must mean acceptance of modern civilization and the same ruinous competition, and destruction of true morality. I should be uninterested in the fact as to who rules. I should expect rulers to rule according to my wish otherwise ... I become a passive resistor against them. Passive resistance is soul-force exerted against physical force. In other words love conquering hatred (Parel, 1997, pp. 133-135).

The Hind Swaraj social order would be characterized by the absence of the nine deadly sins which Gandhiji would ask the people to avoid. These deadly sins are:

(1) Wealth without work.
(2) Pleasure without conscience.
(3) Knowledge without character.
(4) Business without morality.
(5) Science without humanity.
(6) Worship without sacrifice.
(7) Politics without principle.

(8) Failure to regard land as a mother, and agriculture as a way of life.
(9) To hold that literacy or formal education is a great virtue and the good of society depends on literate people.

While studying the writings on *HS* and on Gandhiji in general, one comes across remarks such as "HS does not provide a rigorous, logical social analysis", that Gandhiji was not a model builder, a system expert, that he was not an economist, that he was not an intellectual and so on. We think that such remarks might have been made out of various positive and negative motives. But they are beside the point, they cannot reduce the value of Gandhiji's thought. The light shed, illumination spread may be greater by such 'non-rigorous', writings than that of rigorous writings. The comments such as these should not make us confused about the significance of *HS*.

The thinking on the *HS* world-view did not cease with the demise of Gandhiji. The significant, substantial extension and restatement of the philosophy and action programme of *HS* occurred for many years after 1948. The greatest contribution in this respect was that made by Vinoba Bhave. Through his many books, speeches, and 'padyatra' for about 15 years across the whole of India, Vinoba explained, extended the 'mantras' and 'tantras' of HS. The most visible, impressive advancement of *HS* occurred in the form of bhoodana and gramadana. The *HS* paradigm (along with Sarvodaya, and others) came to be known as 'saamyayoga' in Vinoba's times. Gramadana has been called the most creative thought coming from India. Both bhoodana and gramadana have been both 'mantra' and 'tantra', and revolutionary ideas. Gramadana is a wider and broader vision than that of bhoodana. Similarly, while bhoodana was individual 'dana', gramadana, was a collective experiment.

The progress of bhoodana and gramadana has been very little after the initial years. Gramadana is very much different from the official Panchayat Raj which exists today. The leaders at the summit, politicians, intellectuals are to be blamed for forsaking for the second time the HS-gramadana model when they went in a big way for the market model. They chose a pebble and rejected a diamond. The consequences of this foolhardy step will have to be suffered by the masses. The authorities have advanced the time of extinction of our planet earth, mankind, and human civilization.

HS is an ideal social order. Its aim is to bring about the resurgence of civilization which humans can call their home, home that is auspicious, welfare-enhancing and joyful (*anandavan bhuwan*). In the words of Kusumagraja, a Marathi poet, the aim ought to be *"Jeje jagi jagatt taya, maze mhana, karuna kara"* (whatever lives on this earth, embrace it, accept it, call it mine, and be compassionate). The aim is to make body a temple, to make the family a temple, and establish a homoestasis of the body, family, and society.

In the future, if mankind and human civilization is to survive, it has to make a right choice between the atom and ploughshare, or the atom and the Sermon on the Mount, or the atom and Gandhiji. The choice is between non-violence and non-existence. The crisis created by modern Western civilization can be averted by adopting the values, ideals, etc. of the ancient Indian civilization (AIC) which Gandhiji has called a 'true' civilization suitably modified for making it well-applicable in the present times. Thus, it is imperative to embrace the alternative of *HS* for the survival of mankind.

Another important feature of *HS* is that of violence (*himsa*) and non-violence (*ahimsa*). Non-violence is a foundational feature of HS. There has been a long-standing quest, search for non-violence for the past 2500 to 3000 years by the Indian rishis, sages, saints, munis, yogis. The quest of Buddha and Mahavir has climaxed, flowered in Gandhi and Vinoba. The result of this search was the coming up of the great gem of wisdom, '*Ahimsa permo dharmeha*' (ahimsa is the dharma of highest order), development of the power of non-violence (ahimsa shakti), and evolution of the scope of the meaning of ahimsa.

Gandhiji and *V*inoba have given a gift of survival to mankind in the form of HS. In the chain of researchers and experimenters in ahimsa, Gandhiji occupies the topmost slot. He has added the concepts of 'individual and collective' ahimsa, and 'constructive and agitational ahimsa'.

The HS world-view offers peaceful revolution, as also the revolution for peace, and the revolution without an antagonist is enemy. The revolution in HS says, I do not want blood, I want emancipation (Rakta nako maj, mukti Havi).

In respect of the nature of the future civilization, while the Gandhian school of thought favours a rural, village, arcadian civilization, the Nehruvian school prefers a city or urban civilization. The latter school regards Indian villages as dung-heaps or dung-hills, the sink of ignorance. Gandhian thinkers have insisted that India is to be found not in her few cities but in her about seven lakh villages. An age-old culture is hidden under the encrustment of crudeness, but if encrustment is removed, one would meet the finest specimen of cultured, cultured, finest, free citizens in the villages. Hence the choice of a village civilization. In the *HS* world view, every village would be a *sevagrama*. Both Indian and foreign scholars have accepted that since ages, the village system in India has been working well, India has resided in villages, India has been always predominantly '*gramavasini*'. From this, it is not to be concluded that the *HS* paradigm is relevant only for India. It is not useful for the West. Gandhiji has said that rural life or country life or agricultural life is good for all countries and not only for India.

The choice is to be made also between conventional socialism and Gandhian socialism. The former is not non-violent. *HS* would, therefore, reject it. The first writings on socialism are not Das Capital, Communist Manifesto, etc., they are Gita, Samaveda and Eshavasya Upnishid. Each chapter in Gita states the importance of equality.

For a non-violent way of pursuing the goal of equality, social justice, absence of exploitation, Gandhiji revived the idea of trusteeship. He pointed out that there are many examples of the practice of trusteeship from ancient and historical periods in India. Bharat ruled as a trustee for 14 years from the Ashrama as an ascetic. Shivaji ruled as a trustee of God. The king was always regarded as a trustee of God, the injunction was that he should rule on behalf of God.

In *HS* or Sarvodaya paradigm, there is a profound core in the form of 'mantras' i.e. sacred word(s) such as Jai Jagat, and 'tantras' i.e. means such as bhoodan, gramadana. The aim of *HS* or Sarvodaya is to make our mind, heart, family, village, country, and the world home of joy (aanandavan bhuvana) and the home of the sacred (Mangal bhuvan). This is done by following the essence (tattwa) and light, purity (satva) of tradition. The progressive development of thinking on dharma (dharmavichar) also would occur in Sarvodaya. In Sarvodaya, the method of thinking (chintan) would be integrative or unificatory (samanvaya) the *HS* social order integrates head, heart, and hand. It teaches that man's greatest needs are love and work.

The HS social order would be founded on the essence of all religions and Brahmavidya. Such a social order and its teachings would be like an unbroken stream. Along with the State, there would be a withering away of large-scale industries, many institutions, and exploitation. In such a social order, there would be a worship of five things (panchayatan) namely, Brahma vidya, Gramaswaraj, Shanti Sena, Aacharyakul, and Devanagari script.

A very important doctrine of *HS* is Swadeshi. Its major tenet is "work (act) locally but think globally". The meaning and spirit of Swadeshi is well-expressed in the following somewhat modified wise words of Saint Ramadasa (referred to earlier): "*Chinta, Chintan Karito Vishwache Karya, Seva Karito Gavachi*". (I worry and think about the universe, but I work and serve my villages). The argument is that given his physical features, the man can and should serve his locality and village the best. The desire to serve the area beyond at best, a group of villages. is unnatural. It is not our responsibility to take the burden of the whole world, and to find solutions to all its problems. We have to only see that we spread the 'fragrance' in our surrounding area. There is no conflict between swadeshi and universalism. The sages from the past to the present have talked of a beautiful synthesis of the local and universal. For example, Adi Shankaracharya has said, '*Swadesho bhuvantrayam*' (all three 'lokas' are our swadesh). Sant Tukaram, a saint-poet of Maharashtra of the 17th century has said, "*Aamacha swadesh, bhuwantrayamadhe vasa*" (our swadesh is all the three 'lokas'). While endorsing swadeshi, Vinoba has given the '*mantra*' of '*Jai Jagat*'.

The aim of the *HS* social order definitely is to make people happy, but Gandhi-Vinoba have extended the content of this aim by visualizing that there will also be '*Sukha-saamya*' (similar happiness), '*sama-sukha*' (equality in happiness), and '*sukha-unnayan*' (elevation of happiness), and all this would happen through the gift of love (premadana), and the service of man and society. The goal would be achieved by pursuing the highest, supreme equality in all fields. (Abhidheyam param saamyam), and without opposing, contesting any one (Sarvesham Avirodhen).

The cardinal principles of Vedanta is the foundation of *HS* are as given below:

(i) Whatever and wherever exists is permeated by God (*Ishavasyam idam sarvam, Yat kim cha jagatyam jagat*)
(ii) Brahman and Atman are one, they are not separate.
(iii) Human beings are children of immortality (*Amritasya putraha*).
(iv) There is unity of all religions or paths of the realization of God. (*Ekam sat vipraha bahuda vadanti*).
(v) We must work for the happiness of all (*Sarvetra Sukhinaha Santu...*)
(vi) This planet is one family (*Vasudhaiva Kutumbakam*).
(vii) God lives in the hearts of all living beings (*Ishwara sarvabhootanam rhideshe tishtati*).

HS is the best available paradigm to this date. It is a complete (sampoorna) thought. The individual freedom and social demands are well-integrated in this social order. Sarvodaya-thought is the fruit of old tradition, and the seed of the new tradition.

The content of *HS* may be partially expressed in some illustrative equations as given below:

1) Life = pleasure + sacrifice[2]
2) Minimax Life Style = Minimization of wants + maximum spirituality.
3) Science + Violence = Total annihilation (Sarvanash).
4) Science + spirituality = Sarvodaya (non-violence)
5) Ahimsa = Love + non-killing + not to cause sorrow (suffering) + non-accumulation + giving (dana).
6) Hind swaraj = Vedanta
7) Mere political freedom or political democracy Swaraj.

Two caveats are in order here. First, is it philosophically so rich that it can serve as a redeeming paradigm relevant today? Two, is ahimsa effective? Was ancient Indian civilization really non-violent? In both the Ramayana and the Mahabharata wars, a vast number of people were killed. How can this be taken as an example or adarsha for ahimsa?

About the relevance of *HS*, one may recall the story of yaksha in the Mahabharata. Yaksha asked Yudhistir as to what was the most surprising thing in the world for him? Dharma replied that the most surprising thing is that so many persons have died, and so many are dying daily, and yet everybody carries himself in a way that seems to suggest that he is immortal. Similarly, the cognoscenti know that there is a mountain of quantitative and qualitative evidence to show that all the paradigms implemented so far have failed and yet humanity is still running after those failed systems.

About ahimsa, one can say that it has been effective in some events, but in others it did fail. The following examples can be cited as evidence in favour of the potential effectiveness of ahimsa:

(i) The story of Narada and Valya Koli who later on becomes Valmiki Rishi.
(ii) The story of Buddha Vs. Angulimal, and the raging elephant.
(iii) Gandhiji"s success in quenching the communal conflagration in Naokhali, Calcutta, Bihar, Delhi, during 1946-48.
(iv) Gandhiji's success in many satyagrahas in South Africa and India.
(v) Gandhiji won freedom for India through largely non-violent means.
(vi) The story of surrender by the dacoits before Vinoba and Jayaprakash-Narayan in the 1960s, and 1970s.

Is Indian civilization, culture, and tradition really non-violent? Apparently not, but really yes. Vinoba has said that to get correct understanding of such matters, we need to learn to read our scriptures and our religious books in such a way as to understand symbolism, metaphors, etc. in them. We need to develop the ability so that we are able to unveil the implied, suggested meanings. We should not concentrate our attention on literal meaning. If one does this, one would find that Mahabharata, for example, is a religious book of a poem. The remorse of Yudhishtira, the critique of 'Kshatra dharma' by him, the Shanti-parva in the middle of Mahabharata, only a part of the body of the mongoose becomes golden, predominance of '*shant rasa*', and vairagya rasa in the Mahabharata, Krishna's mediatory role show that the message of the Mahabharata is one of non-violence and peace. Similarly, the remorse of Ashoka and his renouncing of war (yuddha tyaga) also gives the message of ahimsa. The approach of these sources appears to be to ask people to embrace non-violence by showing the futility of violence in solving problems.

In the Mahabharata a moment comes when Rishi Vyasa finds the situation, around him so miserable, so intolerable that he despairs openly saying with his both hands raised, that he was trying to educate people, to make them wise but no one was listening to him. Gandhiji's position towards the end of the war of freedom, and at the end of his life was similar to that of Vyasa. He was trying his best to show the people and leaders the right way to deal with partition, population exodus, and communal riots, but no one would listen to him. Notwithstanding this, he was sure and confident that the path explained by him in *Hind Swaraj* was the only way to tackle most of the short-term and long-term problems which India was facing. The *HS* way was the only alternative available to India and to the world if it is to survive. The following shloka (verse) expresses this superbly:

Na Kaschit Shrunoti me
Sanatano nitya nutanna
Yesha panthaha, yetat karma
Na anya panthha vidyate ayanaya ।

References

Aditya Nigam, Gandhi – The 'Angel of History': Reading Hind Swaraj Today, *Economic and Political Weekly*, March 14, 2009.

Akshaya Kumar, and Madhu Gupta, 'Gandhi's Swaraj as Postnation', *Gandhi Marg*, January-March 2000.

Bhatkal, Ramdas, 'Hind Swaraj: The 'Reader' and the 'Editor'', *Gandhi Marg*, July-September 2009.

Bhole, L.M. 'Samyayoga: Vinoba's Vision of an Alternative Social Order', in Bhole, *Collected Papers on Gandhian Thought*, Amani, Kiel (year of publication not given) (5).

_______, 'Environmental Protection Through Sustainable Social Order', in Bhole, *Collected Papers on Gandhian Thought*, Amani, Kiel (2).

_______, 'Gandhian Model of Non-Violent Social Order', in Bhole, *Collected Papers on Gandhian Thought*, Amani, Kiel (3).

_______, 'Gramaswaraj: Twenty-First Century Imperative' in Bhole, *Collected Papers on Gandhian Thought*, Amani, Kiel (1).

_______, 'The Relevance of Gandhi in Today's World', in Bhole, *Collected Papers on Gandhian Thought*, Amani, Kiel (6).

_______, 'Understanding Gandhi through Romain Rolland's Writings' in Bhole, *Collected Papers on Gandhian Thought*, Amani, Kiel (4).

Cholkar, Parag, *Sabai Bhoomi Gopalki*, Vols. 1-3, Gujarat Vidyapeeth, Ahmedabad, 2010 (Hindi).

Colyber, B., 'Hind Swaraj: A Green Manifesto', *Gandhi Marg*, 17, October-December 1995.

Desai, Jitendra, 'Hind Swaraj, A Small Classic' *Sarvodaya Talisman*, January-February 2009.

Devdutt, 'Hind Swaraj: Context and Text', in Prasad, N. (ed.), *Hind Swaraj: A Fresh Look*, Gandhi Peace Foundation, New Delhi, 1985.

Dhareshwar, Vivek, 'Politics, Experience, and Cognitive Enslavement: Gandhi's Hind Swaraj', *Economic and Political Weekly*, March 20, 2010.

Diamond, J., *Collapse*, Penguin Books. Undated.

Dipankar Gupta, 'Gandhi Before Habermas: The Democratic Consequences of Ahimsa', *Economic and Political Weekly*, March 7, 2009.

Easwaran, Eknath, *Gandhi, The Man*, Jaico, Mumbai, 1997.

Edgar Snow, 'The Message of Gandhi', *Sarvodaya*, March-April, 2005.

Gandhi, M.K., Modern vs. Ancient Civilization, Bhartiya Vidya Bhavan, Mumbai, 1970.

Gandhi, M.K., *Satyagraha in South Africa*, Navajivan, Ahmedabad, 1928.

Gavaskar, M., 'Gandhi's Hind Swaraj: Retrieving the Sacred in the Time of Modernity', *Economic and Political Weekly*, September 5, 2009.

Goldsmith, E., Allen, R., Allaby, M., Davoll, J. and Lawrence, S., 'A Blueprint for Survival', *The Ecologist* 2, 1972.

Gowan, S., Lakey, G., Moyer, W., and Taylor, R., *Moving Towards a New Society*, New Society Press, Philadelphia, 1976.

Huddleston, John, *The Search for a Just Society*, Sterling Paperbacks, New Delhi, 1998.

Kumar, A., and Gupta, M., 'Gandhi's Swaraj as Postnation', *Gandhi Marg*, January-March 2000.

Lunine, M.J., 'Hind Swaraj: A Paradigm and an Agenda for 21st Century Global Swaraj', *Gandhi Marg*, July-September 2009.

Mathai, M.P. and Moolkkattu, John (eds.), Gandhi Marg, Special Issue on Hind Swaraj, July-September 2009.

Paranjape, M., *Decolonization and Development: Hind Swaraj Revisioned*, Sage Publications, New Delhi, 1993.

Parel, A.J. (ed.), *Gandhi: Hind Swaraj and other Writings*, Cambridge University Press, Cambridge, 1997.

Pattanayak, Kishen, 'Failure of Gandhi, Gandhians and Gandhian Intellectuals', in Prasad, N. (ed.), *Hind Swaraj: A Fresh Look*, Gandhi Peace Foundation, New Delhi, 1985.

Prasad, N. (ed.), *Hind Swaraj: A Fresh Look*, Gandhi Peace Foundation, New Delhi, 1985.

Prasad, Nageshwar, 'Introduction' in Prasad, Nageshwar (ed.), *Hind-Swaraj: A Fresh Look*, Gandhi Peace Foundation, New Delhi, 1985.

Prasad, Shambhu, 'Towards an Understanding of Gandhi's views on Science', *EPW*, September 29, 2001.

Radhakrishnan, N., 'Gandhi's concept of Nai Tailim as a Blueprint for Educational Revolution, *Sarvodaya*, Nov.-Dec. 2004.

Radhakrishnan, S., Mahatma Gandhi, Essays and Reflections, Jaico, Mumbai, 1995.

Raja Kalpana, 'Mahatma Gandhi's Guide – His Inner Voice', *Sarvodaya*, May-June, 2005.

Ranjit Chaudhuri, 'Some Reflections on Hind Swaraj', *Gandhi Marg*, July-September 1998.

Rao, K. Raghavendra, 'State and Society: A Swarajist Framework', in Prasad, N. (ed.), *Hind Swaraj: A Fresh Look*, Gandhi Peace Foundation, New Delhi, 1985.

Rao, R., 'Moral Foundation of Hind Swaraj and Nonviolence', in Prasad, N. (ed.), *Hind Swaraj: A Fresh Look*, Gandhi Peace Foundation, New Delhi, 1985.

Roszak, Theodore, *The Making of A Counter Culture*, Faber and Faber,

London, 1970.

Roy, Ramashray, 'Moral Foundation of Hind Swaraj and Non-violence', in Prasad, N. (ed.), *Hind Swaraj: A Fresh Look*, Gandhi Peace Foundation, New Delhi, 1985.

Rudolph, L.I., 'Contesting Civilisations: Gandhi and the Counter Culture', *Gandhi Marg*, January-March, 1992.

Ruskin, John, *Unto This Last*, University Tutorial Press, London, 1862.

Sane Guruji, 'Bharatiya Sanskriti, Continental Prakashan, Pune, 1937 (Marathi).

Schumacher, E.F., *Small Is Beautiful*, Radha Krishna, New Delhi, 1973.

Shaha Kanti, *Gandhi's Hind Swaraj – A Fresh Look.* Other India Press, Mopusa, Goa, 2009.

Susanne Gousan, *et al.*, Moving Towards a New Society, 1976.

Swami Tejomayanand, *Hindu Sanskriti (Hindu Culture)*, Central Chinmaya Mission Trust, Bombay, 1995 (Hindi).

Swami Vivekananda, *To the Youth of India*, Advait Ashram, Calcutta, 1969.

Swaminathan, S., 'Gandhi As Perceived by His Emissary', *Sarvodaya Talisman*, March-April, 2008.

Swaminathan, S., 'Tagore on Gandhi', *Sarvodaya Talisman*, May-June, 2008.

Tagore, R., *Creative Unity*, Macmillan, Madras, 1988.

Tagore, R., *Lectures and Addresses*, Macmillan, Madras, 1980.

Vasto Lanza del, 'Preface to the French Edition (1957), *Gandhi Marg*, July-September 2009.

Vinay Lal, 'The Gandhi Everyone Loves to Hate', *EPW*, October 4, 2008.

Vinoba, Ahimsa Ki Talash, Maitry, Special Issue, *Varsha* 22, Anka 10 (Hindi).

Vinoba, Shikshan-Vichar, Paramdham Prakashan, Wardha, 1965 (Marathi).

_______, Democratic values, Sarva Seva Sangha Prakashan, Varanasi, 1977 (English).

_______, Samyasutre, Paramdham Vidyapeeth Prakashan, Pavaner, 1958 (Hindi).

_______, Samyayogaka Samaj-Darshan, Maitry, Special Issue, *Varsha* 23, Anka 10 (Hindi).

_______, Sarvodaya Aur Samyavad, Sarva Seva Sangha Prakashan, Varanasi, 1968 (Hindi).

_______, Sarvodaya Vichar AAni Swaraj Shastra, Paramdham Vidyapeeth Prakashan, Pavaner, 1956 (Marathi).

_______, Swaraj shastra, Sixth ed., Sarva Seva Sangha Prakashan, Varanasi, 1973.

_______, Vinoba Sahitya, Vols. 1-20, Paramdham Prakashan, Pavaner, Wardha, Undated (Hindi).

Yashaschandra, Sitanshu, 'Hind Swaraj and Hind Svaraj: Changing Contexts of Textual Transmissions', in Suresh Raval, *et al.* (eds.), *Forms of knowledge in India: Critical Revaluations*, Pencraft International, Delhi, 2008.

Index